NELSON'S FIRST LOVE

FANNY'S STORY

Lady Frances Nisbet, *c.* 1804, aged forty-three..

NELSON'S FIRST LOVE
FANNY'S STORY

PATRICK DELAFORCE

AMBERLEY

For my sweet wife with very many thanks for her help with this book

British Library Cataloguing in Publication Data

Delaforce, Patrick, 1923 –
Nelson's first love: Fanny's story

First published 1988

Amberley Publishing
The Hill, Stroud
Gloucestershire
GL5 4ER

www.amberleybooks.com

Copyright © Patrick Delaforce 2011

The right of Patrick Delaforce to be identified as the Author
of this work has been asserted in accordance with the
Copyrights, Designs and Patents Act 1988.

British Library Cataloguing in Publication Data.
A catalogue record for this book is available from the British Library.

ISBN 978-1-4456-0365-0

Typeset in 10pt on 13pt Celeste.
Typesetting and Origination by Amberley Publishing.
Printed in the UK.

CONTENTS

A young Horatio Nelson.

INTRODUCTION

Admiral Lord Horatio Nelson is one of England's famous folk heroes, about whom many famous writers have written: Sir Nicholas Harris Nicolas, Alfred Morrison, George P. B. Naish, Carola Oman, Oliver Warner, Tom Pocock, Sir Arthur Bryant, David Walder, and others. Nelson's famous mistress Lady Emma Hamilton has also had excellent biographies written about her by Hugh Tours, Oliver Warner, and more recently, Jack Russell.

Lady Frances 'Fanny' Nelson, née Woolward, Duchess of Bronte, was Nelson's wife and love for fourteen years. She was of a good family, brought up in the rich plantation life on Nevis in the West Indies. In 1787 she married a completely unknown little naval captain. He was very unpopular locally, had no particular prospects, lived on his pay and was no 'catch' at all. He was nearly thirty at the time of his marriage, not a callow young man as most of his biographers have made out.

Fanny was his loyal devoted wife – and his equally devoted widow – until she died in London in 1831 at the age of 70. Most biographers of Nelson have failed to give her more than a cursory glance, hypnotised as they have been by the dynamic sea captain and his mistress. Fanny was most handsome, highly intelligent, well-read, spoke excellent French, dressed always à la mode, painted watercolours better than most, and played the piano. She wrote entertaining and interesting letters, had a wide circle of friends, was presented at Court and was a favourite with all the Lords of the Admiralty and their wives. She lived a long and extremely interesting life, partly in London, Bath, Paris or Devon, and of course she was a *faithful* wife.

Moreover although she failed to give Nelson *his* child, she did give him her son by her first marriage, Josiah Nisbet, to whom the Admiral was deeply attached. Her stepson was five when Nelson first met him on Nevis. He was a dashing frigate Captain of 20 when Nelson abandoned his wife for the arms of the woman described by Lord Minto as 'a good humoured barmaid'. During those fifteen years Josiah was by Nelson's side much of the time at sea and clearly saved the Admiral's life at Santa Cruz, if not on other occasions. Many times Nelson made it clear that he regarded Josiah as his son. In his will made in March 1798 Nelson left him the sum of £500, or £10,000 if Fanny died before her son. He also made Josiah, who was then 18, a sea captain with a career not less adventurous than

Frances Nelson. This charming miniature by Daniel Orme, produced in 1798, shows what a very attractive woman Fanny Nelson was. It dates from one of the happiest periods of her marriage, when she was devotedly nursing her husband back to health after the loss of his arm..

that of his illustrious step-father, his executor. Josiah not only disapproved of his stepfather's amatory pursuits at the Court of Naples – and made his disapproval known – but he also unfortunately fell in love with the Ambassador's wife himself. As a result he took too many risks at sea, drank too much, enraged his own officers and offended his superiors. Still in April 1800 Nelson wrote that his love for Josiah was very great and that he flattered himself that Josiah would be a good and a great man. This is the strange story of a mother and son and their intimate relationship with England's greatest naval hero.

CHAPTER ONE

PARADISE ON NEVIS

For the first twenty years of my life I lived in Paradise.

Nevis is a small island in the West Indies, rightly called the 'Queen of the Caribee'. It is barely 35 square miles, circular in shape dominated by the Peak, whose summit of over 3,000 feet is always hidden by clouds. No wonder the passing Spaniards on their way to America called it 'nieve' after its snow-capped mountain. Our nearest neighbour was St Christopher or St Kitts, another island in the Leeward group, separated by the 'Narrows'. We were so close that a sloop or fishing boat could make the two mile journey well within the hour. St Eustatius, Montserrat and Antigua are three islands within a day's sail.

The skies were nearly always bright blue and the trade winds from the west kept the temperatures down, except during the hurricane season in August and September. There was the scent of tropical blooms with the philomels singing like nightingales. The air was light and stimulating even on the hottest days as the tradewinds rarely deserted our island.

I have many memories of my childhood. With a governess I visited the town of Charlestown early in the morning before it became too hot. It was close enough to walk there and admire the fine buildings along the shore of the curving bay, and listen to the many noisy hucksters in the negro market. The market women wore violent-coloured dresses – blues and greens, reds and yellows – heads covered with gaudy kerchiefs. Each day I saw the variety of skin colours – darkest ebony, copper, olive, and that strange white with dark, dark blood under the skin. There was a long double row of temporary stalls on market days selling fowl, strange meats, hot soup, oranges, pineapples, vegetables, wild birds, fish, sugar cakes, and household requirements such as caster oil, cloths, handkerchiefs, wood and cheap hand-rolled cigars for the men. The familiar cries filled the air – 'Oyez, Oyez'. 'Bargain, Bargain, here's yo' fine cowfee. Here's yo' pickled peppers. Come see. Only come see. Make you buy. Want any jelly coconut? Any yams? Nice granadilla! Make yo' mouth water. Lady, buy here very cheap – very nice – real.'

The better class negroes and the servants from the white planters' houses came early to secure the best bargains. Sheep were driven into the market along the dusty roads. 'Oyez! Come to the shambles of Mr Columbus Brown. Nice fat lambs and big fat sheep. Cheap!'

Occasionally I would see a white planter in his smart white linen suit and broad panama hat riding to a government office, but rarely any other white women. There was a gay little restaurant in Charlestown which in those days was a rarity and one was considered a little fast to go there.

I remember the famous Nevis baths – this was long before the dreadful Mr Thomas Huggins built the Bath Hotel for £40,000 in 1778 with slave labour. There were rooms for no less than 50 boarders, who came to take the waters. The natural hot bubbling water springs were fed into tanks and at a very early age I would bathe several times a week in them. The mineral waters cured one of rheumatism, gout and agues and acted as a wonderful tonic and restorative. Now the Bath Hotel is famous throughout the Caribbean. The 'haut monde' from London, Bath and Bristol sail out to spend the winter season, admire the Italian rose garden, the goldfish ponds and the turtle crawl. The French cuisine and the wine cellars with the best wines of France, Spain and Portugal are famous. So too is the huge ballroom and, two hundred yards down the ravine, the separate bathhouse built of stone on two floors, fed by the waters from the stream. The crystal clear water is kept at 100 degrees and the bathroom measures thirty feet by twenty, with the separate toilet rooms above.

Some of the plantations near the sea had their private bath tanks filled with sea water carted up from the beach in new rum casks on ox-carts. All my life I have been used to hot water bathing, since my childhood days on Nevis.

On Sundays my governess and I and my father, when he could, all went to church. I was baptised in May 1761 at St George's in Gingerland, which my father preferred to St Paul's in Charlestown. My grandfather William Woolward, a sea captain, was married there to a widow called Anne Smith in June 1724. There were four other churches – St Thomas at Lowland, a mile due north of Charlestown, was the oldest; St John's, Brown Hill, the smallest, to the south of the island; St. James', Windward, in the northeast; and finally St John's Fig Tree, between Gingerland and Charlestown, which featured in my life later on and became the family church. The island was divided into five parishes, each with its own church. Matins on Sunday was attended by nearly everyone and was a remarkable sartorial affair.

I can remember those Sunday mornings so well – the little church, half stone, half timber, romantically poised on the side of the mountain with flaming red shrubs around it. The white planters and their families sat in front, the coloured creoles behind, and the coloured folk at the back. We would wear our best clothes, delicate fabrics with radiant hues, beflounced and beruffled, fringed and ribboned, with floating scarves and sashes of lace and silk. Our bonnets were covered with plumes and flowers. We carried rustling fans to cool, or try to cool, ourselves. The womenfolk would have taken immense pains with their hair. Bunches of curls were half concealed by a mass of 'blonde' or 'tulle'. One's toilette took an hour or more to prepare beforehand. The white creoles kept their porcelain milkmaid skins delicate with buttermilk and spirits of wine. The young white girls on the island were very competitive and I was determined to outdo my cousins Herbert and Morton in prettiness and finery.

Sugar was the main crop upon which the island depended but my family, the Woolwards, were not sugar planters. We did not own one of the Great Houses built of stone standing proudly overlooking the waving sugar cane fields. Our more modest house was close to Charlestown, the busy, bustling capital of the island, on the west side. As my father was Senior Judge of Nevis he needed to be close to the law courts and to the port for conferences across the water at Basseterre, the capital of St Kitts.

He told me when I was a child about the history of Nevis. How Columbus discovered it in 1498 and named our neighbour St Christopher after himself. How Sir Thomas Warner came out from England in 1642 and Anthony Clifton founded the first settlement on Nevis, which was plundered by the Spanish fleet five years later. The terrible hurricane of 1642 destroyed 23 fully laden ships stranded on Nevis beaches, and the capital, Jamestown, was flattened by a huge tidal wave and quite submerged on 30 April 1680. The French navy and army invaded the island in 1706 and carried away nearly 4,000 slaves. The next year saw another furious hurricane which destroyed all the crops, as a result of which the population partly starved and was reduced to 1,100 whites and 3,700 negroes.

My mother was Mary Woolward, or Molly to my father and their friends: She died in childbirth in 1763 when I was two. Her other child, my brother William Manning Woolward, was educated in England like many of the young white boys on the island. My widowed father could not bear to part with me and I grew up with him and was well educated by a series of governesses. Half of St. Kitts was French owned, and even on our much smaller island there were legacies of the 1706 invasion. My father insisted on me learning that elegant language, the Court language, and an important asset in the Caribbean, when a French occupation was always on the cards.

There was a bookshop in Charlestown (as it was renamed after the destruction of Jamestown) owned by young John Anderson. Thomas Howe owned a rather larger one in Basseterre, and David Crawford another on St. Eustatia, the Anglo-Dutch island just beyond St. Kitts. So I was never short of books. Every ship arriving at Charlestown from England brought the latest papers and the Senior Judge on Nevis had a standing order for the London papers. My father was determined that I should have all the attributes of a well brought up young lady. I was taught to sew, and my needlework was a source of great pleasure ever afterwards.

In our small community of two hundred white families we had to create our own entertainment, and music was of course much in demand. I was taught the pianoforte, played it well, and essayed the harp and violin. We acted amateur theatricals every Christmas time – sometimes even Shakespeare but usually something more frivolous. I can remember how when I was thirteen a professional company of actors arrived from England and performed some Shakespeare plays.

One planter's wife taught me how to paint and I also had occasional lessons from a painting teacher in Basseterre, which was ten times the size of Charlestown with many more professionals in the arts. I usually painted watercolours of the plantations, the Great Houses such as Montpelier, and the bustling life in the markets of Charlestown. I have enjoyed painting ever since.

Despite being motherless I was never lonely. I soon took responsibility for ordering meals in our small household and for supervising the negro servants. We always had a friendly negro major domo with whom I discussed all the daily problems. Perhaps I grew up too quickly.

My father's main preoccupation was of course with his legal work. The Judges circuit court sits in March, again in June, and finally in November. The Court of Summary Jurisdiction sits at Charlestown on the 15 February and every alternate month after that. The Magistrates' Court sits at Charlestown, at Newcastle (the second small town in the north of the island) and at Gingerland, two miles inland from Charlestown. My father had two assistant judges to help him and I asked him once who paid for the legal work. He showed me the schedule of the twenty three different responsibilities for which he earned a fee.

Chief Judges fees – Nevis 1732	L	S	D
For every Declaration Action	0	6	0
For every common action	0	3	0
For every writ of Summons	0	3	0
For every witness sworn in Court	0	1	6
For every Judgement	0	3	0
For every Deposition taken out of Court	0	6	0
For the allowance of a Writ of Error	0	6	0
For taking Bail upon a Writ of Error	0	6	0
For returning the Transcript of a Record under his hand & seal	0	14	0
For every Bail taken in Court or out of Court	0	6	0
For the examination of a Feme-covert	2	0	0
For the Probate of every Deed	0	12	0
For the Probate of a Power of Attorney	0	6	0
For the signing of every Execution	0	3	0
For, taxing a Bill of Costs	0	6	0
For acknowledging Satisfaction of a Judgement of Court	0	6	0
For admission of an Infant by his Guardian	0	14	0
For a Writ of Partition	0	6	0
For every Warrant	0	6	0
For the Commitment of any Person	0	6	0

For the Admission of every Attorney of this Court	2	16	0
For the signing every SCIRE FACIAS	0	3	0
For signing every subpoena	0	6	0

The Chief Justice of the Leeward Islands has his court at Antigua, and my father needed to sail to St. Johns harbour, approximately 30 miles away, about three times a year, and he would spend nearly a week away from Nevis.

In addition he was a trading partner in a Charlestown firm called Herbert, Morton and Woolward, which imported and exported merchandise to England and America. This company's fortunes depended entirely on the size of the sugar crop and the price per hundredweight for sugar cane and hogsheads of rum that the English and American factors would pay. Sometimes the firm flourished, and it provided my father, as junior partner, with some extra income. As an only child I grew up aware of the value of money, and this stood me in good stead in later life.

William Woolward was a tall, good looking man, and everybody told me that my mother had been a pretty woman. I was fortunate enough to inherit her pink and white English rose complexion, delicate hands and her fine grey-blue eyes. From my father I derived brown slightly curly hair and a strong physique. I was always tall for my age, and riding and dancing and long walks (after the sun was down) kept me well and healthy. Nevis was a healthy island – the inhabitants rarely came down with fever. They say the trade winds blow all the fevers away. It was only later in the raw East Anglian climate that my health suffered so much.

Heavy drinking among our small society was prevalent. Besides lime juice and water I usually drank a glass of Canary in the evening and perhaps a glass of cold white wine with my evening meal. My father would down one or two Rum Slings before dinner, and another glass or two of French cognac or Madeira or Port afterwards. He would play a hand of whist and liked playing billiards. There were tables shipped in from England in all the Great Houses and all the men played. One would find mahogany four poster beds, settees and sofas, also in fine mahogany – the only wood to defy the West Indian woodworm. The rooms were full of light cane chairs. There were polished floors of pitch pine, display cabinets filled with bibelots, and tables covered with the latest newspapers and magazines from England. Usually there were reading stands, jars of flowers everywhere, a piano of course, and perhaps a harp. The high ceilinged rooms were designed to look coolly elegant. Some of the more erudite planters also had good libraries – an excellent reason for visiting those families. Outside one would find an immense banyan tree in the centre of the courtyard to give shade, its lower branches almost touching the ground. A flower garden would be planted at the side of the house facing the westerly trade winds. Nevis was a heaven for wild flowers. I exclude the cactus, which was of little use but could be utilised when dried, for fire wood. The flaming hydrangea, rose-shaped Arabian jasmine, pink plumieria, bright yellow acacia, the scarlet trumpet flowers, and the purple and white convolvulus all grew naturally, easily and beautifully.

From the gallery on the second floor, in between the white stone pillars there would be a view of a flotilla of white-sailed fishing boats out to sea, or turtles being sought and speared on the beaches. Every verandah was sited for the best views, and sometimes included the sugar grinding mills, which were a trifle mundane but were the lynchpin of the plantation's fortunes. One could see the blue butterflies flittering among the leaves, and higher up in the giant banyans, see and hear the ringed small monkeys. The houses were set in groves of palm and coconut approached by avenues of tropical trees mixed with red and white cedars.

Some of the Great Houses had marble swimming tanks enclosed by a latticed pavilion to allow the trade winds to circulate. The bedrooms had muslin curtains and the stifling but necessary nets against mosquitoes. The rainy season is the winter of the tropics with storms which turn the earth roads into muddy swamps and block the drains with flash floods. The evening fog and mist is even denser in the rainy season.

The day always starts early in the Caribbean. At dawn a coloured servant would wake me with a cup of tea and I would dress and take a short walk with or without my governess before breakfast. This was served at about half past seven and consisted of a mess of rice and banana plantains with a selection of fruit and coffee. In the middle of the morning I would have a glass of cold pineapple juice and discuss and plan the meals of the day with the cook. By then I would have written a letter or two either for local delivery on the island, or for the next packet to England. I would have practised the pianoforte for nearly an hour, and before a late lunch have painted or finished painting a sketch. There were so many subjects to paint in watercolours. I grew skilled at the still lives inside the house and outside: A large banyan tree or a heap of stones massed in a corner of a sugar cane field (the soil on Nevis is mainly clay and the stones come to the surface, impede the young cane and have to be removed), or a pair of negro huts or a planter's still. I found it much harder to paint the animated negro workers in the fields, or at the village shops. Each time I went by sea to Basseterre, to Mrs. Robinson, the best teacher on St. Kitts, the sloop would pass Booby Island, uninhabited save for the pelican colony called "boobies". With a favourable wind it would take two hours to cover the 12 miles from Charlestown. Basseterre was a large town of 8000 inhabitants, more varied architecturally than Charlestown, and I have since painted it from memory. Our own little port of Charlestown teemed with activities, as fishing boats and sloops and schooners came and went. My father would only allow me to sit and paint there if I was accompanied and sitting in the shade. I went everywhere outside our house with a sunshade or parasol. The Nevis hills, Round Hill in the north and Saddle Hill in the south, were also worth painting, and of course all the Great Houses of Mountravers,

Clifton, Hamilton and Nisbet, and the old Government House, later called 'Queens House'. From parts of the island one had exquisite views of St. Kitts, Montserrat, St. Eustatius and Saba. On a clear day – and most days were clear – one could see for ever, and listen to and feel the gentle Trade wind.

From a very tender age the church 'parade' of finery compelled me to dress well, and elegance was a pre-requisite for the belles of Nevis. The coloured worshippers – the trades people and the estate servants of the village – aped the whites in every respect, apart from the choice of colours. We preferred gentle pastel shades; they preferred the primal colours, and who's to say who looked the best? We wore enormous crinolines and bonnets and so did they. We wore real jewelry, they wore false jewellery and coloured swinging bead necklaces. They wore cotton lace and fringe, ribbons streaming from every ample curve, and gaudy shoes. The black men wore smart coats, flowered waistcoats, ruffled neckcloths, tight white trousers and pointed uncomfortable boots a size too small. The bucks and the dandies outdid each other in splendour.

Outside the church would be found the curricles, the phaetons, the gigs, the britzskas, the barouches and the family chaises bringing the planters' families to worship. On a Sunday the small island's dusty roads teemed with the smart carriages going to church, returning from church, going to late luncheons with other planters' families, back for the mid-afternoon siesta and probably out again in the evening.

For very smart social affairs – a large wedding or reception for a visiting dignitary – the military band of St. Kitts would be ferried over from Basseterre by sloop in their smart, tight, and very hot uniforms to play marches and occasion music for dancing. For an evening dance I would wear a skirt of pink satin, flounces of lace, with rosettes on the front, puffed tight sleeves, a corsage of white 'illustion', pink bands with flowers and rosettes. A wreath of pink rosebuds on my head and a best point-lace shawl completed the ensemble. But I could not be seen too often in *that* outfit, so next time it would be a green taffeta, flowing open in front over a white embroidered muslin slip, trimmed with a white fringe. With this I wore a long sash with fringed ends and a white crêpe scarf fringed with green to match the taffeta. Finally I placed an elegant golden fillet on my head. After all, my father had no one else on whom to spend his Judge's dues! There would be round and square dances, alternating with country dances. I think our fashions were much behind those of 'ton' and taste in London. Towards the end of the century when Nevis was a very smart place, the London dances in vogue arrived with the visitors from the London Court. Anyway our young bearded bloods were never great dancers. They seemed to prefer their cognac and hand of cards.

During my first twenty years of Island Paradise – of sheer beautiful self indulgence, beautiful clothes, the admiration of the young bucks and dandies, the minor responsibilities of growing up, of education and the arts – there were few discordant sounds. An occasional duel occurred over cards or too much drink. From time to time there was alarm if a conspiracy of the black slaves was discovered, and this disturbed the peaceful equilibrium, but was always without foundation. The threat of a French invasion was realised several times during the century. But always each year there loomed the possibility of a hurricane and tidal wave. The destruction of Jamestown and of the sugarcane crops was always present in the minds of everyone as the 1st of August drew near.

I was eleven when the terrible hurricane of 1772 struck the islands. Initially the low clouds in the west changed and came scudding over Nevis, and the sea had a strong sullen swell. The wind was so strong that ships in the harbour at anchor and those still unwise enough to be offshore, were driven ashore onto the beaches and rocks. By 9 a.m. on the morning of the 28 July, having had a distracted night, the flood gates of heaven opened and torrential rain fell. We could hear the crash of falling buildings and even the tumbling of stone walls. My father made our small household go down to the cellar clutching our most precious possessions. Timbers of our roof and many others were seized by the wind gusts and carried aloft. We could hear shrieks from the straw native huts, which were the most vulnerable. At half past one there was an earthquake. It is very frightening when you feel the earth move beneath your feet and the whole building quiver. People walking had their cloaks, even their clothes, stripped off their backs and hail stones as big as walnuts bombarded the shelterless. Most estates considered the Rum Cellars and the Molasses Cisterns the safest places of refuge, but some adults and small children were drowned in cellars as torrential rain poured in on top of them. Several other people were killed by falling houses including 20 negroes. Innumerable cattle were killed or blown off cliff tops. One estate manager was snatched by the wind and tossed into the middle of his mule pen, where he stood for two hours in mud and water being knocked about by flying debris. Horse carriages were carried hundreds of yards by the wind. Large tamarind trees were uprooted and hogsheads of sugar were tossed like pancakes into the air. The hurricane was followed by several more earthquakes, luckily quite mild, as the damage done already was hardly believable. The loss of lives, of houses, of ships and cargoes was disastrous. Above all, our precious sugarcane fields were ripped to pieces and then flattened by hail and rain storm. We suffered from the appalling damage for twelve months afterwards.

I was born a restless girl, never able to stay in the same place for any length of time. On Nevis I was for ever organising picnics under the fine old baobab trees covered with "old mans beard" – and excursions to the furthest parts of the island. We would go to the Morning Star estate near Fig Tree, where the estate garrison defeated the French invasion at the turn of the century in a dawn attack (hence the name). We visited the other two little harbours, Indian Castle near St. Georges port in the south east, and New Castle in the north, near the great Nisbet plantations. The banyan and baobab tree groves were favourite places for picnics. So too were the Stone Hill rain reservoir above Gingerland and Saddle Hill Peak and Battery, where our gallant militia defended us from the French, a mile on foot or horseback from Gingerland.

Excursions to St. Kitts or Montserrat or St. Eustatius were easy to arrange. My father's name provided the sea passage and there were relatives or friends to stay with everywhere I went. The boat voyages provided marvellous sights. The sailors would point out the bonita, barracuda, occasional shark and, in the still waters of the Caribbean, just occasionally one could see a huge spotted grouper, frigate man of war, or corvally. The fisherman however wanted to catch Spanish mackerel or tarpon. Flying fish would play ducks and drakes, and along the shore a sleepy turtle would be basking near the water's edge. During the stormy weather months – July to November – the migratory birds, herons and cranes, would come across the Narrows to Nevis. The local birds were golden plover and occasional duck, the Ramier pigeon, waterfowl, quail, and Mountain wood dove, all much in demand for pies. Coots, kites, the killy-killy hawk, the banana bird, the kingfisher, and the delightful humming bird were all to be seen flying in my Paradise.

The menfolk would organise rough shooting for the pot between November and February – teal, white throat, canvas back and the whistling duck. Since they were all members of the local Militia they were meant to be skilled with the use of their firearms! The seabirds were beautiful but inedible – the pelican gulls, terns, and the blackheaded gull called the laughing bird. At dawn and at dusk the birdsong by the shore or on the edges of the rain forest at the foot of Nevis Peak was of great beauty and variety. The natural fruits were superb too. I remember the little boys scrambling up the tall thin smooth coconut trees and shaking down the delicious green fruit. They or their parents would make green wine from the nuts and we would drink the cool fresh cloudy liquid. There were pomegranates and passion fruit and granadillas, from which one could make thirst-quenching iced drinks. We drank lime juice frequently for our health and because it was such a delectable long drink.

One forgot the minor discomfort of life: the grey and black rats, the bats, the caterpillar ants in the bed, the landcrabs scuttling into the house, the horrible buzzing mosquitoes at night, the whistling frogs and the crickets. Luckily there were no dangerous snakes and few scorpions. Coffee and rolls and a plate of delicious fruits at 6 a.m – brought by sweet, grinning, barefooted black maids with names like Hannah and Betsy – woke one up to Paradise. We never lacked for variety of diet. The freshwater fish were superb – red mullet, millions, crayfish, edible goldfish, even mudfish. And our cook did wonders with lobsters, whelks, sea crab and the land crabs. An occasional turtle, green or Hawksbill or the Huckerback – much endangered as a species because they were so tasty and so easy to catch – came to the table.

I must describe some of the culinary delights that Nevis island and our clever mulatto cooks produced for the planter families. The local avocado pear was made into a puree, or a soup, or baked with vinaigrette sauce, or braised with salad oil, salt, peppercorns and onions, or better still, stuffed with creamed shrimps baked in a slow oven. Aubergine soup we made with milk, or stuffed them with minced meat and ate them as a main course. Turtle eggs made an excellent pie, and turtle parmesan was also popular. Lobsters were broiled and eaten with a crayfish sauce or with a devilled sauce, with white wine added and then baked. A crab dish was made with spinach, some lumps of cream cheese cubed and fried bread. A great delicacy was a 6-week-old sucking pig stuffed with corn, bacon, thyme and parsley, baked in a hot oven and basted with olive oil. Another dish was called pixilated pork, a leg of young pig, stuck with cloves and garlic and roasted, then casseroled – delicious! – with spices and white wine. White sea urchins were cooked with lime juice and cayenne pepper and served on brown bread. Turtle stew was made of their fins with rum, lime, onions, green peppers, young pawpaw and hot sauce added, then casseroled. Another way of cooking turtle was to cut the main body into strips and rub them with rum and lime and cook like a real steak.

We improvised with all the local fish, such as snapper and dolphin, crustaceans and semi-wild meats, never with domestic cattle or sheep, so that a beef steak or mutton chop was comparatively rare, but occasional goat waterstew was served. Our black cooks showed natural ingenuity in blending the tasty herbs and spices together. The only luxury was the addition of wine, which had to travel thousands of miles to reach us. The rum, molasses and lime juice of course cost us practically nothing. The crops such as maize, eddoes, yams, cassava and banana-plantains all grew quickly and without much effort. Certain vegetables grew well on Nevis soil – green papaya, pumpkins for soup or stuffed with meat or made into fritters, and breadfruit were popular with the Creoles and with the negro workers on the plantations. Hot pepper sauce was used to accompany either meat or fish dishes. So too was Creole Sauce, a hot blend of tomatoes, lime juice, sweet peppers, onions and seasonings.

We lunched at two p.m., usually quite formally with 3 or 4 courses and a glass of wine and afterwards we were quite ready for a siesta. We read or took a light nap until four p.m. when we would drink a dish of tea in the sitting room, then take a stroll afterwards or a drive in a phaeton with one of my 'beaux' – a leader of 'ton' in our society – vying with each other to take me out and make an impression! For the drive I would have dressed again – one dressed and re-dressed two or three times a day. I wore a white Indian muslin ruffled to the waist sweeping the ground, with wide skirts stretched over a hoop. The bodice, long and tight, exposed my neck, which was then covered with a white silk scarf. My second best bonnet, trimmed either with lilac flowers or feathers, the scoop filled with blonde and mull, was tied under the chin with lilac ribbons. My waist would be encircled by a lilac sash of soft India silk. I wore gloves of course, not too long, in case I had a chance of taking charge of the horse pulling the phaeton.

I remember the typical West Indian post-siesta afternoons on Nevis. The young girls would be reading *Journal des Modes* or dabbling in water colours. An embroidery frame or two would be in evidence. The young men in their jackets and suits with high collar and small necktie would be reading the Racing Calendar (there were races in Basseterre), playing whist or loo, or reading aloud to one or two of the elderly ladies, or holding their knitting wool. The belles and

Nevis. The peak is in the background.

their swains would be flirting in the corners of the room, and the dowagers with fan and smelling salts would be observing them.

That is how I remember my early life on Nevis. The silvery groves of lime trees, the fields of yellow cane. The Great Houses set in their copses. A royal palm on a splendid shining shaft rising to a great height. The spires of churches rising from their romantic nooks, their heavy stone tombs lost in the tangle of palms. The humming birds darting about, living enamel set with jewels. The occasional parrot or macaw, the monkey chatter and the little birds swooping and settling. And always the deep collar of evergreen trees encircling the mountain cone of Nevis.

Paradise indeed.

CHAPTER TWO

PLANTERS, SUGAR AND SLAVES

The economy of Nevis is entirely dependent on the sugar plantations which produce the revenue by the sale of sugar and molasses in hogsheads, distilled rum in puncheons, and lemons, mainly to England and usually through the ports of Bristol and London. The West Indian Society of traders in Bristol with their smart houses in Clifton and Bath, is the central spider and controls the web of small islands in the Caribbean – Nevis, St. Kitts, Antigua, Montserrat and many others.

The Island of Nevis has rarely had more than 1000 white occupants and up to eight times that amount of black slaves and servants. A white family with 2 or 3 children might have between 7 and 14 household black servants. Each would cost about £8 per annum to feed, clothe and maintain. The plantation workers would cost another £7 per annum in land allotment costs, allowances and free molasses. In the year I married for the second time there were 4000 slaves engaged in cultivation of the 300 plantation estates, and another 1500 working in domestic service, as tradesmen, porters, boatmen, or as fishermen. The common field negroes earned £5-8 per annum and the artisans between £8 and £20 a year. The freed coloured classes worked as tradesmen, hucksters, cooks, nurses, sempstresses, grooms, footmen, boilermen, blacksmiths etc.

The field negroes were given allotments to grow basic provisions including fruits and vegetables, to keep goats, hogs and poultry, which they could either eat (to supplement their basic diet) or sell for their own account. They could also sell grass for fodder and firewood. They were paid for Sunday working and allowed per head per week 4-9 pints of flour, corn, peas or beans and 4-8 herrings or other salted fish. They were given free clothing – a blanket, jacket and trousers for men, and a blanket, wrapper and petticoat for women, or 1 suit of woollen and 1 suit of Osnaburghs annually. Infants were given half the adult allowance, and skilled plantation artisans, such as millwrights, masons, carpenters, coopers, and boilermen got a double allowance.

Medical care was free and an allowance was made by each plantation manager of 6/- per head per annum to the Doctor, paid in cash, sugar, or rum! Each estate would have a hospital or 'hothouse' for the care of the sick, although the negroes from the African tribe of Myal cured their sicknesses with herbs and plants.

House slaves were paid three bits per week instead of food from their masters' tables, although most of them obtained both!

The plantation workers built their own houses quite simply and quickly. About a dozen strong sticks or posts were placed firmly in the ground in a circle and were plastered with mud bricks, wattle and thatch to form the roof and sides; certainly sufficient to keep out the rain and withstand the wind, but not of course a hurricane.

It was impossible for anyone brought up on Nevis to realise what a slaveless society is like. The Caribbean economy is based almost entirely on sugar, molasses and rum, which need low cost labour in order to sell the crops for a reasonable price in England and elsewhere. Apart from the Huggins family, who have always treated their slaves abominably (but also have the most efficient estates), the other main planters have always had a reputation for treating their negro workforce fairly – certainly on Nevis.

Once I asked my father and Uncle Herbert to explain to me the finances of a typical estate. I suppose that says something about my character, but being in charge of my father's household from a very early age had made me conscious of income and expenditure! They told me that a good sized plantation would be of 300 acres. Near Charlestown that meant Hamilton (570 acres), the Tobias estate of Stoney Grove (340); in St. Thomas lowland, the Pinneys and Clerkes had Tower Hill (761) but poor production, also Spring Hill (585), Clifton (548) and Paradise of course (300). St. James Windward had the largest on the island, Maddens (1028), Round Hill (980) and Hicks (646). St. Georges Gingerland had Valley (489), Indian Castle (396) and Symonds/Terrain (368) run again by the Pinneys. St. Johns Brown Hill had Low Ground (491) and the Morning Star group of Cane Garden (338) and Dunbars (330). The Herberts had several small estates including Montpelier. The Nisbets had several too, including Mount Pleasant and Nisbett, and the Webbes owned Winter Forest and others.

Nevis had 4,000 acres of sugar cane under cultivation out of 10,000 acres of farming land and usually produced a hogshead of 16 cwt per acre per annum. They both agreed on those figures. Only 40 estates employed about 100 slaves and a further 60 about 50 slaves. The remaining 200 plantations employ about 5 slaves each.

The capital cost of a 300 acre sugar estate was then, in 1787, about £26,000. The sugar mill and coppers cost £8,000; 140 slaves £6,000; 40 good mules, 100 oxen, good grass pen, another £3,000. The original 300 acres would cost, if one was lucky, £30 per acre, or £9,000. The running costs for food, clothing, plantation implements, would be about £800 p.a. and assuming the whole amount of £26,000 was mortgaged at 8% (the current rate) then the annual costs together were about £3,900 a year. The average crop of 160 hogshead of good Muscovado sugar at £15, plus 80 puncheons of rum at £12 each would produce nearly £3,400 p.a. leaving a theoretical balance of £500 a year to offset the perils of rain, drought, hurricanes, a French invasion or wild fluctuations in the trade price of sugar.

For instance in the terrible drought year of 1778 Antigua lost 1,000 negroes, Montserrat 1,200, St. Kitts 400 and little Nevis 350 from want of provisions. The plantations had been ruined by the damage and there was literally no crop and no income, and all the islands were on semi-starvation rations until the sugar cane crop grew again. The following year too, English and American merchants were refusing credit for the provisions needed by the plantations. The bad years were 1772, 1778, 1779 and 1792, when I was in England. The combination of hurricane followed by a drought could almost literally bankrupt the island.

But war was as great a danger as nature to my little Paradise. In 1774, when I was thirteen, we were dependent on American supplies of staples – biscuits, wheat, flour, rice and Indian corn. The Revolution of 1776 disrupted our trade, and for several years we had to pay high prices for staples and plantation supplies, building timber, slaves and animals. Small privateers brought secret supplies from America and we smuggled goods in from Dutch-owned St. Eustatius. There were five ships, each of about 250 tons, with a crew of a dozen, who took our sugar and rum to Bristol and London and brought staples (and luxuries such as wine and cheese) back to the island. They could accept a few passengers and the Captain would charge them £6 each for 'ships share' i.e., food and passage. My cousin George Webbe owned the *Gallant Schemer*, and another cousin James Tobin had a share in one or more of the others – the *Betsy*, *King David*, the *Edward* and the *Nevis*.

Antigua and St Kitts had a much greater sugar production than little Nevis. They had 300 slaves to the square mile and we had only 200, partly due to our poorer soil. St. Kitts had 16,000 slaves to work their 11,000 acres of cane. New African slaves were sold at £70 for men and slightly less for women, but seasoned slaves, who were bred on the island, fetched higher prices. Ordinary plantation slaves sold at prices between £80-£125 for men and £70-£110 for women. Nevis had usually 5 female slaves for every four males. Children and old people made up more than one third of the slave population and the infant mortality was usually as high as half. This sounds a depressing and sad figure but it is roughly the same as for the white population in England. Thomas Williams, the manager of the Pinney estate of Saddle Hill, in his will left me a curious bequest 'Item, I give and bequeath unto Fanny Woolward for ever daughter of William Woolward, a Negro Man called Cato'. This was when I was about ten years of age, and good Cato helped look after me for many years afterwards. Thomas Williams was Aunt Elizabeth Herbert's brother.

The efficient plantation manager kept his workforce fully employed throughout the year. The creole cane matured 15 months after planting and the land lay fallow for 6 months between crops and was manured by cattle droppings. The cycle of planting and harvest overlapped with fallowing, so that the mill was furnished with rope cane in manageable quantities. The mill grinding lasted for 6-7 months, spread over each harvest. The new crop was planted between August and February and the harvest of last year's crop was then made between January and July in the following year.

Usually there were two main working gangs – able-bodied slaves who did the heavy work, and the weeding gang which included younger slaves about 12 years of age, and those less fit. They were mustered at dawn and worked until 9 a.m. when they had an hour for breakfast, then they worked until mid-day. There would be a break of one or one and a half hours before the afternoon spell, which went on until half an hour before sunset. Since grass fuelled the mills, grass picking was essential in the grinding season, so that a ten hour workday for six days a week was usual. But on Saturday nights hundreds of negroes of all ages danced and sang throughout the darkness. Their skill at making music was incredible. A hollow sugar cane or bamboo with holes pierced in it made an imitation fife: a herring barrel or tub covered with a sheepskin made an excellent drum and was called a 'gumbay'. Funerals, weddings and anniversaries were celebrated with a grand ball to music from a violin and tabret. Plantation suppers were superb, with ingredients such as poultry, salt beef, pork, herrings and vegetables with roasted, barbecued or fricasseed rats! I can hear their favourite song to this day, sung interminably through the night,

> Hiphaw! my deaa! you no do like a-me!
> You no jig like a-me! you no twist like a-me!
> Hiphaw! my deaa! you no shake like a-me!
> You no wind like a-me! Go, Yondaa!
> Hiphaw!
> Hiphaw! my deaa! you no jig like a-me!
> You no work him like a-me! You no sweet him like a-me!

This was sung by happy plantation slaves called Mingo, Daphne, Fatima, Fortuna, Chocolate, Scipio and Gingo. My black servants, besides Josiah's mulatto Nanny, were called Black Hannah, Romeo, Mary, and of course Cato.

The creoles of 'The Queen of the Caribees' were composed of about 300 families, and as most of them had been there for a century or more, and white immigrants were rare, the result was that most families were interconnected by marriage.

My family, the Woolwards, were an East Anglian family from near Bury St. Edmunds, of good minor gentry stock. They produced many Rectors and Parsons, usually went to school at Eton College, and became scholars at Kings College, Cambridge. My father told me that a John Woolward was a landowner at Bersted, near Bognor in Sussex, in 1250. Another of the same name was Canon of Windsor. Some of the family became sailors – such as my grandfather William, who came to Nevis very early at the beginning of this century, and his grandson, my first cousin John Woolward of Ramsgate, who became a Commander in the Royal Navy. By marriage we were related to the great merchant family of Manning from whom my brother received his second name. William Manning was one of the most eminent of West India companies with estates in St. Kitts and Nevis. More recently we have become connected with the Herberts, perhaps the most influential family on the island. The family vault at St. George's church, Gingerland, houses the tomb of Edward Herbert of Bristol, buried there in 1724, a merchant who owned ships, plantations and storehouses on Montserrat and Nevis. The Herberts were a Welsh family connected with the Earls of Pembroke. Joseph Herbert was chief Justice of Nevis in 1754 (and was succeeded by my father) and he was grandfather of another Joseph Herbert who became President of the Island. John Richardson Herbert, the present President, is my uncle, as his sister Mary married my father. I have two other Herbert Aunts; Sally who married Magnus Morton, a Judge on Nevis and a colleague of my father's, (their daughter Sally, my cousin, married Captain William Hancock Kelly, who later became a Vice Admiral of the Blue); the other Aunt, Sarah Herbert, never married and kept house for her brother until she died. Uncle Herbert's wife was Elisabeth Williams, whom he married at St. George's Chapel, Mayfair on 3 October 1752. They only had one child, Martha Williams, who later married Andrew Hamilton of Nevis. Both the Williams and the Hamiltons were predictably sugar plantation owners – the Williams on St. Croix and the Hamiltons on Nevis. Uncle Herbert's wife died when I was eight and he has rarely been on good terms with Martha, his daughter. He seemed to prefer his nieces – myself and Parry Herbert (also niece to David Parry, Governor of Barbados). My Uncle was a character and known variously as 'Governor Herbert', 'The Governor', the 'President', or occasionally as 'Mr. H.' He responded nicely to the wiles and charms of his pretty nieces, although in business affairs he was a dominant and successful man. Besides his government stipend he received revenues from two sugar estates and from the trading partnership with my father and Magnus Morton – so that he was possibly the richest man on the island. Certainly Montpelier was the largest and best furnished 'Great House' on the island when I knew it: it has been owned by three generations of Herberts, for over a century.

By my first marriage to Josiah Nisbet, the family doctor to the Woolwards and Herberts, I became closely knit to two other families who had intermarried, the Tobins and the Webbes. All three were plantation owners on Nevis and had trading interests and houses in England. My very good friend Mrs. Fanny Francklyn, who was Josiah's cousin, was born a Webbe.

The Nisbets claimed they were descendants from the Kings of Scotland! Josiah's grandfather Alexander Nisbet married Emilia, daughter of Archibald Douglas, a naval officer, who was fourth son of Francis 7th Earl of Moray – who in turn was 6th in descent from the Regent Moray, son of James V, King of Scotland! Josiah's father, Colonel Walter Nisbet, owned Mount Pleasant plantation, eight miles north of Charlestown on the windward side of the island, and several others including Theds Bay and New Castle altogether about 600 acres. He was a Member of the Council of Nevis. He married Mary, daughter of Josiah Webbe of New River estate and they had five children. The eldest was Walter who was born in 1745 and first married a young widow in 1776 and then Anne Parry in 1784 by whom he had two sons and a daughter. Then came Anne Nisbet, who never married, my Josiah born 7 August 1747, Mary Emilia, who married James Sinclair Lockhart in 1773, and finally James Webb Nisbet born in 1749 who, like his sister Anne, never married.

When Josiah's father died in 1765 he left all the estate to the eldest son Walter, £1,000 each to Josiah and James and £1,500 each to Anne and Mary Emilia. Traditionally the younger sons had to make their own way in life. James was an Assemblyman under Uncle Herbert when Nevis surrendered to the French in 1782, and John Pinney and James Tobin were Nevis Councillors at the time!

The James Tobin family were lifelong friends of the considerable Pinney family of

Bristol, and indeed traded as Pinney and Tobin for twenty years. The Tobins boasted an admiral, a general and a playwright in their family. James Webbe Tobin and his father James were both pamphleteers and thus circulated their views – on slavery amongst other subjects. On Nevis they owned the Stoney Grove Plantation, 340 acres but it was long and narrow and did not have much pastureland. The Tobins owned a house in Endless Street in Salisbury where young John Tobin was born in 1770.

Many many years later I caused a mural plaque to be erected on the right side of the altar in St. John's Church, Figtree on Nevis which linked my three families of Woolward, Herbert and Nisbet sadly – with a fourth family.

William Woolward Esq. of this Island, died Feb 18th 1779. He married Mary, the daughter of Thomas Herbert Esq. to whose joint memory this tablet is erected by their only daughter Frances Herbert who was first married to Josiah Nisbet M.D. and since to Rear Admiral Nelson who for his very distinguished services has been successively created a Knight of the Bath and a Peer of Great Britain by the title of Baron Nelson of the Nile.

Nelson as a rear-admiral painted by Lemuel Abbot in November 1800.

CHAPTER THREE

PARADISE LOST –
DEATHS IN THE FAMILY

In the New Year of 1779 my poor father suffered a minor cut or abrasion on the side of his neck which became infected. A few days later he developed lockjaw. My future husband, Josiah Nisbet, was our family doctor at the time. He did everything he could, but my father died in agony on 18 February, aged only 53. The end was dreadful as he was not able to open his mouth, and thus literally died of starvation. He and I had been together for nearly 20 years and our relationship had been close and loving, so I was very sad to see him buried at St. John's Church.

My father left a will dated 5 November 1778 in which he left £100 to his brother Thomas in England, the residue to me, plus the benefit of his partnership in Herbert, Morton and Woolward. The will was sworn on 20 May 1779 and Administration was granted to the firm's creditors. My uncle explained that the trading firm had no liquid assets of any consequence which were not tied up in trade goods etc.

My brother William was then a Scholar at Caius College Cambridge and could not come to the funeral, so my only near relative on the island was my Uncle, John Richardson Herbert, the President of Nevis. He was the most influential and probably the richest man on the island and with him I went to live. He always treated me most generously.

During my father's lifetime I had promised him not to marry anyone of whom he disapproved. After his death my Uncle took the view that although he had now adopted me he could not really forbid my marriage unless it was obviously unsuitable. I had had innumerable beaux since the age of seventeen, not only from Nevis but from the neighbouring islands as well, as, modesty apart, it was considered that I was possibly the prettiest and the best educated of the young 'Misses'.

Young Daniel Ross was the nephew of Mr. Hercules Ross. That patriotic merchant of Jamaica had sent his slaves to man the batteries of Fort Charles, Port Royal when the French under Admiral D'Estaing were expected. Daniel spent some of his time as a merchant on the little island of St. Eustatius which was partly English, partly Dutch. He dealt in all the commodities which the island planters needed – wood, fine muslins, board, wines, even fine English double Gloucester cheese, which was very well regarded on the islands. He was a nice, lively young man with considerable prospects, and marriage to him would probably have meant living on Jamaica. My father thought highly of him, and if he had lived I would probably have married Daniel and my future life would have been very different. Curiously enough the Rosses were related to Josiah. Hercules Ross had married a Miss Parish. Her brothers James and Edward were planters on Nevis, and came from a good family in Aberdeen, although a branch of the family lived in Hamburg. The Parish family as well as the Rosses were related by marriage to the large Nisbet family.

My heart was given to strong, handsome Josiah. He was older than I and had been educated at Edinburgh University. He had studied medicine under William Robertson SSTP and as 'ex India Occidentali' wrote a 32 page thesis in 1768 for his medical doctorate. Professor Cullen MD was his tutor and Josiah dedicated the thesis to him. It was published as *Dissertatio Medica in Auguralis de Rheumatismo Acuto*. It was published by Balfour, Aud and Smellie 'pro gradu Doctoris'. Josiah's doctorate was awarded him by John Gregory MD and Alexander Baron SPD.

Josiah then became an Apothecary at Coventry for a year or two and returned to Nevis in 1771. As the second son he had no hand in running the large family plantations, which was Walter Nisbet's responsibility. On our small island the non-planters often had two or more activities. For instance my father, besides being a judge, was a trader with two other merchants. He was also a surveyor. Once in 1767 [9 June] he surveyed the estate of Mr. R. Coker for probate. The Parson, the Rev. William Jones, who was paid his stipend in sugar, perforce had to trade in sugar with Mr. John Pinney in Bristol in order to earn payments in cash or goods.

Josiah, besides being a good doctor was one of the official Receivers for estates that were wound up or needed valuations. He was an Arbitrator with Morton and Hodgzard. In 1776 Josiah was called in by Mr. John Stanley, the King's legal representative for the Islands, to resolve a trade dispute between Mills and Swarston and a planter called Mr. Thomson. It was his responsibility to adjust the Accounts and arbitrate between the various parties, for which he charged a bill of £120. In 1777 he was responsible for purchasing six mules for Mr. Joseph Williams' estate against payment by bill of exchange of £156.

Josiah had studied rheumatism for his Doctorate because of his previous experience of the therapeutical values our hot mineral water springs on Nevis provided for sufferers. His knowledge of Botany stood him in good stead on the island. He discovered that shrubs called the Horse Nicker and the Ringworm bush provided cures for ringworm, that casuarina shrub cured dysentery, as did Fat Pork roots and leaves: purging cassia was a laxative, as was the syrup of the tamarind bush. The fitweed shrub provided a good native medicinal tonic. He was forever prowling round the sand dunes looking for seagrape on the shore, and exploring the white mangrove swamps growing in the salt meadows, looking for shrubs called Womens tongues, Allamanda, wild orchids, avoids, aloes and bromeliads. He would come back with posies of wild flowers for me and shrub leaves for his own medicinal concoctions.

Besides his dual income from being a Doctor and Receiver/ Arbitrator Josiah had been left £1,000 on the death of his father. He might also in due course have had some small expectations in the considerable Nisbet estates.

At the time I was not aware that the subject of my choice of suitor was arousing much excitement on the island! John Pinney wrote to Robert Robertson Jones in Bristol on 30 June 1779

> There has been a great contest between Dr. Nisbet and [Daniel] Ross to gain the affections of Fanny Woolward – she always gave a preference to the former, the Father warmly espoused the cause of the latter. Considerable bets have been laid. Stocks have occasionally rose and fallen. Words dropt by the young lady and her assurance to her Father that she would not marry contrary to his wishes have frequently changed the opinions of people who were not in the secret – she certainly gave Mr. Archibald great cause to believe she would be decided in favour of Ross which induced him to lay George Webbe 100 Guineas amongst other bets: all of which he will now lose as the young lady since her Fathers death ... hath discarded Ross and declared in favour of Nisbet who are to be married very soon which I believe will not be very pleasing to my friend Walter [Nisbet] ... Ross has been extremely unfortunate lately and has suffered great hardships. He went up to St. Lucia in a Dutch flag of truce with an address from this island [Nevis] to Admiral Barrington and Governor Grant. On the way home landed at Dominica was seized and carried off to Martinique. James Nisbet sticks close to the eldest Miss Wharton ...

So I married my first true love – Dr. Josiah Nisbet at St. John's Church, Figtree on 28 June 1779, and was given away by my Uncle Herbert in a ceremony attended by all the white families and many of the negro families on the island. The service was performed by the Rev. William Jones and a superb reception was held at the Great House of Montpelier.

Fig Tree Church, Nevis, where Horatio Nelson and Francis Herbert Nisbet were married.

We were ecstatically happy in every possible way for many months, until towards the end of the year Josiah started to behave rather strangely, and suffered from delusions and fevers. I consulted Mr. Archibald, who at one point thought that Josiah was suffering from Yellow Fever. Josiah himself in his more lucid moments diagnosed a severe attack of sunstroke, which was a possibility since he spent much time outside on horseback visiting patients, or in his forays on to the beaches and into the swamps in search of natural medicines. I thought perhaps that he had taken a toxic dose of one of the many shrubs. For instance the Manchineal trees which grow along the banks of the Bath stream are known to be poisonous, as rain dripping from them scalds the grass and is known as 'dew from the trees'. I believe he had been making experiments with these dangerous concoctions and had poisoned his system.

His condition failed to improve and after consultation with Uncle Herbert, Walter Nisbet and Dr. Archibald, we decided to take ship for England for other medical opinions and for the benefit of its milder climate.

The West Indian planters have owned houses in Bristol, Clifton, Bath and Salisbury for many generations. The Nisbet family were living either at Camalthan House near Glasgow (Josiah's sister Mary Emilia had married James Lockhart) or in Kirkby, Overcar, Yorkshire. Josiah hoped to continue his practice as a doctor and to utilise his commercial experience and when we were asked to stay in Salisbury, Wiltshire we accepted that kind offer. Josiah's mother was born Mary Webbe, and her brother George Webbe and his wife asked us to live with them in Salisbury. George Webbe had married an heiress, a Miss Windham, with a fortune of £105,000 and the Manor House, Stratford-sub-Castra. John and James Tobin's mother was also a Webbe and the Tobins lived in a house in Endless Street in Salisbury. Moreover Uncle Herbert had a property near the Cathedral Close called Sherborne House, and the hospitable Pinneys who lived near Bristol also offered us shelter.

Josiah and I sadly took sail for Plymouth and were greeted with much affection and sympathy on our arrival in Salisbury. The George Webbe family made us very welcome, not only for poor Josiah's sake but because now I was distinctly 'enceinte'.

Little Josiah was born in Salisbury in May 1780. Our hosts had just lost their eldest son Joseph who had died the year before aged 27 and was buried in Salisbury. Our arrival helped take their minds off their sad loss and when my small son was born it was for them a happy distraction. The birth however was not easy and the local doctor and my husband warned me that future births might be difficult.

For a while we were happy again. The cool spring rain appeared to benefit my husband, although the local doctors could offer no reassurance of any kind. We made plans to send young Josiah to Mr. Butt who ran a famous school in Salisbury for small children. We talked to James Tobin who wrote Essays and Tracts on the treatment of slaves in the West Indies which had a wide circulation. The prosperity of the islands depended on the slave trade, which I believed to be immoral, and from which my Uncle, and my husband's family, my hosts all derived their comfortable living.

The West Indians were always generous and I remember one particular occasion. A poor old Count William was lodged in Salisbury gaol for a debt of his son John. Mrs. Webbe gave him £20 for proper clothes and George Webbe asked all his friends, John Richardson Herbert, my Uncle, John Pinney, John Stanley and Walter Nisbet to subscribe money – which they all did – to get the old man out of prison.

Looking after my sweet little infant son so pre-occupied me that I failed to realise that my husband's health was deteriorating. On the 5 October 1781 he died in his sleep aged only 34. It seemed unfair of my Maker to take away so abruptly from this life my young strong husband, on whom I and his son so completely depended. Our house in the Cathedral Close was dark and sad around its despondent occupiers. At the funeral the church was packed with our friends and family – Nisbets, Webbs, Tobins, Pinneys, all came to pay their tributes and last respects. I caused a tablet made of marble to be placed on the south wall of the chancel of St. Lawrence Church in Stratford sub Castra,

> Josiah Nisbet/of the Island of Nevis/Born 7th Augst 1747, died 5th Octr 1781/
> This monument was erected to his memory by his affectionate wife Frances
> Nisbet."

The Nisbet coat of arms was painted over the top of the memorial 'Vis Fortibus Arma' with a boar's head with tusks.

The *Salisbury Journal* carried this pathetic notice on 15th July,

CLOSE of SALISBURY

> To be SOLD by AUCTION, by C. LONG on Tuesday the 16th July instant (1782) and following day. All the neat Mahogany and other FURNITURE, some curious China jars and other china, bedsteads, beds and bedding, a well-toned harpsichord in a neat mahogany case etc., etc. of Dr. NESBIT, deceased. The sale to begin each morning at half past ten o'clock. The goods to be viewed Monday preceding the sale and Catalogues to be had at the place of sale at the principal inns and of the Auctioneer in Salisbury.

Josiah died intestate and John Burke, Crown lawyer for the Leeward Islands, decided the estate could only be settled by Chancery.

To compound our problems the French navy had seized St. Kitts after the garrison of 600 soldiers under General Fraser and 350 militia had fought nobly at Brimston Hill. They surrendered on 8 February 1782 and St. Kitts was yielded to Count Dillon by Governor Sir Thomas Shirley. The French war had started the year before my father died, and Nevis underwent great miseries for five years with soaring prices. My Uncle Herbert, as President, the two Nisbet brothers, James and Richard, and John Pinney, as Assemblymen, negotiated a separate surrender to Admiral de Grasse. It was at Ward Estate near St. Paul's, Charlestown, that he received the contributions levied on the island. The Marquis de Bouillé became the French Gouverneur, and Admiral de Grasse had his headquarters at Bath Plain.

During 1782 and 1783 – until the Treaty of Versailles was signed, my many friends and relatives were virtually prisoners on the island, although the French invaders behaved most correctly. Not only was trade much diminished with Bristol and London, but also remittances from the island were non-existent. Josiah's estate on the island was frozen and Mr. John Stanley, the Receiver, could do little to help me or my little son. I arranged with kind John Pinney to draw on George Webbe or Walter Nisbet's account. For instance when I was in London on 13 September 1783 John Pinney recorded 'I have paid Mrs. Nisbet on your a/c £20 and the remainder on her application.' My brother-in-law James Nisbet, then on Nevis, planned to leave when Walter returned to the island with his new bride. He was in Grafton Street, London at the time and duly married Miss Ann Parry, daughter of the Governor of Barbados in April 1784. His first marriage had been disastrous. His wife disappeared suddenly and ran away with another man. Walter was fortunate that his two younger brothers James and Richard could run the large estates in his absence. They were in partnership with Mr. Joseph Gill and had trading connections with our brother-in-law James Lockhart in Glasgow.

Mr. and Mrs. John Pinney of Nevis had sent their elder children to school in Salisbury. In late July, Jane Pinney, who was married to William Burt Weekes, asked him to bring the Pinney children up to London to meet their parents. I had arranged to meet and greet the Pinneys on their arrival at the Weekes' house in London. The Pinneys received their children as total strangers so much had they grown and altered during their education in Salisbury. I exclaimed "Good God! Don't you know them. They are your children!" Mrs. Pinney was so upset she set her head-dress in a blaze by the candle in front of where she was sitting. Mr. Pinney sat stupefied by the double shock – of his grown up strange children and wife ablaze.

Meanwhile they had brought me a message from my kind Uncle Herbert, who asked me to come back to run his Great House at Montpelier for him. (He had been widowed for many years and he failed to get on with his only daughter). He also offered me and Josiah a permanent home until he retired from Nevis.

So just before Christmas I took ship for Nevis with my three-year-old son, the French having by then quit the island. Mr. John Pinney wrote from London to Uncle Herbert in April 1784

> I believe your good niece Mrs. Josiah Nisbet little expected so sudden an alteration when she left this country in December last. My best wishes always attend her – she is your child by adoption and your kindness will alleviate the distress of her mind. The anxieties and feelings of a mother for the welfare of an only child must be great. Remember me kindly to your Daughter & Sisters & believe me to be as I really am …

So I returned to Paradise on Nevis, having been away four years and not yet accustomed to the deaths of my adored Father and Husband.

CHAPTER FOUR

PARADISE REGAINED –
THE LITTLE CAPTAIN

I arrived back on Nevis at Christmas 1783 to live with my Uncle Herbert and to take care of Montpelier for him. There was constant entertainment and bustle as visitors from the neighbouring islands of St. Kitts, Antigua and St. Eustatius arrived on political or commercial affairs with the President and his Council. And of course nearly every week there would be a visit from a Naval vessel's officers. From the cliff tops of Nevis one could see ships scurrying through the Narrows, little sloops and schooners, brigs and fat commercial ships carrying our sugar to England. The Royal Navy could be trusted to have its frigates patrolling the islands.

As a result I never lacked for admirers – not only from the sugar planters, including my rejected suitor of a few years back, young Daniel Ross, but also the visiting ships' Captains. One of them was Captain Sutherland, who was very smitten. On many occasions during '84 I was almost tempted by his blandishments. The problem, I said to myself, is that if one married a handsome sailor he would have sailed away by the time that one decided whether one really loved him or not. My cousin Sally Morton was flirting with an Irish Naval Captain, and we discussed this together. With the young planters one knew everything about them and had probably grown up with them. Our families had known each other for several generations. We were such a close-knit island family that in a way, we knew each other almost too well! These young Naval officers were dashing because, irrespective of their physical attributes, they had an air of mystery, because one was simply ignorant of their background. And that mystery can often be misconstrued as something romantic – when it might turn out to be completely humdrum and plebian.

Anyway I had much on my mind. Josiah was then four and growing up fast. My Uncle was very busy but planning to retire to London in a few years. Life at Montpelier was never dull.

On 6 January the frigate HMS *Boreas*, 28 guns, spent three days in Charlestown harbour, then three days in February, and again three days in March. On each occasion the controversial Captain spent some time at Montpelier and met Uncle Herbert, who disapproved of his policies but approved of him very much as a man.

Captain Nelson arrived on our peaceful scene at Nevis with a most devastating impact. Theoretically, and no doubt illegally, the American merchant traders were

HMS *Boreas*, 28 guns, off the coast of Nevis in 1786.

defying the Navigation laws and actively trading with the individual Leeward Islands thus breaking the monopoly of Great Britain. Every Leeward trader, including rich Uncle Herbert, connived at these infringements, as the Americans could and did supply goods required more quickly and cheaply. They also bought our sugar and cotton at reasonable prices. Captain Nelson and Cuthbert Collingwood (later to be made Vice Admiral and a Baronet) were agreed that the English Navigation laws *must* be respected. On a cruise to the islands of St. Kitts and Nevis they seized four American vessels lying in Nevis roads. One was the *Hercules*, another the *Nancy Pleasant*. When the American ships' masters went on shore they were met by a lawyer who had been briefed by our angry Nevis merchants, who had raised a large sum of money for them to sue Captain Nelson for assault and imprisonment. They were claiming the huge sum of £40,000 damages. To avoid arrest Nelson had to stay aboard the *Boreas* for two months until the trial came on. Eventually the Treasury in London wrote and supported Nelson and Collingwood, and promised to pay the legal expenses of their defence. There were also congratulations to Sir Richard Hughes and his Naval Captains for their resolute zeal in protecting Great Britain's commerce.

My Uncle Herbert, who stood to lose the most, offered Nelson bail of £10,000 if he chose to suffer arrest. He said that this young officer Nelson was only doing his duty, and could not be blamed in any way.

So there were storm clouds surrounding the little Naval Captain when he eventually came ashore!

When the *Boreas* visited Nevis in January I had been staying in Basseterre with my friends William Payne Georges and his wife. He was not only Chief Justice of HM Court of King's Bench of the Leeward Isles, but also of St. Kitts, and had always had a high regard for my father. He was the Colony Agent of St. Kitts, and was the second most important man on the island. (Sir Thomas Shirley was the Governor). He kept a good table and he and his wife were always most hospitable to me and treated me like a daughter. My cousin Parry Herbert wrote me a note sent over by sloop across the Narrows,

> We have at last seen the Captain of the *Boreas*, of whom so much has been said. He came up, just before dinner, much heated, and was very silent: yet seemed, according to the old adage, to think the more. He declined drinking any wine, but after dinner, when the President, as usual, gave the following toasts, 'the King', 'the Queen' and Royal Family and 'Lord Hood' this strange man regularly filled his glass and observed that those were always bumper toasts with him, which having drank, he uniformly passed the bottle and relapsed into his former taciturnity. It was impossible, during this visit for any of us to make out his real character: there was such a reserve and sternness in his behaviour, with occasional sallies, though very transient, of a superior mind. Being placed by him, I endeavoured to rouse his attention by showing him all the civilities in my power: but I drew out little more than 'Yes' and 'No'. If you, Fanny, had been there, we think you would have made something of him: for you have been in the habit of attending to these odd sort of people.

My cousin was quite correct. As the President's niece I was expected to entertain all my Uncle's guests, however peculiar or taciturn they might be. I was never away from Montpelier for more than a couple of days since he relied on me more and more to run Montpelier for him. 'Dear Fanny' he would say of me, 'as dear to me as a child, perhaps dearer, who must have his own way in everything.' Most wealthy old widowers tend to want and to get their own way, and Uncle Herbert was no exception.

Eventually the young Captain of the *Boreas* did arrive on 11 March at Nevis, which he described as 'this place being in paradise'. First he encountered my son Josiah, very early that morning. He and Parry Herbert had arrived at Charlestown harbour at first light and reached Montpelier before breakfast was announced. Uncle Herbert wrote of the encounter afterwards 'Good God! If I did not find that great little man of whom everybody is so afraid, playing in the next room, *under the dining-table* with Mrs. Nisbet's child'. Josiah made friends with the little

Captain, who later became his step-father and whom he called 'father'. After our marriage, Horatio used to refer to Josiah as his 'son-in-law', and himself as my son's 'father-in-law'.

The Captain of the *Boreas* was not at first glance a handsome or a distinguished man. I judged him to be a year or two older than myself. He was of slim build, almost frail, and scarcely an inch taller than I. He had a long strong nose, marked eyebrows, and the most lovely honest eyes – almost as though he contemplated and was within reach of visions. As I later found out, my little Captain was a visionary, with ideals and concepts such as honour and loyalty – patriotism and respect for the Royal Family. He looked as though he might be humorous, but was not in any way. He was the most serious and dedicated man that ever I did meet. He had a lofty intellectual forehead and as a contrast most sensual wide lips. He had a great deal of his own hair, always powdered white on social occasions. Later on, as he became more senior and more responsible his face in repose became sad and melancholy. His uniform was rarely band-box smart and always looked practical and well-used. Certainly no popinjay. Horatio Nelson had none of the courtier's graces and his manners were abrupt and awkward – perhaps from so many years cooped up aboard small ships. His voice was difficult at first to appreciate – it was rather highpitched, distinctly nasal, with a Norfolk drawl, which my East Anglian forbears possess, but with which I was not familiar.

After his encounter with Josiah I thanked him politely 'for the great partiality he had shown to my little boy'. Thereafter he came frequently – or as frequently as his duties would allow him – to see me at Montpelier. He wrote to his brother, the Rev. William Nelson, who had been the Chaplain on the *Boreas* – a pure sinecure – on 3 May, 'I am just come from Nevis where I have been visiting Miss Parry Herbert and a young widow: the two latter known to Charles Boyles', (Lieutenant on the *Raisonable*, who eventually became Admiral of the Blue). Charles was a merry young man, also from Norfolk, whom I hoped would marry my cousin Parry. A few weeks later Nelson wrote to his brother on 28 June 'Entre nous, Do not be surprised to hear I am a Benedict for if at all, it will be before a month – do not tell.'

I soon discovered that Nelson was reputed to be a most active and dedicated young officer – quite out of the ordinary – always serious with slightly eccentric manners and no known vices. He was brusque almost to the point of rudeness with the opposite sex, as my cousin remarked. A most modest drinker by Plantation and Navy standard, he rarely gambled or played cards.

At first I thought he was rude, but after a few visits I realised it was a shyness with our sex, and as a consequence he had a direct boyish gaucherie, as though in the field of romance he had not learned any particular rules. Although when I first met him he was senior captain on the Leeward Island station at the age of twenty seven, he had had little chance of distinguishing himself at sea. He had not been in any battles. A few years earlier he had sailed in an ill-fated expedition against the Spaniards in Nicaragua, and had been with an expedition to the North

Pole. Once he had said to one of his naval friends 'I will be a Hero confiding in Providence, I will brave every danger', and it was clear to me that that indeed was to be his destiny.

He had some patronage from his Uncle Maurice Suckling, Comptroller of the Navy, and more frequently from the famous Lord Hood. He would talk for hours to anybody who knew the rudiments of naval tactics and strategy, often using abstract thoughts and words of 'honour' and 'glory' and 'service to my King and Country', which lesser mortals would never dare use in colloquial conversations.

Nelson's friend Cuthbert Collingwood of the *Mediator* confided in me in his quiet and serious manner that I had achieved a 'bloodless conquest' of the senior Captain on the station. Nelson preferred Cuthbert to his brother Wilfred, who was, poor lad, soon to die of tuberculosis. Cuthbert eventually rose to great rank as Vice Admiral despite a reputation for ill-luck, and always remained Nelson's firm friend. Since June he had been staying at Montpelier on his frequent visits to the island.

At this point – just before the hurricane season started in the Leewards – I had to take stock of my feelings about Captain Nelson. I had had many conversations with my Uncle and my cousin, but advice is difficult to give and rarely taken – particularly on the most delicate subject of all – love and marriage! Initially I had found it very difficult to get to know what was behind the façade of a small, homespun captain. It certainly was not love at first sight, nor even, after reflection, at second sight. He was not particularly handsome, nor gallant, nor had he any prospects that I could see in the Navy. He had nothing but his naval pay and no likelihood of receiving any legacies from his extremely modest Norfolk family of parsons and tradesmen. As a sailor he would want to be at sea to promote his career, and would undoubtedly once on shore, 'on the beach', pine to be back at sea. Definitely he was no catch at all, and this I made politely clear to him. Nevis was my home, and after my sad experiences in Salisbury, I was not at all eager to return to England.

As far as I had any plans at all they were encompassed by the next eighteen months when it was my duty to stay and look after my Uncle Herbert. In addition I had to admit to myself that life on Nevis was extremely enjoyable. For what it was worth I was considered to be the first lady on the island, running the President's 'salon' for him. I missed having a husband and poor Josiah was still in my thoughts, and I missed having a father for his son Josiah, who was now a lively handful.

I refused to correspond with the little Captain despite Captain Collingwood's confirmation of the obvious. Nevertheless before he sailed to Barbados in mid-August he 'spoke' for me, not only to my Uncle as protocol demanded, but also, of course, to me. I promised him nothing of any consequence. My Uncle Herbert was at the time much preoccupied with putting up the first windmill on the Montpelier estate, to replace the cattle mills. Power was needed to turn the rollers which crushed the sugar cane. His friends scoffed at such a new-fangled invention. Cattle were more reliable, but slow and needed pasturage, and replacement when they died. The Trade Winds however blow for ever on Nevis! In addition his sister, my Aunt Sarah, who had lived with him most of her life, died after a long illness on the 5 September. So Captain Nelson received a politely non-committal letter from my Uncle. But we had both under-estimated the little Captain's determination. He started writing long passionate letters to me and eventually I felt that I had to respond, although initially my letters were lukewarm, and so we drifted into an understanding.

He wrote to his Uncle William Suckling on 14 November,

My dear Sir, Not a scrap of a pen have I by the last Packet from any relation in England; but, however, you see I don't think I am forgot, more especially when I open a business, which, perhaps, you will smile at, in the first instance, and say "this Horatio is for ever in love." My present attachment is of pretty long standing, but I was determined to be fixed before I broke this matter to any person. The lady is a Mrs. Nisbet, widow of a Dr. Nisbet, who died eighteen months after her marriage, and has left her with a son. From her infancy (for her father and mother died when she was only two years of age) she has been brought up by her mother's brother, Mr. Herbert, President of Nevis, a gentleman whose fortune and character must be well known to all the West Indian Merchants, therefore I shall say nothing upon that head. Her age is twenty-two; and her personal accomplishment you will suppose *I think* equal to any person's I ever saw; but, without vanity, her mental accomplishments are superior to most people's of either sex; and we shall come together as two persons most sincerely attached to each other from friendship. Her son is under her guardianship, but totally independent of her.

But I must describe Herbert to you, that you may know exactly how I stand; for when we apply for advice, we must tell all circumstances. Herbert is very rich and very proud, – he has an only daughter, and this niece, who he looks upon in the same light, if not higher. I have lived at his house, when at Nevis, since June last, and am a great favourite of his. I have told him I am as poor as Job; but he tells me he likes me, and I am descended from a good family, which his pride likes, but he also says "Nelson I am proud, and I must live like myself, therefore I can't do much in my life-time; when I die she shall have twenty thousand pounds; and if my daughter dies before me, she shall possess the major part of my property. I intend going to England in 1787, and remaining there my lifetime; therefore, if you two can live happily together till that event takes place, you have my consent." This is exactly my situation with him; and I know the way to get him to give me most, is not to appear to want it; thus circumstanced, who can I apply to but you? The regard you have ever expressed for me leads me to hope you will do something. My future happiness, I give you my honour, is now in your power: if you cannot afford to give me anything for ever, you will, I am sure, trust to me, that if ever I can afford it, I will return it to some part of your family. I think Herbert will be brought to give her two or three hundred a year during his life; and if you will either *give* me, I will call it – I think you will do it – either one hundred a year, for a few years, or a thousand pounds, how happy you will make a couple who will pray for you for ever. Don't disappoint me, or my heart will break: trust to my honour to do a good turn for some other person if it is in my power. I can say no more, but trust implicitly to your goodness, and pray let me know of your generous action by the first Packet.

I shall send by this Packet some queries, which I must beg you will get your solicitor to answer, for there are divided opinions in this Country as to the rights of Admirals, Captains, etc., seizing Vessels to the King's use under the Navigation Laws.

Best wishes for the happiness of every part of your family, and may they enjoy the happiness 'tis so much in your power to give me; but on every occasion believe that I am, Your most affectionate,
Horatio Nelson.

From Antigua on 15 December on the *Boreas* he wrote to his brother the Rev. William Nelson,

My dear Brother, You are so good a correspondent, that I fear I miss answering all your letters, but let me beg this may not hinder your exactness; for I do not, be assured, miss intentionally. You will have heard from my Father and Mr. Suckling – indeed, I think it was hinted to you, before the hurricane months – that I am in a fair way of changing my situation. The dear object you must like. Her sense, polite manners, and to you I may say, beauty, you will much admire: and although at present we may not be a rich couple, yet I have not the least doubt but we shall be a happy pair: – the fault must be mine if we are not. Your rum, etc. I shall certainly procure, and everything you want from hence. I wish you were fixed in your house, for really you begin to be too old to walk about the world without a fixed residence of your own. Marry *Ellen*, and then you are settled for life; but in all this you will please yourself, I know.

I told you long ago, Miss Rosy was married to Major Browne of the 67th. They live at St. John's, and were they to stay there till doomsday I should not rise so far to visit them. I have the Leeward Station still, but direct as usual to Barbadoes. We are put in here by bad weather, having sprung our mainmast, and hurt the Ship a good deal. We are all well on board, and everybody desires their kind remembrance to the Bishop. You are still upon the Books as Chaplain. You will accumulate a fortune if you proceed this way. You shall give me a horse, however. Remember me kindly to Mrs. Bolton and her family when you see them; to the Walpoles, and all my old acquaintances. Bless you, and believe I am, with great truth, Your affectionate Brother, Horatio Nelson.

Herbert, President of Nevis, says you seem a good fellow; he will make a cask of remarkable fine rum for you double-proof.

Nelson wrote two weeks later on New Year's Day 1786 to his brother William,

My dear Brother, Although I wrote to my Father and your Honour by the Packet which sailed from St. Kitt's only two days ago, yet as I have received a letter from you since my last, I shall send another across the Atlantic, to say I am well, and as merry as I wish. So I must be, you will conclude, sitting by the woman who will be my wife; and every day am I more than ever convinced of the propriety of my choice, and I shall be happy with her. You will esteem her for herself when you know her; for she possesses sense far superior to half the people of our acquaintance, and her manners are Mrs. Moutray's. The Admiral lives in a Boarding house at Barbadoes, not much in the style of a British Admiral. Lady H., with her daughter, Mrs. Browne, in St. John's, Antigua. They all pack off next May, certainly, and I hope most devoutly they will take the Admiral with them, but he wishes much to remain another Station. He is too much of a fiddler for me.

Am I to think you are in Norfolk, or at Bath? You may push for Miss Dorothea, and then you will soon be a Bishop, without any interest but money, which is indeed the strongest of any. To everybody that asks after me, say, "how d'ye?" To Mrs. Bolton, Edmund, etc. etc. love and kind remembrances. Adieu, and believe me to be, your most affectionate Brother, Horatio Nelson. Mr. Herbert says he will make some fine rum for you, and you must mind and have the Norfolk turkeys, fat, ready for eating. A merry Christmas, and a happy new year. To my father and Kate give my kind love.

During the eighteen months of our engagement Horatio rarely managed to visit Nevis, but there was by now little doubt in my mind that he would make me a loving husband and Josiah an equally loving father. However in May all the officers of the *Boreas* came ashore at Nevis and used the natural hot baths for rheumatism (and gout!) Horatio stayed at Montpelier as usual and visited the Saddle Hall Peak and Battery to watch for the approach of the 'enemy'. We would walk or ride there together from Gingerland. A most romantic loving time – the Trade Winds whispered – we were happy together.

The *Boreas* obtained fresh drinking water from the lagoon at Cotton Ground, later known as Nelson Springs. Horatio told me that he was disturbed that his Uncle William Suckling was proposing to re-marry, since he was likely to be Horatio's prime source of financial help. Neither of us were making much progress with my Uncle Herbert, who proposed great things for me and for Josiah, but did not so dispose them.

My cousin Sally Morton married Captain William Kelly on 23 March in Nevis, and Horatio managed to be present.

I remember one letter I wrote in April after receiving a rather distant letter from Horatio, 'I will not begin by scolding you, although you really deserve it, for sending me such a letter. Had I not know the warmth of your Heart by this time, I might have judged you had never seen me. However I have fixed my resolve of not saying more.

In November 1786 the HMS *Pegasus* of 28 guns joined the Station from Nova Scotia under command of Prince William Henry, later Duke of Clarence, and came under Horatio's command. He also had the *Solebay*, Captain Holloway, *Maidstone*, 32 guns, and *Rattler* under Captain Wilfred Collingwood, in his squadron.

The twenty-two-year old Prince brought problems with him for Horatio to solve. He was not a natural commander and had reacted adversely to his older, and more experienced first lieutenant Isaac Schomberg. The problem was simply that Horatio had so much respect for the Royal Family that he felt he had to support the Prince, even though in fact the wretched first lieutenant was performing his difficult duties perfectly correctly. Schomberg and the other officers of the *Pegasus* were all demanding courts martial for themselves, so that they could leave their unhappy

Prince William, Duke of Clarence. This engraving shows the prince in about 1782, when he first met Nelson.

ship. The Prince, an excitable and difficult young man, was in awe of his father, King George III, and was most uneasy in case the Royal wrath descended from London.

To Horatio's great credit he calmed the dangerous situation down, and made lifelong friends with the Prince into the bargain. They re-fought the naval battles in which our Admirals Barrington, Byron, Rodney and Hood had defeated the French, not that Nelson was there, but he had closely studied the tactics employed by both sides. The Prince was an inveterate Romantic and convinced himself that Horatio was not only deeply in love with me, but was already married to me! When the luckless Horatio protested that the wedding date was undetermined, his new Royal friend insisted on the role of Father of the Bride and wanted to give Nelson's intended away at the wedding. On a visit to St. Kitts Horatio wrote 'The Prince admires Mrs. William Georges very much. I have had a severe scolding from her *but as you was the cause* I felt perfectly easy. A neglected female does not easily forgive.' Tongues were wagging about our protracted engagement even though we had made it clear that my Uncle Herbert intended to retire to London during '87 – and that the wedding date depended on that occurrence. Horatio and the Prince spent the 3rd week of February on Nevis, when I met the Prince for the first time. On 6 March Horatio wrote urgently to say that the Prince's future sailings had now been planned via Nevis, the Virgins, and a call at English Harbour, Antigua. Then finally to Grenada before HRH returned to Halifax, *and* the refitted *Boreas* took passage back to England in mid-May. So everyone's hands were forced – mine, Horatio's and Uncle Herbert's. Nevis society went mad with excitement. Not because Uncle Herbert's favourite niece (and Josiah Nisbet's widow) was marrying again, but because King George s naval son was visiting the Island and giving away in marriage a Nevis girl to that unpopular but 'great little Captain'.

It also dramatically crystallized Uncle Herbert's plans, since he realised that once the pageantry and drama of the Prince's visit and my wedding was over, he would be bereft of a housekeeper/companion. He then made plans to hand over the estates to a manager, which was easily done, since all day to day routine plans had long since been well delegated, and booked a passage to England.

I had five days notice to prepare for the grandest wedding the Island had ever seen and might ever see again, before Horatio and I enjoyed a week's honeymoon on Nevis. The custom was prevalent of marriage ceremonies taking place in the Great Houses on the island, and we asked the Rev. William Jones of Figtree Church, St. John's to officiate. Several hundred guests were asked and they accepted with alacrity, including friends from St. Kitts who chartered a sloop for the day. My Uncle Herbert did not stint on wines or foods, served on a special dinner service of Royal Worcester plate cast in England for the occasion.

The President had caused £800 to be voted by the Council for the royal festivities. No less than 100 male guests came to the dinner and 70 ladies for the Ball afterwards. Poor Horatio only had his young cousin, midshipman Maurice Suckling, attending – to represent his family. It was a very happy affair and Josiah enjoyed every moment of it. I wore a magnificent Limerick lace dress of the finest quality. Horatio and the Prince were both in blue and white and gold full-dress uniform, and the silks and satins of the assembled wedding guests were up to the standard of St. James' Court.

The large blonde Hanoverian was an arrogant, determined and difficult young man and offended many people he met, but he seemed to like and appreciate me. He congratulated Horatio on 'having borne off the principal favourite of the island', which was handsome of him. I danced minuets with him and with Horatio and once even with my old Uncle Herbert, and enjoyed every minute.

Many years later the Prince wrote of how much he enjoyed dancing with 'the Widow Nisbet' and how he had spent many happy hours at Montpelier where he found her to be 'a pretty and sensible woman with whom poor Nelson was head and ears in love.'

Meanwhile the church parish register had been written up.

I, William Jones, Clerk, Rector of the Parishes of Saint John and Saint Thomas in the said Island do hereby certify that Horatio Nelson Esq., Captain of His Majesty's Ship the BOREAS and Frances Herbert Nisbet, widow were married this eleventh day of March in the year of our Lord, one thousand seven hundred & eighty seven, according to the Canons and Constitutions of the Church of England at the dwelling house of the Honourable John Richardson Herbert President of His Majesty's Council & Deputy Ordinary of the said Island in the aforesaid Parish of Saint John. Given under my hand the day and Year above written Will Jones. This marriage was solemnised between us in the presence of
William
Horatio Nelson
Frances Herbert Nisbet.

Horatio and I spent a week getting to know each other. I was the more experienced since I had been married and loved before by poor Josiah. Horatio was as direct and tender and thoughtful in his love making as one might expect of him. We had been engaged and mostly apart for a year and a half. All too soon we had to part yet again (a shape of things to come).

It was interesting for me to ascertain what Horatio's friends thought of his marriage. James Wallis, his First Lieutenant, approved and described me as 'the amiable and beautiful Mrs. Nesbit.' He was a lady's man and made advances to the *Boreas* purser's wife, and others! The Prince approved of me, which was handsome of him. Captain Thomas Pringle of the *Daedalus* was most friendly towards me, but disapproved of Nelson's marriage, 'it is a national loss that such an officer should marry: had it not been for that circumstance, I foresaw Nelson would become the greatest man in the Service.' We were all very young at the time and perhaps more prone to rash prophecies, but Thomas was proved quite wrong! After our wedding

Horatio wrote to Captain Locker on the *Boreas* on the way to Tortola (21 March) 'I am married to an amiable woman that far makes amends for everything indeed till I married her I never knew happiness. And I am morally certain she will continue to make me a happy man for the rest of my days I shall have great pleasure in introducing you to her.' Just before we sailed back to England (7 May) he wrote to Prince William 'President Herbert is near going and it is impossible to a female in a few hours – never yet having made the *Boreas* her home.'

One of the Norfolk midshipmen wrote home how surprised he was that the Captain of the *Boreas* had not taken his bride home in his own ship – 'she, a pretty and attractive woman and a general favourite – though lately married he went home in his Frigate and she in a Merchant ship ... he was then so ill that it was not expected that he could live to reach England and he had a puncheon of rum for his body in case he should die during the voyage.'

It was a difficult decision for me to make. Horatio, although ill of a fever, wanted me to sail with him on the small *Boreas* but my Uncle Herbert, old and ailing, with Martha Herbert, his daughter, and Parry Herbert, his niece, wanted me – perhaps selfishly – to accompany him. In many ways he treated me as his daughter and not Martha, and we had become very close since my return to the island. I thought that I might not see Uncle Herbert again and that I would have a lifetime of happiness ahead of me with Horatio, so we all sailed home together on the *Roehampton*, a large and luxurious West Indian man.

Thus ended a chapter of my life – 'Paradise Regained'. I never went back to Nevis again.

The entrance gates to the Montpelier estate on Nevis island..

CHAPTER FIVE

HORATIO'S LOVE LETTERS TO ME

My husband was a dedicated correspondent and wrote over two hundred and fifty letters to me, starting from his courtship and continuing throughout our marriage until a certain 'événement' occurred fifteen happy years later. During that period his love for me was paramount, as some of these early letters demonstrate.

Mid August 1785, *Boreas* before sailing for Barbadoes

My dear Mrs Nisbit,

To say how anxious I have been, and am, to receive a line from Mr. Herbert, would be far beyond the descriptive powers of my pen. Most fervently do I hope his answer will be of such a tendency as to convey real pleasure, not only to myself but also to you. For most sincerely do I love you, and I think that my affection is not only founded upon the principles of reason but also upon the basis of mutual attachment. Indeed My charming Fanny, did I posses a Million, my greatest pride and pleasure would be to share it with you; and as to living in a Cottage with you, I should esteem it superior to living in a palace with any other I have yet met with.

My age is enough to make me seriously reflect upon what I have offered, and commonsense tells me what a Good choice I have made. The more I weigh you in my mind, the more reason I find to admire both your head and heart. But come, don't say "What a vain young Man is this! 'tis a modest way of telling me I have given a proof of my sense by accepting him". No! To Your heart do I own myself most indebted, yet I trust you approved of me for this obvious reason – "He esteems me, therefore he is the person I ought to expect most happiness from, by a return of affection" ... My temper you know as well as myself, for by longer acquaintance you will find I possess not the Art of concealing it. My situation and family I have not endeavoured to concial. Don't think me rude by this entering into a correspondence with you. Consider that separation from the objects we esteem loses some of its stings by a mutual unreserved correspondence ...

Boreas, English Harbour, 11 September, 1785.

Indeed, my dear Fanny, I had buoyed myself up with hopes that the Admiral's Schooner would have given me a line from you; but the tidings she brought of the release of poor Mrs. Sarah Herbert, from this world, sufficiently apologize for your not thinking of an absentee. Yet this believe from my heart, that I partake in all the sorrows you experience; and I comfort myself, that however great your grief at this moment may be, at losing a person who was so deservedly dear to you, as your good Aunt; yet, when reason takes place, you must rather have pleasure in knowing she is released from those torments she had undergone for months past. Time even has, and in the present instance I trust may have, a tendency to soften grief into a pleasing remembrance; and her unspotted character must afford you real comfort. Call Religion to your aid; and it will convince you, that her conduct in this world was such as insures everlasting happiness in that which is to come.

I have received a letter from Mr. Herbert, in answer to that which I left at Nevis for him. My greatest wish is to be united to you; and the foundation of all conjugal happiness real love and esteem, is, I trust, what you believe I possess in the strongest degree towards you. I think Mr. Herbert loves you too well, not to let you marry the man of your choice, although he may not be so rich as some others, provided his character and situation in life render such an union eligible. I declare solemnly, that did I not conceive I had the full possession of your heart, no consideration should make me accept your hand. We know that riches do not always insure happiness; and the world is convinced that I am superior to pecuniary considerations in my public and private life; as in both instances I might have been rich. But I will have done, leaving all my present feelings to operate in your breast: – only of this truth be convinced, that I am, your affectionate, Horatio Nelson.

P.S. Do I ask too much, when I venture to hope for a line? or otherwise I may suppose my letters may be looked on as troublesome.

Boreas, English Harbour, 25 Feb 1786

My Dear Fanny,

We landed Mr. H. C. Adye yesterday afternoon at St. John's; and after a disagreeable night, here we arrived this morning. Captain Collingwood is gone into the Country, therefore from this place I sail at daylight. You are too good and indulgent; I both know and feel it; but my whole life shall ever be devoted to make you completely happy, whatever whims may sometimes take me. We are none of us perfect, and myself probably much less so than you deserve. I am, etc. Horatio Nelson.

Off the Island of Deseada, 3 March 1786

Separated from you, what pleasure can I feel? none, be assured; all my happiness is centred with thee; and where thou art not, there I am not happy. Every day, hour, and act, convince me of it. With my heart filled with the purest and most tender affection, do I write this: for were it not so, you know me well enough to be certain, that even at this moment I would tell you of it. I daily thank God, who ordained that I should be attached to you. He has, I firmly believe, intended it as a blessing to me; and I am well convinced you will not disappoint his beneficent intentions.

Fortune, that is, money, is the only thing I regret the want of, and that only for the sake of my affectionate Fanny. But the Almighty, who brings us together, will, I doubt not, take ample care of us and prosper all our undertakings. No dangers shall deter me from pursuing every honourable means of providing handsomely for you and yours; and again let me repeat, *that my dear Josiah shall ever by considered by me as one of my own.* That Omnipotent Being, who sees and knows what passes in all hearts, knows what I have written to be my undisguised sentiments towards the little fellow. I am uneasy, but not unwell. Nothing but the Admiral's orders to be at Barbados at a given time, hindered me from coming down after my letters. Sir Richard Hughes, I am certain would have overlooked my disobedience of orders, and have thought I had served the friend, who had neglected to bring my letters, very properly. But I cannot bear the idea of disobeying orders: I should not like to have mine disobeyed: therefore I came on. However, it was a toss-up, I assure you.

9 March.

At last we are arrived; and as we came into the bay on one side, the "Adamant" made her appearance on the other. Captain Knox has brought me one letter from Antigua; for which one, although I know there are more, I retract all my mischievous wishes; and I have received several at this place from my sister and brother; the former from Bath, where my old friend Scriviner desires to be kindly remembered to me. I don't think my dear sister knows of my intentions of altering my situation, or she would have mentioned it. My friend Mountray is still there: but I have not a line. It is wonderful, and I cannot account for it. I know myself to be so steady in my friendships, that I cannot bear the least coolness or inattention in others. My brother takes it for granted I am a married man, and in consequence desires his love. From my uncle Suckling I have a very kind letter, saying he will do everything in his power to add to my happiness; and if I should want it that he will give me pecuniary assistance. It is strongly reported that we are to sail from this Country in June next: if that is to be the case my time is short. All this affects my spirits, and will not allow me to feel so pleasant as I wish; and makes me the more regret that I had not paid greater attention to getting money. But I will have done with this subject. You must write often, and long letters. I am, etc. Horatio Nelson.

Horatio brought back with him two pairs of dancing pumps, a new hat and ribbons for my riding outfit, and some harpsichord strings.

Boreas, Carlisle Bay, 25 March 1786

My dear Fanny,

Most probably, when the Packet arrives, the Admiral's Schooner will be so soon hurried away, that I shall not have a moment's time to write ... The Inhabitants here are heartily tired of my company. I am ready to give them my room; and they may assure themselves I will not trouble them one moment longer than I can help: for although my person is with them, my heart, thoughts, and affections are far off. Upwards of a month from Nevis. When I sailed, I hoped by this time to have been there again: but how uncertain are human expectations, and how vain the idea of fixing periods for happiness. I am anxious, yet sometimes fear to receive Mr. Herbert's answer to my letter: yet why I should fear, I know not; for I conceive I wrote nothing but what was proper and right. What signify professions of friendship, if they are never to be put to the test? You, my dear Fanny, are all I care about: if you are satisfied, you will readily believe me, when I say, I shall. But I will give up the subject, and hope for the best.

The Admiral lives very retired. I have twice dined with him. We are good friends, nor do I think I should soon disagree with him. He seems ready to do everything I can wish him, and only wants to be well informed. The Governor [David Parry] and Mrs. Parry are very civil: they have given me a general invitation, and always appear glad to see me. For the last week a French Man-of-War has been here: and going about with them so much in the sun has given me violent headaches. I shall expect you will send me a long epistle.

29 March.

I am involved in Law, and have Custom-House etc. etc. upon me: but I fear not, being conscious of the rectitude of my intentions. The Admiral is highly pleased with my conduct here, as you will believe, by sending me such fine lines with a white hat. I well know I am not of abilities to deserve what he has said of me: but I take it as they are meant, to show his regard for me; and his politeness and attention to me are great: nor shall I forget it. I like the man, although not all his acts. If you should show the lines to any person, I desire it may not be to any Officers of the Squadron with you, as the compliment is paid to me at their expense. You will understand this as meant to extend to the very near relations of the parties: indeed, I do not wish to have them shown to any one. How is my dear Josiah? Pray give him a kiss for me. Bless you; and believe that I am, with the purest affection, yours most sincerely, Horatio Nelson.

Boreas, Carlisle Bay, 17 April 1786

My dearest Fanny,

I have been looking out anxiously for some time past, for the "Adamant" and "Berbice", making sure of the pleasure of receiving a letter – but it is not to happen: therefore I must write what I know, and not answers to what you send. My letters from my sister and brother are very kind; and, from the former, filled with every sentiment of affection for you. I am involved in Law: and although everything will go as I wish it, yet I fear it will keep me this fortnight. I shall wish the Vessels at the devil, and the whole Continent of America to boot.

Lord Hood has the command at Portsmouth. I had a letter from him by the Packet. I am all anxiety to hear and know what I have to hope for from Leeward.

23 April

All the Squadron are now here holding Court Martials, which will finish tomorrow, when they return to their respective Stations, except poor me, who am kept to take care of two Yankees; I wish they were a hundred fathoms under water: and when I am likely to be released, I have not the smallest idea ... On Tuesday or Wednesday the "Adamant" sails for Antigua with Sir Richard – so much for the Flag-ship; I should be sorry to have one: a Captain in her is never his own master. I am so much out of temper with this Island, that I would rather sacrifice anything than stay. I have been upon the best terms with the Admiral, and I declare I think I could ever remain so. He is always remarkably kind and civil to every one: I told him that no one could think otherwise but you, and I hoped you would be angry with him for keeping me away so long. Whenever I can settle about my prizes here, I shall sail directly for Nevis.

How is my little Josiah? – I sent yesterday, the moment the Admiral told me the Schooner was going to Nevis, for nobody but myself knew it, as polite a note as I was able to. The servant brought word back, there was no answer; not even "much obliged", "thank you", or any other word but what I have told you: I may be uncivilly treated once, and then it is my misfortune: but if I put it in any person's power to be so a second time, it's my fault. – Farewell for a little time; and bless you, with all my heart and soul;

– and do believe, and never doubt, but that I am, with the most sincere affection, ever your Horatio Nelson.

Boreas, 4 May 1786, Barbarous Island.

My dearest Fanny,

Never, never, do I believe, shall I get away from this detestable spot. Had I not seized any Americans, I should now have been with you: but I should have neglected my duty, which I think your regard for me is too great, for you to have wished me to have done. Duty is the great business of a Sea-officer. All private considerations must give way to it, however painful it is. But I trust that time will not have lessened me in the opinion of her, whom it shall be the business of my future life to make happy. Bless you, bless you. Ever, with the greatest affection, your Horatio Nelson.

Boreas, England Harbour, 19 August 1786.

My dearest Fanny,

Having seen in this day's newspaper, that a Vessel cleared out from St. John's to Nevis a few days ago, I feel vexed not to have had a letter in the Office for you: however, if I can help it, I will not be behindhand again. To write letters to you is the next greatest pleasure I feel to receiving them from you. What I experience when I read such as I am sure are the pure sentiments of your heart, my poor pen cannot express, nor indeed would I give much for any pen or head that could describe feelings of that kind: they are worth but little when that can happen. My heart yearns to you – it is with you; my mind dwells upon nought else but you. Absent from you, I feel no pleasure: it is you, my dearest Fanny, who are everything to me. Without you, I care not for this world; for I have found lately nothing in it but vexation and trouble.

These, you are well convinced, *are my present sentiments; God Almighty grant they may never change. Nor do I think they will:* indeed, there is, as far as human knowledge can judge, *a moral certainty they cannot;* for it must be real affection that brings us together, not interest or compulsion, which make so many unhappy.

I have not been able to get even a cottage upon a hill, not-withstanding my utmost endeavours; and therefore have been kept here, most woefully pinched by mosquitoes, for my sins, perhaps; so the generous inhabitants of Antigua think, I suppose: not one of whom has been here, or has asked to leave English Harbour. But I give them credit for not paying attention to me to another cause that I am a faithful servant to that Country which most of them detest, and to which all their actions are inimical: I wish not for a better proof from them of my having done my duty. These gentlemen I shall in my mind hold very cheap in future: but I will have done with such trash. I am not that jolly fellow, who, for a feast and aplenty of wine, would sacrifice the dearest interest of his Country; they are fond of those gentry.

Leave all Antigua by itself, 'tis not fit company for the other parts of the letter.

Monday, (21 August) seven in the Evening.

As you begin to know something about Sailors, have you not often heard, that salt water and absence always wash away love? Now, I am such a heretic as not to believe that Faith; for behold, every morning since my arrival, I have had six pails of salt water at daylight poured upon my head, and instead of finding what the Seamen say to be true, I perceive the contrary effect; and if it goes on so contrary to the prescription, you must see me before my fixed time. At first, I bore absence tolerably, but now it is almost insupportable; and by-and-by I expect it will be quite so. But patience is a virtue; and I must exercise it upon this occasion, whatever it costs my feelings. I am alone in the Commanding Officer's house, while my ship is fitting, and from sunset until bed-time, I have not a human creature to speak to: you will feel a little for me, I think. I did not use to be over-fond of sitting alone. The moment old "Boreas" is habitable in my cabin, I shall fly to it, to avoid mosquitoes and melancholies. Hundreds of the former are now devouring me through all my clothes. You will, however, find I am better; though when you see me, I shall be like an Egyptian mummy, for the heat is intolerable. But I walk a mile out at night without fatigue, and all day I am housed. A quart of goat's milk is also taken every day, and I enjoy English sleep, always barring mosquitoes, which all Frank Lepée's care with my net cannot keep out at present.

What nonsense I am sending you: but I flatter myself the most trivial article concerning me, you feel interested in. I judge from myself; and I would rather have what passes in your mind, than all the news you could tell me which did not concern you. Mr. Horsford, our neighbour, came to visit me, making many apologies for his neglect, and pressing me much to come to his house, which has "Boreas" in view. Also the Comtroller of the Customs, with fine speeches: he may go back whistling, if he pleases. I cannot add anything further, for I do not know if you would read more than a sheet full.

Boreas, English Harbour, (August 1786)

My dearest Fanny,

What can I say? Nothing, if I speak of the pleasure I felt at receiving your kind and affectionate letter; my thoughts are too big for utterance: you must suppose that everything which is tender, kind, and truly affectionate has possession of my whole fram[e]. Words are not capable of conveying an idea of my feelings: nothing but reciprocity is equal to it; I flatter myself it is so. I have begun this letter, and left off, a dozen times, and found I did not know one word from another. Well, on the Saturday morning after the "Berbice" Schooner left me, Mr. Lightfoot came and paid me a visit, with an apology, of his having been confined to his house, or he would have done it before: that, not writing, he meant it as a mark of attention. He prevailed upon me to sleep at his house on Monday last, the day I dined with Sir Thomas Shirley [Governor of the Leeward Islands]. This great attention made amends for his long neglect, and I forgot all anger; I can forgive sometimes, you will allow. I only came from thence this morning; it is nine miles, and with writing ever since my arrival, I feel a little tired, therefore expect nothing but sheer stupidity.

I have also seen the great Mr.; he says, he understood and believed I was gone to England – whistle for that! The Country air has certainly done me service. I am not getting very fat, my make will not allow it: but I can tell you, and I know your tender heart will rejoice, that I have no more complaint in my lungs than Captain Maynard, and not the least pain in my breast. Pray present my best respects to Dr. Jefferies; I am very much flattered indeed by his good opinion. Although I am just from salt water, yet, as I am in a hurry to get the "Berbice" away, that she may reach Nevis by the evening, I must finish this thing, for letter I cannot call it. I have a newspaper for Miss Parry Herbert; it is all I have to offer that is worth her acceptance and I know she is as fond of a bit of news as myself. Pray give my compliments to her, and love to Josiah. I am, etc. Horatio Nelson.

English Harbour, 23 September 1786.

On the 9th of October, barring something extraordinary you will certainly see H.N. again; and, I need not say, if it be possible, with a stronger affection than when he left you. My letter is short, but my mind could say the paper full; therefore, don't let that be a reason for your writing either a short letter, or making the lines very wide from each other ... Believe that I am ever the same Horatio.

Off Antigua, 12 December 1786.

Our Young Prince is a gallant man: he is indeed volatile, but always with great good nature. There were two balls during his stay, and some of the old ladies were mortified that HRH would not dance with them; but he says, he is determined to enjoy the privilege of all other men, that of asking any lady he pleases.

Wednesday. We arrived here this morning at daylight. His Royal Highness dined with me, and of course the Governor. I can tell you a piece of news, which is, that the Prince is fully determined, and has made me promise him, that he shall be at our wedding; and he says he will give you to me. His Royal

Highness has not yet been in a private house to visit, and is determined never to do it, except in this instance. You know I will ever strive to bear such a character, as may render it no discredit to any man to take notice of me. There is no action in my whole life, but what is honourable; and I am the more happy at this time on that account; for I would, if possible, or in my power, have no man near the Prince, who can have the smallest impeachment as to character: for as an individual I love him, as a Prince I honour and revere him. My telling you this history is as to myself: my thoughts on all subjects are open to you. We shall certainly go to Barbadoes from this Island, and when I shall see you, is not possible for me to guess: *so much for marrying a Sailor. We are often separated, but I trust our affections are not by any means on that account diminished.* Our Country has the first demand for our services; and private convenience, or happiness, must ever give way to the Public good. Give my love to Josiah. Heaven bless, and return you safe to Your most affectionate, Horatio Nelson.

1 January 1787.

How vain are human expectations. I was in hopes to have remained quiet all this week: but to-day we dine with Sir Thomas Shirley; to-morrow the Prince has a party; on Wednesday he gives a dinner Saint John's to the Regiment; in the evening is a Mulatto ball; on Thursday a cock-fight, and we dine in Colonel Crosbie's brother's and a ball: on Friday somewhere, but I forget; on Saturday at Mr. Edward Byam's, the President. If we get well through all this, I shall be fit for anything; but I hope most sincerely the "Commodore" will arrive before the whole is carried into execution: in many instances it is better to serve than command; and this is one of them. If the "Commodore" does not come down and relieve me, I think it likely we shall remain here all this month at least; for the Ship's company of the "Pegasus" are sick, and I cannot with propriety leave His Royal Highness by himself.

Should Sir Richard Bickerton come down, and I think he must be at Barbadoes, and send me to Nevis, I will bless him: yet I would sooner die than ask any favour. If he is polite, he will do it without; if not, he would perhaps refuse me with asking, and I should not like the mortification. What is it to attend on Princes? Let me attend on you, and I am satisfied. Some are born for attendants on great men: I rather think that it is not my particular province. His Royal Highness often tells me, he believes I am married; for he never saw a lover so easy, or say so little of the object he has a regard for. When I tell him I certainly am not, he says, "Then he is sure I must have a great esteem for you, and that it is not what is (vulgarly), I do not much like the use of that word, called love." He is right: *my love is founded on esteem, the only foundation that can make the passion last.* I need not tell you, what you so well know, that I wish I had a fortune to settle on you: but I trust I have a good name, and that certain events will bring the other about: it is my not my fault. You can marry me only from a sincere affection; therefore I ought to make you a good husband, and I hope it will turn out that I shall. You are never absent from my mind in any place or company. I never wished for riches, but to give them to you; and my small share shall be yours to the extreme. A happy New Year; and that many of them may attend you, is the most fervent wish of your affectionate Horatio Nelson

Boreas, Montserrat, 11 February 1787.

Boreas, Sandy Point, St. Kitts, 6th March 1787

How uncertain are the movements of us sailors. His Royal Highness is rather unwell: therefore I have given up the idea of visiting Tortola for the present. Today we dine with Mr. [William] Georges [the Chief Justice] at his country house. I am now feeling most awkwardly: his Royal Highness has been with me all this morning and has told me that no things here are changed, if I am not married when we go to Nevis it is hardly probable he should see me there again: that I had promised him not to be married, unless he was present: that he wished to be there, to show his esteem for me, and should be much mortified if impediments were thrown in the way. He intends this as a mark of honour to me: as such I wish to receive it. Indeed his Royal Highness's behaviours throughout has been that of a friend, instead of a person so elevated above me. He told me this morning that since he had been under my command he has been happy: and that I should find him sincere in his friendship. Heaven bless you: I need scarcely say how much I am your affect. H.N.

After our marriage on Nevis and our return to England Horatio wrote to his friend Captain Locker 'Mrs. Nelson's lungs are so much affected by the smoke of London that I cannot think of placing her in that situation of living so near London, however desirable'. He was always so thoughtful and careful of my health, which suffered much after leaving the West Indies climate. Captain Locker has a most pleasant house in Kensington. We stayed initially at No. 10 Great Marlborough Street, and when Horatio returned to the *Boreas* at the Nore I stayed with Uncle Herbert at his mansion, No. 6 Princes Street, in Cavendish Square.

* * *

Horatio sailed off early in 1793 to the Mediterranean in the *Agamemnon* with Josiah and several other Norfolk lads as midshipmen. He wrote to me at least once a week. Off Toulon on the 4 August

How I long to have a letter from you: next to being with you, it is the greatest pleasure I can receive. The being united to such a good woman, I look back to

as the happiest period of my life: and as I cannot here show my affection to
you, I do it doubly to Josiah who deserves it, as well on his own account as on
yours for he is a real good boy and most affectionately loves me ...

That autumn after the visit to Naples he realised that I was beginning to fret at his
absence and wrote in October 'My dear Fanny, I received a letter from Mr. Maurice
Suckling yesterday and was indeed truly sorry to hear you were not perfectly well.
Why should you alarm yourself? I am well, your son is well and we are as comfortable
in every respect as the nature of our service will admit.' And a little later

> I need not, I am certain, say, that all my joy is placed in you. I have none
> separated from you: you are present to my imagination be where I will. I am
> convinced you feel interested in every action of my life: and my exultation
> in victory is twofold knowing that you partake of it. Only recollect that a
> brave man dies but once, a coward all his life long. We cannot escape death:
> and should it happen to me in this place, remember it is the will of Him in
> whose hands are the issues of life and death ...

He was always interested in my activities and also in the continuing saga of my first
husband's estate, complicated by the fact that he had died intestate in Salisbury.

In December 1793 he wrote 'I am glad you are improving in your music and you
must have a good instrument, we can afford that I am sure. Has Fraser etc. paid
you or how will that be settled now that they are bankrupt?' I shortly afterwards
purchased a fine pianoforte for £25.

In the autumn of the following year (September 1794), after his wounds and
loss of the sight of one eye on Bastia, Horatio wrote

> I expect to see you in the fall of the year, and although I shall not bring with
> me either riches or honours yet I flatter myself I shall bring an unblemished
> character. It always rejoices me to hear that you are comfortable and that
> my friends are attentive to you. I hope we shall find some snug cottage,
> whenever we may be obliged to quit the Parsonage ... I shall return to the
> plough with redoubled glee ... some little cottage

Ever since I met him on Nevis, Horatio had the sailor's dream of a pretty little cottage in
the countryside. Once achieved, he like all Sailors, dreamed of command at sea again!

The next summer (25 August 1795) my 'old Mediterranean man' wrote

> I shall be glad to hear John Stanley is arrived and I beg you will write to
> him and request his interference that the legacy be paid. It is scandalous to
> withhold the scanty pittance from you: Your letters dear Fanny are not only
> affectionate but full of news. You used to say you could not write letters but
> very few people write so well – this without flattery.

I always tried to make my letters interesting to my husband. I could not of course comment *knowledgeably* on his naval activities, but I could and did praise him on many occasions. I always sent him naval gossip because he wanted to know what was being reported to me by my friends and what the papers were saying. He relished news (and gossip) about our mutual friends in Norfolk or Bath, and my comments about his family and, above all, his father.

By now my Uncle Herbert's estate was proving difficult to resolve. He had died in London at the end of 1793 but my legacy took several years and many letters before it was eventually paid.

On 24 April 1796 as Horatio was being made Commodore, he wrote 'Rest assured my dear Fanny of my unabated and steady affection which if possible is increasing by that propriety of conduct which I know you are pursuing. I thank you for telling me of the gown you are making to receive me in but for fear you should not have finished it I have one, lawn I fancy, and worked the most elegantly I ever saw...'

After the battle of Cape St. Vincent he wrote to me (27 May 1797)

Though we can afford no more than a Cottage – yet with a contented mind, my dearest Fanny, my Chains, Medals and Ribbons are all-sufficient. We must be contented with a little, and the cottage near Norwich, or any other place you like better will I assure you satisfy me. Do not mention this matter of the Royal Favour to anyone except my Father...

Shortly after the terrible action of Santa Cruz, Horatio, now with a shattered arm, spent three months with me in England, having his wound treated by doctors and by me. He told Lavinia Bingham, who had married George Spencer, First Lord of the Admiralty – a pretty, elegant, perhaps untrustworthy woman that I was beautiful and accomplished, that my tenderness to him was angelic, and that I dressed his wounds and had saved his life. Lady Spencer later said of us that 'at dinner his (Nelson's) attentions to his wife were those of a lover. He handed her to dinner and sat by her apologising to me by saying he was so little with his wife that he would not voluntarily lose an instant of her society.' There was no doubt in my mind and in the mind of our friends that we were as devoted a married couple ten years after our marriage as at the romantic beginning on Nevis. Horatio wrote to Lord St. Vincent before the end of that year 'I find my domestic happiness perfect. I am possessed of everything that is valuable in a wife and I hope time will bring me about again but I have suffered great misery' [with his wound] ... dreadful.

My husband admitted to me on many occasions that his vanity was often overwhelming. On 24 May 1798 he had allowed his first-rater the *Vanguard* with Captain Berry to be dismasted in a great storm, and he wrote to me

I ought not to call what has happened to the *Vanguard* by the cold name of accident. I believe firmly that it was the Almighty's goodness to check my consummate vanity. I hope it has made me a better officer as I feel confident it has made me a better man. I kiss with all humility the rod. Figure to yourself a vain man on Sunday evening at sunset walking in his cabin with a Squadron about him who looked up to their chief to lead them to glory and in whom this chief placed the firmest reliance that the proudest ships in equal number belonging to France would have bowed their flags and with a very rich prize laying for him. Figure to yourself this proud conceited man when the sun rose on Monday morning his ship dismasted, his fleet dispersed and himself in such distress that the meanest frigate out of France would have been a very unwelcome guest. But it has pleased Almighty God to bring us into a safe port.

Poor Horatio needed a deeply loving wife in whom to confide his humiliation in such stark, revealing words and the depth of his despair. Captain Ball in the *Alexander* took *Vanguard* in tow into a small island harbour off Sardinia.

After the battle of the Nile, Horatio wrote many times to me from Naples. 'I must endeavour to convey to you something of what passed but if it were so affecting to those who were only united to me by bonds of friendship what must it be *to my dearest wife, my friend, my everything which is most dear to me in this world?'*

In the great cabin of the *Foudroyant* (1800) in Naples Bay were many new publications sent from England by me for Horatio and his officers to read the latest news. There Lady Knight asked him whether the battle of the Nile was the happiest day of his life, to which my husband replied 'No, the happiest was that on which I married Lady Nelson'.

In this portrait by Leonardi Guzzardi Nelson wears a decoration in his hat that was presented to him by the Sultan of Turkey to commemorate the battle of the Nile. The wound that Nelson recieved to his forehead in that action still hurt when this portrait was made in 1799, and it is due to this that his hat is pushed back in this portrait.

CHAPTER SIX

THE NELSON FAMILY

At the time we were married, Horatio had been at sea in the *Boreas* for three years and much had happened in the Nelson family in Norfolk during his absence. He had of course told me much about his elderly widowed father, the Reverend Edmund Nelson, who was Rector of Burnham Thorpe, Burnham St. Albert with Alp and Burnham Norton in the northern part of Norfolk, a few miles from the North Sea. The children of Edmund and Catherine neé Suckling, had all been born and baptised in the parish church of All Saints, Burnham Thorpe, about a mile from the Parsonage House. Horatio had been motherless since 1768 when he was nine. He was naturally very fond of his father (who was sixty-six when I first met him) – a tall man with a long, irregular shaped face, strong nose, warm eyes, and mane of white hair. He talked and wrote as though he were delivering a sermon without a trace of humour! A man to whom I became very attached and whom I attended until his death. It was difficult to realise that his wife had conceived eleven children in seventeen years.

His elder brother William, a large and heavy looking curate called 'The Rector', was possessed of most rough unsaintly manners: he was a bore, and greedy, always asking for favours from his more successful brother. (The sinecure Chaplainship on the *Boreas* was a typical example. Horatio, to my surprise, kept the wretched William dishonestly on his ships' books long after William had had enough of life at sea and returned home).

In Horatio's absence in 1786 brother William had married Sarah Yonge, daughter of a Devon vicar, eight years older than himself. My sister-in-law was a small woman who never ceased talking usually gossip. The only good thing in my opinion about this tedious couple was their daughter Charlotte, with whom I remained friends all my life. She was a sweet, kind, lively child who later married into Lord Hood's family. Horatio was devoted to his elder brother and they exchanged letters all their life – but I must confess that I never liked him. Once I wrote to Horatio 'The various passions that torment the Rector discomposes our good father who has been describing them to me. First of all ambition, pride and a selfish disposition.'

His eldest brother Maurice left home early and spent all his life at the Auditor's office in the Excise and then in the Admiralty. Maurice was the most amiable and unassuming member of the Nelson family, with whom I was always friendly. He

Revd Edmund
Nelson

was not at all ambitious, other than to become a Commissioner in his Office. He never married but lived with a blind woman, Mrs. Sarah Ford, at Laleham near Windsor, who was known affectionately as 'Poor Blindy'. I am not sure how the Reverends in the family accepted this unusual arrangement. He was Horatio's favourite brother, never made any demands on anybody, was always poor (he had a salary of £300 a year in 1800 when he was 47) and later on – when I was in need of a friend – remained my friend.

Horatio's three sisters were quite another matter. Susanna, early apprenticed as a milliner, inherited some money and married Thomas Bolton, a corn and coal merchant of Norwich, when she was twenty-six. 'Sukey', as she was sometimes known, quickly became a formidable matron with chin and nose to match. She was the mother of four ill-mannered daughters, Catherine and Susan, Anne and Elizabeth, a son George, who died aged twelve as a midshipman, and another son Thomas, who survived. Mr. Bolton was a gambler and even my father-in-law referred to 'VERY HIGH PLAY, HIGHER than ever.' As a result Mr. Bolton borrowed

Burnham Thorpe – the Nelson family home.

money from me (later even from Lady Hamilton) to pay his perpetual debts. Of the daughters my father-in-law wrote 'True Boltons, I pity them that marry them but no man will venture.' I once wrote of Thomas Bolton 'My maid tells me that they say at Ipswich his family is supported from the Gaming Table – true it is that he is always there so his family says, but they call it the *Coffee* House!'

Horatio's youngest sister was Catherine, otherwise known as 'Kate' or 'Kitty' who was born in 1767 and married George Matcham, a most interesting man known as 'G.M.' He was an East Indian nabob, a man of means, an explorer and author – a charming, restless man moving from one property to another. He was a keen and knowledgeable gardener and put Barton roses into the Parsonage garden. In twelve years of marriage they produced eight children and four more were yet to come. Kitty was always full of praise for her brother, and critical of me. Initially they lived at Barton Hall near Norwich, a comfortable house and pleasant park with many servants and much entertainment. The other daughter, poor Anne, who had trained in London in a lace warehouse died unmarried in Bath, in her twenty first year, as a result of a chill caught after a dance.

The Walpole family of Wolterton in Norfolk were cousins of the Nelsons. Horatio Walpole, the second Baron, and his Lady, were always friendly and sympathetic to me: they were far removed from the William, Susanna and Catherine Nelson families in style and manners. Horatio's mother's family, the Sucklings, were directly related to the Walpoles.

The annual visitation to the Walpoles at Wolterton was initially a matter of some importance. Our father (as Horatio and I always called my father-in-law) wrote to his daughter Mrs. Matcham, 'Be so good as to buy for Mrs. Nelson a plain Hansom Bonnett such as she may wear at Wolterton if need be, or what you would for yourself buy for dining, visits etc. Send it down and if any covering for the neck by way of a cloak is needfull add that also. Place them to my account.'

On his return from the West Indies Horatio had to meet *his* new relations: William's wife, Susanna's husband and Catherine's husband and their various modest establishments in Norfolk. It meant that we both met the 'other halves' at the same time and formed our own conclusions. Horatio, who was very much a family man, approved of the way that I started to care for his old father and to act as his companion when his son was away. I think he preferred my company to that of his children. His principal pleasure seemed to be hearing good reports of his famous son and writing homely letters to his dear HOR!

It was difficult to realise that this old man – whom I was to know extremely well for more than twenty years (until his death in Bath in 1802) had ever been young! I knew that I had married his favourite son – a sensual little Naval officer: despite his cloth his father must have been of a similar nature – long ago.

The Nelsons had never been a distinguished family. They produced many village parsons. Horatio's two grandfathers were East Anglian clergy as were two of his great uncles and no less then eight cousins – in addition to his father, and Horatio's own two brothers. The girls in the family usually married local trades-people. It was difficult to understand from where my husband derived his naval skills, his determination, and above all his incredible bravery – not, that is clear, from the Nelson family. His mother I was told had been a strong minded, forthright woman and her brother, Horatio's uncle, Captain Maurice Suckling of Woodton Hall in Norfolk, was a distinguished sailor. He had commanded HMS *Dreadnought* of 60 guns in 1759 in a famous engagement in the West Indies. After that he commanded the *Raisonnable* of 64 guns and took little Horatio, aged twelve, to sea with him as a midshipman. The Captain became Comptroller of the Navy, and died in July 1778.

Mr. William Suckling inherited the Captain's estates. He had a handsome mansion in Kentish Town. He was an influential official in the Customs and Navy office and the only relative of Horatio's who had both means and influence. He was generous not only to Horatio but to me, and I was always happy to visit the Kentish Town establishment. When he eventually died in 1799, when Horatio was inactive at the Court of Naples, he was made an executor and left a small legacy of £100. 'I love his memory' my husband wrote, 'and am not sorry that he has forgot me, except as his executor, in which I will be faithful. I loved my dear uncle for his own worth.'

Mainly for Horatio's sake I constantly entertained his sisters' children during their school holidays, either at Round Wood, or a London house, or occasionally in Bath. I preferred William's two children, Charlotte at school in Kensington, and

Captain Maurice Suckling, Nelson's uncle, who took 12 year-old Horatio to sea in 1770.

Horace at Eton College. Charlotte wrote to Horatio (5 February 1799) 'My aunt Nelson has recommended a school to Mama in London called Camden House which I reckon very much of ... I am now learning a grand march on your victory and another called "Lady Nelsons Fancy" which I hope you will like ...'

CHAPTER SEVEN

MARRIED LIFE IN NORFOLK
1787-1793

I am not sure what I expected life to be like in England with my new husband. He had no idea what the Admiralty might have in store for him when the *Boreas* was finally paid off. Naturally he hoped for another appointment at sea (although I was obviously less enthusiastic). We had very little money, although we could count on much hospitality, not only from Uncle Herbert in London, but also from West Indian friends scattered in the West Country at Bath, Clifton, Bristol and Salisbury. The Webbes, Tobins and Pinneys would always look after us (for a limited amount of time). When it came to the point Horatio's oft-repeated dream of a pretty little cottage meant lodging with his old father in his cold, large vicarage in Norfolk.

Just after his arrival in England, Horatio wrote to his old sea-Daddy, Captain William Locker (9 July) 'My dear wife is much obliged by your kind enquiries I have no doubt but you will like her upon acqaintance for although I must be partial yet she possesses great good sense and good temper.'

The stately *Roehampton* with its West Indian contingent duly arrived and berthed at the end of August '87, and as Horatio's victualling of the *Boreas* at the Nore was not scheduled to finish until the end of September, Josiah and I continued our Nevis life by going to live in London with Uncle Herbert and my cousin Parry Herbert. Horatio had by now developed a severe cold and fever and I shortly followed suit. There is no doubt that the hot-house plants of the Caribbean do not transplant healthily to the English shores. Apart from temporary cures at the Spa towns and seaside resorts such as Exmouth, I was never to regain the same health and vitality that I had been accustomed to in the West Indies. London with its fogs and vapours was the worst place for me (although short stays to visit the Court and theatre were possible); the East Anglian winter of damp cold and biting winds was almost unbearable despite many extra layers of clothes. No one brought up in London or East Anglia could understand the difference! Even Horatio, never fit at the best of times, knew how sublime the West Indian climate was by comparison. Of Bath he wrote 'This is little Jamaica to any other part of England.'

Josiah adapted himself much better to the rigours of the English climate. He had not been long enough in the West Indies for his blood to become thin, and his stepfather reported frequently years later 'Josiah is never ill'.

Horatio was not only busy with the *Boreas*, but was involved in the distribution of much booty of presents and purchases he had obtained in his Caribbean cruises – mainly rum, wine and tropical fruits. I had visited London before when I was a young widow in the two years after Josiah's birth, so now for the time being we took modest lodging near Uncle Herbert in Marylebone – at No. 10 Great Marlborough Street and then at No.6 Princes Street. We spent Christmas with my Uncle and cousin at No. 5 Cavendish Square and he extended his usual lavish hospitality to us.

Horatio's business with the *Boreas*, with the smuggled luxuries, and with the Admiralty finished, we resumed our honeymoon. Although neither of us was particularly fit, we went to Bath for a fortnight of taking the spa waters. There we met several West Indian friends and Horatio some 'sea-folks'. We then went to Bristol and stayed with the Tobins and the Pinneys, spent another fortnight in Bath and then in early May had a very happy month in Exmouth, the oldest resort in Devon. It was ideal spring weather and we were young lovers again. As a result, that part of the world made a deep impression on me; (Twenty years later I made it my home). In mid summer we returned to London where Josiah rejoined us from school, and stayed with Uncle Herbert who was happy to see us united again.

Prince William Henry had come back into our lives again. The *Pegasus* had returned safely to Plymouth from its cruises to Canada and the West Indies. We had visited him briefly on the 26 April on his return and Horatio reported favourably on the ship, its discipline and on its Royal Commander. Since I knew the Prince thought highly of the 'widow Nisbet' to whom he had been 'Father' at Montpelier a year back, I suggested to Horatio that HRH might have a situation for me in the Royal Household. A letter was sent but nothing favourable emerged.

Meantime I had written polite letters to Horatio's father and immediate family in Norfolk, and in August we went on a grand tour to meet them all. I wore what I thought was suitable for a first occasion – a highwaisted dress, graceful flower-decked turban, and looked distinctly handsome (or so I was told) and more suited to the Bath Pump Room society. The kind old Rector took to me at once despite his forebodings (and I was to look after him for the next fourteen years, although I had no inkling of that at the time.)

My husband's half pay as Captain 'on the beach' was eight shillings per day. We both of us through our Uncles received an annual allowance of £100 which combined worked out at nearly seven pounds a week. We were certainly not impecunious, but with Josiah's clothes, board and lodging to be considered, we had to be thrifty. We had been planning to spend the winter in France where it would be warmer, cheaper, and better for our learning of the language – he said he 'experienced great inconvenience from not understanding the language'. However when the Rector of Burnham Thorpe, Burnham St. Albert-with-Alp and Burnham Norton offered us a home with him at his large Parsonage House, we accepted at once: I had not the slightest idea of how cold the East Anglian weather can be. There were three rooms available to us 'somewhat like a Bath lodging' – a guest chamber, bedroom, and a little dressing room which Josiah used when he was there with us in his school holidays. They were the coldest set of rooms we had ever conceived of, four miles from the North Sea. We huddled together at night for warmth – almost for survival. Our days were simply spent. Our small family rose between 6 and 7 a.m. dined at 4 p.m. and were in bed by nine o'clock. I was careful not to alter the old man's daily regime but often discreetly interfered with the cooking arrangements.

The Reverend Edmund wrote of me 'I believe she will form a valuable part of our family connections' and later hoped for 'a little society and an instrument' with which I could 'pass away an hour'. 'She does not openly complain' he wrote. 'Her attention to me demands my esteem and to her Good Husband she is all he can expect'. Horatio and I were very much in love and we spent all the time together. We had winter walks through the snowy lanes, an occasional visit to a hostelry, many visits to Horatio's relatives, and attendance at Sunday church services. I would accompany the old Rector if he visited his parishoners. Occasionally we would go to a Sessions Ball at Norwich, to the Aylsham Assembly or the Lynn Feast. On the 2 October each year there was a minor festival at the parsonage House to commemorate Captain Maurice Suckling's victory over the French in 1759 in the West Indies when he commanded the *Dreadnought*. In the spring we would go birds-nesting together, and Horatio would cultivate his father's garden and dig up plots – even plant shrubs. If the weather was inclement he would study charts, draw up plans and write many letters. At the same time I would do my needlework and embroidery, paint if the light was good, and one or other would read aloud to our father. I missed having a musical instrument. With our slender resources I could not ask for what I wanted. I had to wait a few years before Horatio's prize money and my legacies warranted the purchase of a pianoforte for £25.

My husband was the kindest, most considerate father young Josiah could have had. He played with him constantly indoors and out, helped him with his three Rs, made dams on the local streams for model ships, and told him stories.

Horatio decided to buy a riding pony. His brother and his brother-in-law had left a horse at the Parsonage House stables for both of us to ride and to use with a dog-cart. On 26 April 1789 he went to the local fair and purchased 'a Gallwey, a little pony' and in due course came home with it expecting much interest and perhaps praise as well. During his absence at the fair, two men had visited the parsonage 'in their appearance resembling Bow-Street officers of the law'. They had forced their way into the house demanding to see my husband. When I told them politely that he was not available they asked me whether I was his wife, to which I assented. They then presented me with a document bidding me to 'give it to "Captain Nelson".' It was a writ served on behalf of the angry American sea-captains whom Horatio had taken off Nevis. Now they were claiming damages of £20,000 as a result of his honesty and inflexibility towards the Maritime laws. It was a most distressing interlude for me and Horatio at once wrote to the Admiralty and obtained their Lordships' protection. He made immediate plans to leave for France if the Admiralty failed to defend him. He intended that Maurice Nelson would take me (and presumably Josiah too) to join him ten days later. Horatio once spoke of the Russian service. I had never known him quite so angry and so desperate. However, Captain Thomas Pringle had word from George Rose, the Secretary of the Treasury, that he would be supported by the Treasury, so all was well.

Meanwhile, restless as ever, he wrote letters to Prince William Henry, to the First Lord, Earl of Chatham, Commodore Cornwallis, and to Lord Hood. The latter refused to pass Horatio's name upwards with his blessing. The amazing reason was that 'The King was impressed with an unfavourable opinion of Nelson'. This was a bitter blow and resulted from the Palace taking the view that Nelson was responsible for Prince William's trouble-making cruises in the West Indies, some of which had had minor repercussions. The criticism struck Horatio to the heart as it was completely unfounded. He and I were on the best of terms with Prince William, and all our friends in the Navy knew that to be so.

After this rebuff Horatio pursued country pastimes – coursing, occasional game bird shooting, riding Tycho (the pony) and more gardening. The Parsonage had 30 acres around it, mostly pastureland with occasional woods.

In 1790 the Reverend Edmund kindly vacated the Parsonage for us and moved to a cottage nearby at Burnham Ulph, and wrote of 'Poor Mrs. Nelson still kept in the same harry of spirits and uncertainty as she has been for the last six months'.

Horatio became a member of the Gregorians. He wrote to Mr. Pillans, 'Grandmaster of the Ancient Order of Gregorians', which flourished at Norwich and owned masonic items such as a snuff box. He studied the lot of the agricultural poor in Norfolk and wrote to the Prince that there was 'not quite twopence a day for each person – water only – for beer our poor labourers never taste unless they are tempted'. The Prime Minister told the House of Commons that 'we might reasonably expect fifteen years of peace' and the Navy was reduced to 15,000 men. Dismal news indeed for a professional naval officer.

Apart from my health which suffered from the harsh cold winds and the damp winter (the Parsonage was never warm), I was happy, even though I could see that Horatio, now in the prime of the career, a Post-Captain of thirty three, was wasting away 'on the beach'. I wanted with all my heart for him to stay with me in the Parsonage. The eternal dilemma for a sailor's wife! Towards the end of '92 the clouds of war with France were fast gathering, despite William Pitt's earlier prophecy, and by the New Year Horatio was sure that he was about to get a command. He became a different man. Interviews with Lord Chatham and Lord Hood followed, and the press-gangs were soon out scouring Norfolk for the 74 gun *Agamemnon*. Young midshipmen joined the ship, including my son Josiah, a schoolboy no longer.

Just before Horatio sailed he wrote to me from Chatham (15 March) about Uncle Herbert's legacy 'the not tying up any of the money left you I consider as a

Nelson was struck in the face by gravel thrown up by a French round shot during the battle of Calvi, 12 July 1794.

confidence reposed in me and I shall take care that this is not misplaced.' With me he was always considerate and polite, even in the midst of the intense excitement of a sea-command after five years 'on the beach'.

My husband was at sea again in 1794, although after his exploits on land at Bastia and Calvi in conjunction with the Army, he was emulating the best of the Royal Marine tradition – that of fighting the enemy on land and at sea.

My letters to him that autumn were written partly from Mr. William Suckling's comfortable house in Kentish Town in north London, not far from Hampstead Heath, and from New King Street in Bath where our father and I had retired for the winter season.

From my early days on Nevis with Horatio I discovered that he was a natural 'matchmaker' with a liking for a bit of gossip, particularly about members of his family, and about our mutual friends of the West India Station. He was always avid for news of naval affairs that I might glean from the Lords of the Admiralty and the 'Bath' Admirals, Sir Andrew Snape Hammond who became Comptroller of the Navy, Lord and Lady Hood and his brother Lord Bridport, Admiral Cosby and Admiral Sir Richard Bickerton (who married my good friend Anne Athill).

During that autumn and Christmas Horatio was suffering from the loss of an eye sustained on 12 July at the siege of Calvi. I knew that he would be in the forefront (with Josiah) of the fighting, and from a distance of a thousand miles away was naturally deeply worried. As usual he made light of his injury.

During October my hopes were raised that he might return to me and dock at Portsmouth – but alas that was not to be.

I always took care to send him *good* news so that in addition to his daily worries and duties he need not worry about me or our father I am including this letter as an example of how I used to write to him.

Kentish Town, 30 September 1794

My Dearest Husband,

Yesterday was your birthday, Mr. Suckling drank it with no small pleasure, gave some of his best wines and a Norfolk man deserved two geese. We were cheerful. Mr. Rumsey and family were of the party. *Mr. Mentz* as usual intreated his best respects to you and said many handsome things which I received with pleasure knowing how deserving you were of them. A happy birthday for me, the next I hope we shall be together.

Your letter and *my son's* of the 5th September I have received and look every day for one telling me you are coming. Everybody that Mr. S and Maurice has asked if they know who are the captains that are coming home seems to say, you of course, that the ship must want much rest. Maurice came here last Sunday. He is much wanted at the Navy Office, but I do not know that they have offered him what would make it worth his while to quit his present post. Father is well. Mr. and Mrs. and Miss Suckling send

Frances Nelson. From a
watercolour drawing by
G. P. Harding after
Edridge.

their love to you. If any little thing falls in your way bring it for Miss S. as a
keepsake. I feel for her. An attachment between her and Captain Whigley:
he is on the Continent, her father knows it. He is to sell out. Don't take
notice of it, it is not known. How is Frank [Lépee, Nelson's servant]? I have
seen his beautiful china.

The West Indies is now a scene of mortality. Never was such a fever there
before. An officer who was tried for not knowing his own things has seen
most of the Court Martial dead before the trial was over. The hurricane they
have had I hope will be of service to them. Guadeloupe is not yet retaken.
Capt. Roberts is a prisoner, recovered his wound. I am glad Maurice Suckling
is well. Pray take care of yourself. How I shall rejoice to see you. You must
save yourself as much as you possibly can. Sir Andrew Hammond [the
comptroller] has a house at Hampstead. I shall call on Lady H. and the first
time I can on Lady Hood. Lord Hood has had leave to come by land or in his
ship. The French have ships cruising.

Mrs. Matcham I have not heard from since I came to town but Maurice
tells me they went to Tunbridge. Surely there never was such an unsettled
man. The journey I hope will be of service to her. You may depend upon
it, it is a violent cold she has caught. Capt. Suckling embarks again for the
Continent. They are all well. Suckling, Nelson and the two clergymen of
Aylsham are very good friends. Mr. S. says he liked to have my letters sent
to him for then he knew you were well. He is very much interested about

you. Our Station, for his half pay is £130 yearly and profitable one now. He is grown stout.

Your assurances of health and I hope the prospect of soon seeing my dear husband and child has made me happy beyond expression. It has given health for before you wrote me you were well and Calvi was taken, I was fallen into the same way I was last year, now I am quite well. Mr. Suckling behaves in kindest manner. Miss Suckling I shall always have a sincere regard for. Mrs. S. is equally kind. My dear son's letter did contain news. I thank him for it and hope he is quite right in what he says.

Lord Southampton is gone to demand the Princess of Brunswick for a wife for the Prince of Wales, everybody congratulates themselves on the change he is going to make; Mrs. Fizherbert has been long dismissed. Her violence of temper and some improprieties gave disgust. Everybody are full of the wicked design that a French watchmaker had to take away the life of our King.

They were three concerned, the French man, who had made a tube, which upon blowing with his mouth a poisoned arrow was to have struck our King, a saddler and a chemist in Fleet Street. The saddler's conscience tormented him. He went and disclosed it. They are all taken up. The Playhouse was to have been the scene of wickedness, the signal for the watchmaker a call of not. I wish these French away I never liked them.

Admiral Nelson, painted by Lemuel Abbot.

CHAPTER EIGHT

NELSON'S LOVE FOR HIS 'SON-IN-LAW'

From that March morning in '85 in Charlestown when my husband first met my son and for the next fifteen years they maintained a close paternal and filial relationship. Nelson wrote of Josiah as 'my son-in-law' and Josiah wrote to his stepfather as 'Father'. His diminutive name was 'Jiah'. It was a very loving time for both of them.

When Josiah was six Horatio wrote to me (25 February 1786) 'Josiah I dare say makes a wonderful progress in his book [Learning how to read]. The greatest favour you can at present grant me is to learn him to read. Give my kind love to him and do rest assured my excellent ––, fill up the blank that I am with the purest affection your Horatio Nelson.' Three weeks later (3 March) he wrote 'No dangers shall deter me from pursuing every honourable means of providing handsomely for you and yours and again let me repeat that my dear Josiah shall ever be considered by me as one of my own. That Omnipotent Being who sees and knows what passes in all hearts knows what I have written, to be my undisguised sentiments towards the little fellow ...' Presents followed including a young grey parrot!

Dr. Jeffreys was the island doctor on Nevis and with the recent appalling deaths of my father and Josiah's father I made sure that my son had regular medical checks. He was a strong and sturdy child and was told that there was no cause for worry.

By the following year we had returned to London and Josiah's education had to be considered, particularly since our finances were slender and his father's estate had not been resolved. Nelson's brother the Rev. William recommended a school nearby at Hillborough – that was on 29 October 1787 when we were staying at Uncle Herbert's London house. Moreover Mrs. William Nelson kindly offered to help in any way she could. Horatio wrote to his brother in the following January

Our little boy, Josiah, shall be at Hillborough on Tues. or Wed. next escorted by Frank [Lépee] who I have desired to stay two or three days till the child becomes reconciled. I am assured of your and Mrs. Nelsons goodness to him that is you will *not* allow him to do as he pleases: its mistaken kindness where it happens. I wish him at school to have the same weekly allowance as the other boys and whatever else may be proper for him. We have been very unwell and shall go to Bath as soon as I can.

Horatio was a wonderful father for Josiah. He had infinite patience and never had a cross word for him. He even helped him acquire a love of plants and flowers. Eventually his Uncle Walter Nisbet on Nevis and John Ward, Judge of the Vice Admiralty Court settled my late husband's estate, which meant that the interest of the legacy was paid to me for young Josiah's education. The death of Uncle Herbert in London and his substantial legacy to me coincided with Horatio's promotion to command the *Agamemnon* ship of the line *and* take Josiah aboard as a small midshipman – nearly 13 years old! I could not bear to let them both go off to war together – the little Captain and my forlorn little son at his side. I went to the Nore to inspect their quarters on the great 74 gun ship. Josiah was in good company with little Hoste, Weatherhead, and cousin Bolton – all of his age and known to him from his recent years spent in Norfolk.

Every letter Horatio sent me contained news of my son. In mid-January, a year after they had sailed, he wrote 'I never was better in health so is Josiah ... I think if the Lockharts [Josiah's aunt and uncle in commerce in Scotland] will get Josiah a good place he has sense enough to give up the sea although he is [aged 14] already a good seaman. He desires his love.'

I think that Horatio never remembered that the Woolwards had a nautical background extending over centuries. Far better for Josiah to be near his loving stepfather, growing up adventurously (which is what he seemed to want) rather than a new life hundreds of miles away from me in the cold North.

In mid-summer he wrote of Josiah, who had been in the thick of the fighting in Calvi

> Josiah is very well, amazingly grown and will be a handsome young man and I have no fears but he will be a good one. He is affectionate but warm in his disposition which nothing can cool so well as being at sea where nobody have entirely their own way. The only treasure to you I shall expect to bring back is Josiah and myself. (14th July) Your son came to dine with me and is on shore at Calvi. (18th August) J. is very well and a clever smart young *man* so I must call him his sense demands it. Josiah is never sick, Hoste, Bolton and Suckling were ill. (26th August) J. went with Hoste and myself to Pisa for the day. He will be an excellent officer.

There were no secrets between the three of us. Horatio showed all my letters to Josiah, so that he knew in detail of my life and thoughts. Like most boys he was a most indifferent correspondent!

Horatio wrote to his family and friends about Josiah's progress. 27 September 1794, 'Josiah says he is 5 feet 1 inch tall now. (October) At Leghorn for repairs, 70 crew sick will seek a French master for himself, Josiah and Hoste ... all on shore for a day to have a good dinner, wine etc. come on board at sunset.' 10 October off Gourjean Bay, *Agamemnon* to Commodore William Locker 'Josiah is very well and thanks you for your inquiries after him' and later 'Josiah is a fine young man and a brave fellow' (21 March 1795).

Horatio commissioned a portrait of himself to be painted at Leghorn to be sent to Mr. Maurice Suckling; not only did Josiah not like the finished portrait but he also refused to be painted himself! (17 January 1795) 'As for Josiah I have no doubt but he will be a comfort to both of us: his understanding is excellent and his disposition really good: he is a seaman every inch of him.' (2 March) Leghorn. Josiah was very well 'just buying a jacket and complains things are very dear'. (14 March) Josiah and Hoste with Bolton were his aides de camp in the battle in March when the *Ca Ira*, 80 guns, and *Censeur*, 74 guns, were taken by Nelson and behaved with great courage, 'Josiah thinks there is no great danger from a Frenchman's shot!' Horatio had been made a Colonel of Marines and was entitled to a uniform with plain gold epaulettes with bullion. Josiah wanted a set for himself! (2 June) 'J's teeth are good: his cough as usual but I believe it is a great deal habit: it neither affects his eating or growth. He will brag himself a great stout boy.' (September 1795) 'Josiah will be a good officer I have no doubt but I fear will never be troubled with the graces. He is the same disposition as when an infant. He is in extraordinary good health never sick.'

Another winter and Christmas came and went. In the spring of '96 Horatio wrote to his brother William from Genoa, still with deep snow lying, and intensely cold 'I am grown old and battered to pieces and require some repairs. Josiah is very well and often inquires after you.' The following month, 'Josiah is not learned in the French language for although we have Frenchmen on board they cannot speak English therefore not much can be got from them as masters.' Horatio kept an eye on Josiah's finances, 'I hope by your account the legacy will be paid soon at least the interest. The fancy that it could be omitted for want of a word in the will would fall before a jury. The contention of the donor [Uncle Herbert] was clear and in respect to Josiah is particularly so for it says the interest is to go towards his education. Josiah well, full of business.' Later, 'Josiah is well, teeth good, 5 feet 4 ½ inches in height.'

In mid-summer off Leghorn, Horatio wrote 'Josiah has not served his time and it is impossible as far as I know of the service to get him made a lieutenant and this war will not last till his time is out when I know it will be difficult to promote him but I cannot help it, I wish I could.' I knew that midshipmen had to do six years at sea before they could qualify to take the examination for promotion to lieutenant. He had by now served a little over three and a half years at sea. 23 August 1796, 'You seem to think Josiah is a master of language. I must say he is the same exactly as when an infant and likes apples and port wine but it will be difficult to make him speak French much more Italian. However I hope his heart is good and that is the principal.' Horatio wrote to his brother William, from the *Captain* between Bastia and Leghorn 'Josiah thanks you all for your inquiries: he is not the least altered.'

That winter still with the in-shore squadron Josiah had a chance of going with Nelson on a 'most important mission' in the captured *La Minerve* of 42 guns. He chose to stay on the *Captain* while Horatio sailed to save the English garrison on Elba. Horatio's comment was 'His knowledge of the world is as forward as I wish it.' Horatio was away on this expedition for two months; he was involved in encounters with Spanish frigates, met and liked Sir Gilbert Minto, attended Captain Freemantle's wedding and later wrote that they 'very nearly escaped visiting a Spanish prison'.

My husband's role in the fleet victory over the Spaniards off Cape St. Vincent is well-known. By disobeying Sir John Jervis' orders, the *Captain* and gallant Troubridge in the *Culloden* brilliantly broke the Spanish line. His friend Collingwood in the *Excellent* bravely supported my husband and Troubridge and between them they were responsible for a famous victory. Horatio and Josiah were in the thick of the hand to hand fighting on the captured Spanish ships. Horatio wrote to me quickly 'I am well, Josiah is well' which is what I hoped to

Sir John Jervis was created earl of St Vincent for the victory Nelson inspired at Cape St Vincent.

hear. The *Captain* was so battered that Nelson transferred to the *Irresistible* and a little later wrote to me dated 3 March 1797 from Lisbon

> I have sent Josiah with Captain Edward Berry on a sloop, who wished to have him and he will learn more with him than he could with me, and he must be broke of being at my elbow. *I assure you I love him and I am confident its reciprocal.* His understanding is manly and his heart is as good as we can wish, but the same shyness is still visible, it is his nature and cannot be altered, but how much better than if he was forward. All from the *Captain* are promoted and I regret Josiah has not served his time. I have wrote to Maurice [Nelson, at the Admiralty] to see if he cannot get a little cheating for him (by entering his name on the books of a ship fictitiously) it might be done and would be invaluable ... for if the war lasts another year he must be made at least a lieutenant, and I hope farther. *His abilities are superior to many who command ships.* Captain Berry gives me very good account of him.

To my great surprise and joy, Horatio wrote to me (2 April) 'When you write to Josiah you may address yourself to Lieutenant Nisbet and I hope he will be a Captain if the war lasts till October next' and later (12 April) 'Josiah is a Lieutenant, Sir John Jervis gave him a commission April 8 which is gone home for confirmation. He is now officer of the watch' (back on the *Captain*).

A few months later in midsummer after the appalling fiasco of the gallant night attack on Santa Cruz, where Horatio was severely wounded and lost an arm, he wrote to me left handed (5th August) 'I know it will add much to your pleasure in finding that Josiah under God's providence was principally instrumental in saving my life ... Good Earl St. Vincent have made Josiah a Master and Commander. I shall come to Bath the moment permission come from the Admir. for me to strike my flag.' Even in his weeks of acute pain and discomfort he advanced Josiah's promotion with Lord St. Vincent (on 24 July). Young Hoste was made a lieutenant on the death of John Weatherhead, his great friend on the *Theseus* – there had been two hundred and fifty British casualties and no success to report. He wrote again to Earl St. Vincent in August

> I am become a burthen to my friends and useless to my Country but by my letter wrote the 24th, you will perceive my anxiety for the promotion of my son-in-law Josiah Nisbet. When I leave your command I become dead to the world: I go hence and am no more seen ... the Boy is under obligations to me but he repaid me by bringing me from the Mole of Santa Cruz. I hope you will be able to give me a frigate to convey the remains of my carcase to England ...

My poor sorely wounded husband came home to be nursed and cared for but – indomitable and brave as ever – was at sea in the spring of 1798 in the Mediterranean. On 21 March, just before he sailed, he made a new Will and left *to my son in law Josiah Nesbit five hundred pounds* ... I give and devise unto my dear wife Dame Frances Herbert Nelson all my freehold and copyhold lands, tenements and hereditaments to hold to her heirs and assigns for ever and I also give to my said wife all the rest of, and residue my personal estate and effects but in case my dear wife shall happen to depart this life in my lifetime or in case she shall survive me and shall die without having made any will or disposition of the estate and property hereby by me devised to her then and in either of the said cases I do give to my said son-in-law Josiah Nesbit the legacy or sum of ten thousand pounds instead of the said sum of five hundred pounds herein before by me given to him and I appoint my said wife sole executor of this my will but in either of the before mentioned events I do appoint *the said Josiah Nesbit, executor of this my will,* witnessed at Bishops Court, Chancery Lane by Thomas Combe, Thomas Smith, William Ryder.

The happy and devoted father to son relationship continued for the next eighteen months. On the 15 April 1799 I was constrained to write to Josiah

Have you received the Medal I sent you. I will enclose this letter to My Lord – fearing it might fall into other hands – *I never had a secret from him.* My dear Josiah, I have written of late very frequently to you and as I generally take my fetters to the foreign Post Office I hope you may have received them. I received a letter from My Lord Nelson dated Jan. 25th *when he mentions your improvements with tenderness and kindness his love for you is very great, he flatters himself he shall see you a good and great man.* It is in your power to be both therefore God pray you disappoint me not – you are very young and cannot know the World, be satisfied of this faith and implicitly follow the directions of My Husband who is truly a Good Man and his Military achievements has stamped his character greatly all over the world. You are more conspicuous than you imagine, be assured you are much envied from having such a father to bring you forward who has every desire to do it ...

My dear Josiah take yourself to account every day. Don't excuse any foible. I do assure you your first lieutenant has always wrote of you in a handsome manner, I have seen his letters to his mother. Silence on this subject ... God bless you and believe me your affectionate mother.

Until the events at the sinister, steamy Court of Naples took place, and the subsequent stormy homecoming, my husband and my son continued to enjoy a loving relationship. I was never able to give Horatio *his son,* although not through lack of endeavour. But I was able to give him *my* son.

CHAPTER NINE

JOSIAH AT SEA –
HIS ACCOUNT (1805)

A few weeks ago my step-father died. He was expecting to be killed and had faced sudden death on many previous occasions. At Trafalgar he tempted Fate once too often.

On the afternoon of the 21 October 1805 my step-father, Admiral Lord Horatio Nelson, died aboard HMS *Victory* at the battle of Trafalgar. The French and Spanish fleet were mainly destroyed: eighteen out of thirty three ships were taken or burned and a further four captured two weeks later. The remaining eleven ships escaped to Cadiz. It was a famous naval victory which will effect Europe for years to come. My step-father was a proud and alas a vain man. During the action he wore on his left breast the stars of the four Orders of Knighthood to which he was entitled. He presented an easy target to any enemy sharpshooter within range of the *Victory*. The 74 gun *Redoubtable* engaged the *Victory* closely, and at 1.35 that afternoon my step-father was shot and mortally wounded by a French sharpshooter.

I wish I had been there with him.

But I must start at the beginning. I cannot remember what my real father looked like, for he died when I was two. We had been living in Salisbury and my father had never recovered from the sunstroke illness suffered on Nevis island. I cannot now recall our voyage back to the island, but the childhood years were completely happy. My mother was keeping house for her Uncle John Herbert. The Nisbet estate of Mount Pleasant and the Herbert estate of Montpelier were ideal places for a small child to grow up in.

In 1785 when I was five, I remember at Montpelier impatiently waiting for breakfast to be served. I was always hungry and therefore always first at table. Just after daybreak on a spring morning there was a noise as my cousin Parry Herbert arrived at the house. She had just come by sea from England on the HMS *Boreas*, and was helped down from the carriage by a man, whom I thought of, at the time, as being a funny little naval officer. I could tell by then the difference between the officers and the ratings! One of my favourite games was to walk round the harbour in Charlestown examining all the ships. There were merchantmen berthed – English and American – and sometimes a Naval sloop or even a frigate. For instance I learned to count the gun ports showing on the side of the navy ships – the *Boreas* only had 28 guns.

When he was not looking I studied this strange sea-captain and soon recognised him. My great-uncle Herbert had been fulminating about the English commander of the *Boreas*, who had captured four American merchantmen lying in Nevis sea-roads. I did not understand great-uncle Herbert's point, but I knew we were not at war with America, and could not understand the reason for this peaceful battle.

Anyway this little Captain soon became my friend and also – just as Important – my mother's friend. Two years later when I was seven (and she was twenty six) my mother married the Commander of the *Boreas*. I looked in awe at a large blonde man – one of the King's sons – Prince William Henry, who was commanding the *Pegasus* (also of 28 guns), who was at the wedding. He seemed to be friends both with my new step-father and my mother. A week after the wedding my mother and I took ship to England whilst Captain Nelson sailed back in the *Boreas* to Portsmouth arriving there in July 1787.

Soon I was sent off to boarding school and came home in the three school holidays. Home was now at Burnham Thorpe in Norfolk, where my mother shared a house with my new stepfather, and his father, the village parson. Nelson was very good to me and took me fishing. He always referred to me as 'my son-in-law'. He and I, and the boot and knife boy, Williamson by name, damned a stream and sailed a lovely model ship of the line which my step-father had made. He showed me his nautical charts and read extracts to me of Dampier's *Voyages*. Although it was always cold in Norfolk – my mother and I had thin blood after life in the tropics – I enjoyed my school holidays. My mother played her pianoforte, painted her pretty water-colours, and tried to correct my French. I admired her fine needlework. (At that time, although a large rather loutish schoolboy, I was brought up to be polite at home). When I was a bit older my step-father took me out coursing and we chased every hare in Norfolk. I noticed that he caught just as many heavy colds as my mother and I did. Even I could tell that he was restless at home and wanted another command at sea. Just after Christmas 1793 he was told that he was to get a ship –his first ship of the line. He wrote to my mother from London 'Post nubila Phoebus – your son will explain the motto. After clouds come sunshine'. Even I knew that! By now Captain Nelson was like a god to me. He obviously made my mother very happy and he took immense trouble with me. It was always clear to the three of us that I would go to sea and become, I hoped, as good a captain as my step-father seemed to me to be.

The *Agamemnon* was one of the finest two decker Sixty-Fours in the Service and as Nelson wrote to my mother at the time 'with the character of sailing most remarkably well.' There were other youngsters known to me – Maurice Suckling, a cousin, and George Andrews, whom I had met on Nevis, and Nelson's nephew George Bolton who joined the *Agamemnon* with me as midshipmen. It is often reported that a midshipman is the lowest form of animal life. Perfectly true – we were disliked by the seamen and usually despised, sometimes pitied, by the officers.

Of course I was sick as a dog at Spithead. The rumour on board was that the little Captain was also sick. He had not been to sea for over five years and that must have made a difference. Getting one's 'sea-legs' they called it. By mid-summer, as part of Lord Hood's fleet, we anchored off Cadiz, where Nelson went to see a bullfight which he and all the Navy officers detested.

Captain Nelson's advice to his midshipmen was 'First you must always implicitly obey orders without attempting to form opinion of your own respecting their propriety: secondly you must consider every man as your enemy who speaks ill of your King and thirdly, you must hate a Frenchman as you do the devil.' As I grew older and more experienced it became clear to me when I commanded a frigate that the first tenet could be most dangerous and irresponsible, i.e., blind obedience! The second tenet was suspect during the reign of the Georges, and eventually when my mother and I lived in France, we made many Parisian friends.

The midshipmen were given specific duties. For instance, whenever the ship's powder room was visited (it was of course kept under lock and key) one of us would attend the light room and make sure that no naked flame was ever used, and that powder was logged in and out before action stations. We had to attend the Store Room, since the Steward was not allowed to serve stores, food or slops except at fixed times. There was constant friction with the Purser and his men, who were always regarded as robbers by the whole ship's crew – usually with good cause. Midshipmen were in the thick of battle. Two of my friends were killed in action as serving midshipmen – James Goodench and Thomas Lund – and another, Samuel Gamble, was wounded. We often had much responsibility but of course no authority. Captain Nelson passed on to us the regulations for keeping a Ship of War, which I applied to my commands of the *Dolphin*, *La Bonne Citoyenne* and the *Thalia* in later years.

For piping the hammocks up, morning at	half past seven
To begin washing the ship	Five
For the people to wash	Tues/Friday
For washing between decks	Wed/Sat
For the pursers steward to serve, morning at	Five
Provisions twice a day, evening at	Four
For going to the holds, morning at	Five
For all storeroom keys to be returned evening at	Six
For hoisting in the boats, evening at	Six
For piping the hammocks down (sunset)	Six
For liberty to be granted to the ships company to go out of the ship	Sunday

The *Agamemnon* needed a crew of well over 400 to man it. For four years as midshipman I was part of Captain Nelson's efficient ship of war. I learned my sailing skills under a fine set of officers. Martin Hinton was the First. The other lieutenants were Wenman Allison, Thomas Edmond, Joseph Bullen, George Andrews (who later became Post Captain) William Lucas, Maurice Suckling (my step-father's cousin) Edward Chetham, Peter Spicer, James Summers, James Noble, Henry Compton, James M'Arthur (who later became Lord Hood's secretary) and last, but certainly not least, Edward Berry. He became a great friend of my step-father and of my mother. Later he was made an Admiral and knighted. The sailing master was Mr. John Wilson, and the purser was Mr. Thomas Fellowes (regarded by all, perhaps unjustly, as wily and mercenary.) Joseph King was the sturdy boatswain who had been on the *Valliant* and the *Boreas* under Nelson. The Surgeon is one of the most important men on board ship. For most of the time they have little to do except drink. Many of them are butchers in their trade. We were fortunate with Mr. John Roxburgh, our Scots surgeon, who was well liked and was polite to the child-midshipmen.

My step-father's sailor servant was Frank Lépee, who was meant to keep an eye on me from time to time. He was so often in his cups that it was surprising that Nelson put up with him so long. He was eventually succeeded by Tom Allen, whom I knew and liked from Burnham Thorpe days. He was not much better – a stunted little blackhaired runt with bad manners and quite illiterate (at least he could not read my mother's letters to Nelson when they arrived in the Captain's large cabin!)

We were in many actions in the Mediterranean and many of the ship's complement died in action or of wounds received. Sickness and occasional scurvy reduced our numbers still further. At the battle with the *Ca Ira* we could only muster 344 to action stations. When we reached Naples harbour we had over seventy sick and ill (not wounded).

After the brief visit to Naples the *Agamemnon* failed to find the French squadron and sailed for Leghorn and thence to Toulon, where we arrived on 5 October 1793. From there Lord Hood sent us back to Sardinia and then to Tunis. At the end of October we had a brisk action and chased the *Melpomene*, a fast French frigate of 40 guns. We damaged her badly and would have sunk or captured her but a French squadron of frigates, a corvette and a brig appeared, so we called off the fight. It was warm work and the *Melpomene* did a lot of damage – our topmast, mainmast and mizzen mast had been badly damaged. The Froggies were faster but we outgunned them and nearly took them. We spent most of November and December in Tunis looking at a large French convoy at anchor which we were not allowed to attack. We all knew that the Captain was furious with his orders. By Christmas 1793 we were back in Leghorn, south of the Gulf of Genoa. There we were told that Lord Hood had been forced to abandon Toulon, which seemed like a disaster at the time, although the arsenal had been blown up, nine French naval ships burned, a dozen frigates and four ships of the line captured. It was said that 15,000 French Royalists from Toulon had been saved from the Revolutionaries and brought mainly to Leghorn. The Neapolitan Army had behaved disgracefully and had retreated ignominiously.

Next Lord Hood ordered the *Agamemnon* to Corsica. Our Captain told us that we were to hold the area round Calvi in the Northwest of the island with the Army, and land a naval force. We had half a dozen coastal raids in which I took part. Cutting out, burning or capturing – vessels loaded with wine – capturing local forts, castles, and a mill.

On 12 October 1793 I had written to my mother

> On the Agamemnon, Dear Mother, I have been very well since I wrote you last and hope you have been so. I hope Mr. Nelson is very well. I still like being at sea and think I always shall. We have been at Toulon which I think a very strong place. The Spaniards have ran away every time they have engaged the French and have behaved with the utmost barbarity to all those who laid down their arms and also the Neapolitans have behaved very cruelly in some cases. Josiah Nisbet.

30 December 1793 I wrote

> We are now at Leghorn and have just heard of Toulons being evacuated by Lord Hood. He burnt fifteen sail of the line and carried out with him the "Commerce" of Marseilles and two ships of the line and seven frigates. Lord Hood is laying at anchor with nine miles off Toulon. I heard we had very few killed. We had not time to blow up La Malque. The SCIPION a French ship of the line blew up on the 23rd November in the road supposed to set on fire wilfully etc. etc. Josiah Nisbet.

I was meant to start studying the exams for promotion to lieutenant but there was so much excitement going on that my studies were slow, although I could not take the exam until I had been at sea for six years.

Siege of Bastia (Corsica), April–May 1794. Bastia was captured by Lord Hood's fleet. HMS *Victory* is clearly visible in this drawing by N. Pocock.

Captain Horatio Nelson, 1794.
(*National Maritime museum*).

By now I was taller and broader than my step-father – the largest of the midshipmen, so there was never much risk of being bullied either because of my strength or because of my favoured connection. In any case I was becoming a good sailor.

Nelson had decided to take the town of Bastia by storm with our fleet of six frigates. He had rather rashly promised Lord Hood that we could take the place with a combined force of 1,300 including an Army regiment. During the attack Nelson was wounded in the back. After a siege lasting seven weeks, Bastia fell. On 22 May 1794 Nelson wrote to my mother from the Camp at Bastia 'Josiah came to me and has been with me at the head of the British Grenadier taking possession of forts and posts sufficient to have prevented our success had they been fought well. 1,200 men quitted the first post we went to ...' It was certainly hot work. Nelson thoroughly enjoyed our combined operations on land in co-operation with our Army. He called them 'our fiorenzo army.'

On 30 June 1794 I wrote to my mother 'I am much obliged to you for your remembrance to me. I am glad to hear the hobby [horse] is well. I will thank you to remember me to Mr. Nelson.' I never became much of a correspondent and the missives to my mother have not improved much since I was fourteen.

On 20 September 1794 I wrote on the back of my step-father's letter to my Mother 'I hope you are well. We are now at anchor in Genoa mole. We expect to come home shortly with the Victory or with the convoy. I am your dutiful son Josiah N.'

The *Agamemnon* then sailed west to Gibraltar to refit. Nelson had the bit between his teeth and 'Naval Expeditions' were to continue. In the middle of June our fleet – three men of war and sixteen transport and storeships – was anchored off Calvi, the fortress on the Northwest coast of Corsica. During the attack on 12 July my step-father was quite badly wounded by an enemy shell and splinters hit his face and breast. He bravely continued his leadership of the siege, and the garrison surrendered on 10 August: shortly afterwards he realised that he had lost the sight of his right eye.

In October 1794 Lord Hood sailed for Gibraltar and then home to Portsmouth, but the *Agamemnon* stayed behind on blockade duty between Golfe Jouan, Leghorn, Porto Ferrajo in Elba and San Fiorenzo in Corsica.

I was nearly fifteen and my mother wrote to my step-father about me as 'my young man' instead of 'my child'. Nelson reported home quite favourably 'His understanding is excellent and his disposition really good. He is a seaman, every inch of him.' But Nelson also told me that he detected in me signs of what he called 'a warm disposition', by which he meant that I was rather headstrong and wanting my way too much for the good of my career. As events later turned out, he was quite right!

We had shore leave from time to time at the port of Leghorn where we refitted and revictualled the ship. Nelson took me to the opera and introduced me to the Pollards, Levant merchants, and Mr. John Udney the British Consul. He also took time to have his portrait painted for my mother by a local artist.

That spring of 1795 Nelson wrote to his father at Bath 'Remember me with sincerest affection to my dear wife and say Josiah is very well and a very good boy.' My mother wrote to my step-father 'My child! I figure him to myself – good and obedient to you and I hope tells you all his secrets. If he does, you will keep him good.' My mother did not realise that to a young midshipman the Captain takes the place of God. Despite our close relationship it was impossible for me to talk to him of my problems. I was however protected from the usual wardroom bullying (although I could now take care of myself) but nevertheless it was an invidious situation. Young Hoste in particular was jealous of me and we had a keen rivalry, since we are both ambitious for promotion. He was always suffering accidents – breaking limbs etc. – which he took with great good humour.

In early March '95 a French fleet was sighted out of Toulon heading for Corsica. The blockading fleet was under the command of Admiral William Hotham, and Vice Admiral Samuel Goodall commanded the division to whom Nelson reported. We chased the French fleet, and eventually on 14 March we had a long running battle with the 80 gun *Ca Ira*, which had been dismasted by incompetent handling by its French crew and taken in tow by a frigate. The Captain persevered as audaciously as ever, like a terrier after a bull, because the *Ca Ira* was protected by the huge *Sans Culotte* of 120 guns and the *Jean Bart*. It was an incredible little battle since we were quite alone and totally outgunned. When the *Ca Ira* was a perfect wreck, Admiral Hotham signalled from afar off to the *Agamemnon* to

Nelson's 64-gun *Agamemnon* (right) batters the 80-gun *ça Ira* (centre) in the battle of Hyères, March 1795.

discontinue the attack. The next morning we caught up again and in a brisk action in which two English ships were disabled, we captured the great *Ca Ira* and the *Censeur*. The French ships had a casualty list of 750 and the *Agamemnon*, despite two strong close engagements, had but 13 wounded. It was my first serious action with large ships of the line. Nelson was all for chasing after the main French fleet but Admiral Hotham was too cautious.

My step-father wrote on the 25 March 1795 to his brother Reverend William

Our late Action with the French Fleet ... I am most perfectly well, as is Josiah, and that Agamemnon is as ready as ever to give the French another meeting ... the only line of Battle Ship who got singly into Action on the 13th when I had the honour of engaging the Ca Ira, absolutely large enough to take Agamemnon in her hold. I never saw such a ship before ... We killed on board Ca Ira on the 13th, one hundred and ten whilst only seven were slightly wounded on board Agamemnon. On the 14th although one of the Van-ships and in close Action on one side and distant Action on the other for upwards of three hours, we had only six men slightly wounded. Our sails were ribbons and all our ropes were ends. If you see Hoste's father in your travels I beg you will say what a good young men [sic] – I love him dearly and both him and Josiah are as brave fellows as ever walked ...

Nelson wrote to my mother (28 March 1795) 'Josiah is very busy at this moment in watering the ship but the wars will be over long before he has served his time and then he must wait a long time for promotion.'

Nothing much happened for a while, although we were told of Lord Hood's retirement from service at sea. He was nearly 70 and he and his Lady became firm friends of my mother. He then became Governor of Greenwich Hospital for another 20 years.

In July '95 we sailed from San Fiorenzo with a small squadron of five frigates, and halfway between Genoa and Nice fell in with the French fleet of nearly 30 ships. We ran for our lives. Not even Nelson could take on those odds. We only just managed to get back to rejoin our main fleet. On the 13th we met up with the French fleet and a running battle took place off Hyères, but the French escaped with the loss of the *Alcide* which struck, caught fire and blew up. Cautious Admiral Hotham then called off the pursuit, much to my step-father's chagrin. Next week we were back in Genoa; Hotham left Nelson in charge of a squadron of eight little frigates – HMS *Ariadne, Inconstant, Lowestoffe, Meleager, Romulus, Southampton, Speedy* and *Tartar*. At the end of August off Alassio, half way between Nice and Genoa, the squadron had a brisk little action and captured a corvette *La Reserve*, two galleys, a large gunboat and six small trading vessels.

In September we attacked three large Turkish merchantmen: two escaped into Genoa but one was captured, however we lost heavily in casualties.

Most of our Fleet had funny nicknames given to them. The 74 gun *Bellerophon* was called the *Bully Ruffian*. We were called *Eggs and Bacon* and the *Polyphemus* naturally was *Polly infamous*!

Early in 1796 the *Eggs and Bacon* came under command of Sir John Jervis, the new Commander in Chief, who had a reputation as a strict disciplinarian but a record of distinguished service mainly in the West Indies. In the spring

HMS *Agamemnon* off the coast of Italy in the autumn of 1795. An engraving from the *Naval Chronicle*. Midshipman Josiah Nisbet was aboard.

Nelson, now 38, was promoted to Commodore and flew his Broad Pennant on the *Agamemnon*. On 11 June he shifted to the *Captain*, a 74 gun ship of the line: Mr. Edward Berry was the First Lieutenant and Midshipman Nisbet, now nearly 16, was part of the complement. I was sorry to say goodbye to the old *Eggs and Bacon*. She had been my home for three years – constantly at sea. I was often seasick, often in action, – and nearly always happy.

We took aboard the *Captain* the Wynne family – refugees from Florence – whom Nelson christened *the Amiables*. There were no less then five daughters, one of whom fell in love with Captain Thomas Fremantle. But they had little truck with young midshipmen!

Soon after I joined the *Captain* the ship was sent to Ajaccio, but Nelson transferred to the *Diadem* of 64 guns and sailed to Bastia to receive secret orders from Admiral Jervis. Calvi, Bastia and Ajaccio were to be evacuated, and we had to take our troops from Elba. Boney's armies were on the move again and our mainland allies – royalist French, Corsicans and Neapolitans proved unreliable and no match for the experienced French troops.

Sir John Jervis was determined to bring the Spanish fleet into a grand battle and on 14 February 1797 the two grand fleets met 25 miles west of St. Vincent – a Portuguese headland. The English fleet and 15 sail of the line with no less than 6 ships of 90 guns or more. Our *Captain* was one of Admiral Jervis' eight 74 gun ships. In addition there was a Sixty-Four, four frigates, a sloop and a cutter. The Spanish Grand Fleet consisted of no less than 27 ships of the line, ten frigates and a brig. In broad terms we were out-gunned by more than two to one. All of our ships were veterans of the West Indies or the Mediterranean and no-one, least of all my step-father, was in any doubt as to the outcome. Admiral Jervis decided to break through their long straggling line – seven miles between their leading and their last ship. The *Culloden*, Captain Troubridge, led the charge through the Spanish line, which was successful. But our Nelson performed a most unorthodox manoeuver. We were the third from the rear of the British line and as soon as the *Captain* was through the Spaniards – in defiance of orders – we turned back and led a small unofficial squadron of the *Culloden* and the *Blenheim*, 90 guns, and went hell for leather at the huge *Santissima Trinidad* – flagship of Don Jose de Cordoba with 136 guns – double our size. It was the bravest, maddest act you can imagine. To do him justice Admiral Jervis saw *and* recognised Nelson's brilliant move and ordered the *Excellent*, *Prince George* and *Orion* to support us.

After an hour's savage gunfire we were in very bad shape. Our wheel had been shot away: our fore topmast was lost. As Nelson wrote 'Not a sail, shroud or rope was left'. It was very warm work. He also saw another opportunity (the *Culloden* and ourselves were effectively crippled by now.) He ordered our Captain Miller to lay alongside the *San Nicolas* of 80 guns, put the helm down, and we sent a boarding party led by Commander Miller (a *passenger* on the *Captain*). All the old *Eggs and Bacon* crew, including myself, responded – with my step-father in the van – and after fifteen minutes of bloody cut and thrust we took the ship.

HMS *Captain* (centre). As her crew climb her bowsprit ready to board, Nelson's pendant ship ranges alongside the Spanish *San Nicolas* at the battle of Cape St Vincent (14 February 1797). Lt Nisbet fought well.

Simultaneously – and this is almost unbelievable – we became entangled with the huge *San Josef* of 112 guns and we boarded her from the now burning *San Nicolas*.

I thought to myself that if we stayed on the *San Nicolas* we would be burned alive, if we returned to the *Captain* she was probably sinking anyway – so we *had* to board the vast *San Josef*! As Nelson said 'Westminster Abbey or Glorious Victory'. I thought it was neither of these. I expected a Spanish cutlass in the ribs and a quick watery grave. Nevertheless in all the annals of British naval victories, not one has been quite so foolhardy and successful as was Nelson's on that day. The *San Josef* struck and Nelson received the surrender of the Spanish Dons. Don Francisco Xavier Winthuysen, the Admiral, was below decks, nearly dead, and his Flag Captain handed over the Spanish flag to Nelson. The three ships were inextricably linked – the battered *Captain* dwarfed by the two enormous Spanish leviathans. It was an amazing spectacle greeted with cheers by the *Victory* and every other English ship.

By five o'clock on that February afternoon, St. Valentine's Day – almost dusk – all the firing had stopped. The victory was ours but not overwhelmingly so. We had captured four Spanish ships, admittedly two of them large first-raters, but the vast majority had escaped to Cadiz. The *Captain* had over sixty casualties, dead and wounded, and was in a bad state. Her Captain, too, as usual had been wounded, but not seriously. The old *Agamemnon*'s who distinguished themselves included Captain Berry, Francis Cook, John Sykes and coxwain, John Thompson, and burly William Fearney the bargeman. We lost that day Major William Norris

The boarding of the *San Nicolas* at the
battle of St Vincent.

Battle aboard the Spanish ship *San Josef* at the battle of St Vincent, 'bloody cut and
thrust'.

Commodore Nelson receiving the sword of the dying Spanish Admiral on the quarter deck of the *San Josef*.

of the Marines, James Goodeach, a midshipman, and 22 others. Our ship the *Captain* expended no less than 146 barrels of powder during the long action. As a fleet action it was modest, but nevertheless Admiral Jervis was made Earl of St. Vincent, the other Admirals present made baronets, and my brave step-father, who deserved everything, was given the Order of the Bath! In the usual course of seniority he was made a Rear-Admiral of the Blue.

A month later my step-father took us off to a disastrous and vainglorious attack on Santa Cruz, a seaport and capital of Tenerife and the Canary Islands – a *thousand* miles away from St. Vincent. The intention was to intercept the Spanish bullion fleet from Mexico on their way to Spain or the rest of the Spanish Grand Fleet sent to the Canaries to greet and guard the treasure fleet on their homeward run. The storming of the capital Santa Cruz was considered the key to the overall plan. The treasure ships must call in there on their return voyage, *very* heavily laden.

Where my step-father went, so I followed. He decided to take the 74 gun *Theseus* with Captain Ralph Miller and on 27 May we transferred ship from the *Captain* – we being the Admiral, his 'son-in-law', and other members of the old *Agamemnon*. On the way to Santa Cruz we made a limited attack on 3 July on Cadiz and bombarded the town. One of the reasons given for this rather pointless onslaught was to distract our fleet's attentions from the consequences of the Nore and Spithead naval crew mutinies. Four mutineers were court martialled, sentenced and hanged on the 9 July in full view of the Spanish fleet in Cadiz. On the 15th Nelson's squadron of nine ships set sail for the Canaries, to attack Santa Cruz.

By now I was 17 and by dint of hard work, some good fortune and by being the gallant Admiral Nelson's 'son-in-law' had taken and passed my examinations for lieutenant. After two failed attempts to land our raiding parties on the rocky island shores of Santa Cruz, I found myself on 24 July, Officer of the Watch on the *Theseus*.

I was summoned to my step-father's cabin, where I found him sorting and burning my mother's letters to him. It was at once evident that he thought our operation was to be a desperate venture. I was of course dressed ready for embarkation with the ship's landing party. 'Should we both fall, Josiah, what would become of your poor mother? The care of the *Theseus* falls to you. Stay, therefore and take charge of her' he said. To which I answered 'Sir, the ship must take care of herself. I will go with you to-night if never again.' I loved my adopted father and there was no moment of doubt for me – where he went, so did I. My thoughts and motives were quite uncomplicated. For the last five years I had followed him – blindly, faithfully – through moments of extreme danger. He seemed to bear on his small fragile body the wounds which should perhaps have come to my much larger and more vulnerable (but younger) target. He wrote that he thought the venture was now a forlorn hope, from which he himself never expected to return.

Three hundred and fifty of us from the *Theseus* formed the raiding party to land not on the beaches nearby, but on the mole of the town of Santa Cruz, on a dark, rough and stormy night. About 900 sailors and marines made that foolhardy attack, doomed to failure from the onset. The Spanish garrison had been observing us with amazement for three days and nights: they had forty guns trained on the mole-head all the time.

My friend William Hoste, midshipman of the *Theseus*, and John Weatherhead, a lieutenant like me – all three of us Norfolk lads who had joined the good old *Eggs and Bacon* over four years ago – were involved in this night attack. Hoste had had bad luck – typhoid at the siege of Calvi, a broken leg and malaria at Leghorn had kept his promotion back.

My step-father, brave: and foolhardy as ever, that is for a middle aged Admiral of 38, led the central division of boats towards the mole of Santa Cruz, which was defended by nearly 500 Spanish troops. In the face of rockets which illuminated the night, our forces were torn apart by grape-shot and canister. Although eventually we spiked the six 24 pounder guns on the mole, we were nearly all by then killed or wounded, and Nelson was blasted by a grape-shot which almost took his right arm off. It was a bloody shambles. I was as scared as everyone else – but failing to see his little gallant figure ahead of me in the dark horrible confusion, I searched for him and discovered him senseless and bleeding on the ground and carried him on my back to a boat. He was placed gently on the bottom, came to, saw his blood everywhere, and nearly fainted again. I placed my hat on his breast to that he could not see his own wounds and talked to him. 'I am shot through the arm. I am a dead man' he cried out. A sailor called Lovell pulled off his shirt to form a sling and helped to adjust a tourniquet, otherwise he would have bled to death in front of our eyes. The boat's crew were on the mole with the attack, but I found and brought back five tars and after some delay, pushed the stranded boat afloat again. I took an oar myself and shouted to the coxswain to go as close to the mole battery guns – but *under* them – as possible to get out to sea. Nelson was still conscious as we saw the cutter of the *Fox* sink with a hundred men on board. We picked up some survivors as we battled out towards the *Theseus*. En route after half an hour we came close to the *Seahorse* but the Admiral refused to let me board her in case he would alarm Captain Fremantle's *wife* who was on board. Eventually we reached the *Theseus* and Nelson with two legs and one arm hauled himself aboard. The French surgeon Ronicet who had followed us from the *Eggs and Bacon* to the *Captain* thence to the *Theseus* amputated Nelson's arm the next night.

The landing party who reached the main market square of Santa Cruz were surrounded and forced to surrender. Fortunately the Governor of the Canaries was a humane and chivalrous man and returned to us unharmed the captives of the landing force. Two hundred and fifty officers, seamen and marines were killed or wounded in this gallant but totally pointless fiasco. The Governor even victualled our squadron before we sailed away with our tail between our legs.

A wounded Nelson is rescued by Josiah.

Before the action on the 24 July, Nelson wrote to Jervis

My dear Sir, I shall not enter on the subject while we are not in possession of Santa Cruz: your partiality will give me credit that all has hitherto been done which was possible, but without effect. This night, I, humble as I am, command the whole, destined to land under the batteries of the Town and tomorrow my head will probably be crowned with either laurel or cypress. I have only to recommend Josiah Nisbet to you and my Country. With every affectionate wish for your health, and every blessing in the world believe me your most faithful Horatio Nelson.

The Duke of Clarence, should I fall, in the service of my King and Country will, I am confident, take a lively interest for my son-in-law, on his name being mentioned.

A few days later, badly wounded and just convalescent, he wrote to Jervis

My dear Sir, I am become a burden to my friends and useless to my Country but by my letter wrote the 24th, you will perceive my anxiety for the promotion of my son-in-law Josiah Nisbet. When I leave your command I become dead to the World; I go hence, and am no more seen. If from poor (Captain) Bowen's loss, you think it proper to oblige me, I rest confident you will do it: the Boy is under obligations to me, but he repaid me by bringing me from the Mole of Santa Cruz. I hope you will be able to give me a frigate to convey the remains of my carcase to England. God bless you my dear Sir H.N.

After the tragic fiasco of Santa Cruz, my step-father returned to England and spent some months with my mother, initially in Bath to have his injured arm stump attended to, and then in London attending Levées and walking the corridors of power. His health rapidly recovered, and although the newspapers made no bones about our defeat in Tenerife, his reputation suffered little. So little that on 29 March 1798, when he was 39, he hoisted his Admiral's blue pennant on the 74 gun *Vanguard* at Spithead as flagship, with the *Orion* 74 guns, *Alexander* 74 guns and several frigates, to join Lord St. Vincent at Lisbon and Gibraltar.

Meanwhile, perhaps as a result of saving Nelson's life at Santa Cruz, and his enthusiastic and kind letters about me to the Commander in Chief, I was given, much to my astonishment, command of the old 24 gun frigate HMS *Dolphin*, now a hospital ship. I had been lieutenant on the *Theseus* for a relatively short time and a frigate command at the age of 18 was thus remarkable good fortune. My friend William Hoste commented rather enviously 'Pretty quick promotion.' Being a large, well built young man, taking after my father, I looked much older than my true age.

On 16 August (1797) Nelson wrote to my mother 'Good Earl St. Vincent has made Josiah, master and commander of the Dolphin hospital ship'.

Sketch by William Bromley of Lieutenant Josiah Nisbet holding Nelson – badly wounded – in his worst defeat. In two attacks, over 250 casualties, out of 1,000 were lost in the attack on Santa Cruz.

Lieutenant William Webly of HMS *Zealous* painted Tenerife Harbour. The town of Santa Cruz is on the left and the British squadron is on the right. Castillo de Paso Alto is in the centre.

Lord St. Vincent wrote to Admiral Nelson in April 1798

My dear Admiral, I do assure you the Captain of the Dolphin has acquitted himself marvellously well in three instances. In getting his ship out and joining us off Cadiz soon after we arrived: in conducting a convoy of transports with troops from Gibraltar to Lisbon; and lately in pushing out to protect the stragglers of the convoy from England in very bad weather: and he also improves in manners and conversation and is amply stored with abilities which only want cultivation to render him a very good character.

By the time Nelson met Lord St. Vincent off Lisbon on 30th April I had already achieved three small actions in-shore.

Later on I joined a squadron under Commodore John Duckworth and the *Dolphin* sailed for Fornello and helped the capture of the island of Minorca. The ship's carpenter John Olva resigned his warrant rather than work under me!

During May a terrible storm almost destroyed the *Vanguard* at sea, losing all the masts and sails and shipping so much water that the lower deck had to be scuttled to prevent the ship sinking. My poor step-father nearly lost his ship at sea. The smaller frigates including the *Dolphin* ran before the wind to safety. The squadron was scattered but eventually we joined up again in the lee of Gibraltar Rock.

Bonaparte's fleet was out of Toulon – somewhere in the Mediterranean – no one knew where, and Nelson scoured every port as far east as Alexandria (and Aboukir Bay) before he found them and finally defeated them.

The dramatic events at Santa Cruz will always be deeply imprinted on my mind. By then I had been at Nelson's side in many sea actions and he had been not only my hero but also that of every ship's company he commanded. The ratings always knew that he cared for them – for their welfare and safety, their diet and medical care (unlike many naval commanders who were quite indifferent to the welfare of their men). As a result they knew that whatever raging battle or blustering storm he sailed them into, he would be in the thick of it, always leading the attack. They grumbled perhaps at the extra danger – and there was danger everywhere my gallant step-father sailed – but under his command they were sure to emerge relatively unscathed. Part of his fame and glory passed immediately down the line to his men, so that his exploits became theirs. The officers too knew that they would receive calm, cool, decisive orders in the face of any peril – never any panic, never passing on his problems. He always accepted total responsibility. They might have smiled at his views on Westminster Abbey, glory, fame, titles (yes, these were subjects discussed on the lower decks), but if Nelson decided to sail his ships and his men into the jaws of Hell, the whole squadron or fleet would put on full canvas to make sure they all kept in station and laughed and joked as they did so. It was pure magic that he created amidst the often tedious weeks and months of escort duty, or being in the inshore squadron bottling up Boney's ships. We all knew that even on those uneventful cruises it was a privilege to sail under his command.

CHAPTER TEN

ROUND WOOD – IPSWICH – FANNY'S STORY

After Horatio had recovered from the loss of his arm at Santa Cruz, he insisted that he bring to fruition his dream – the purchase of a little cottage in the countryside.

We had enlisted the help of the Bolton family and others in the search, including the Rector, who produced large decaying mansions – quite unsuitable.

Round Wood, a house on the Rushmere road about two miles from Cornhill on the outskirts of Ipswich, seemed quite suitable. So in the autumn of '97 Horatio arranged for it to be bought at auction for £2,000, but as it was occupied by a Captain Edge, I could not move in with our father until the following May. The Sale particulars described it as 'A modern built messiage consisting of a small hall, dairy, cellar, 3 wine vaults, 4 good bed chambers, 2 dressing rooms and 2 servants chambers etc.' It was a plain pleasant house with a grey slate roof and white stucco walls with several long windows opening on to the lawn. Its wine cellars were kept full of excellent wine on Horatio's orders. In the grounds were a large barn, stalls, a cow house and other offices. The well planted gardens contained fine old elm and chestnut trees with a yew hedge. Fifty acres of rich arable land in the parishes of St. Margaret, and Wix Ufford were included in the price. Mr. Fuller was our tenant at the farm and he wanted to continue the lease with his famous new landlord.

Since there was a possibility that the empty houses in Suffolk might be converted into barracks in case of a French invasion I had furniture put into the house promptly. The Rev. Edmund was delighted with the house (which was damp and needed painting) although the garden needed more trees to shelter the house, the garden walls were tumbling down and the water pump needed repairs! I wrote 'All looks like a gentlemans house.'

Louisa Berry and other friends helped me and my father-in-law make the gardens shipshape. We ordered flowers from a local nurseryman, including carnations named 'Admiral Nelson' for which I paid 10/6d – the name was irresistible!

The County gentry were suspicious of us. Horatio had only recently been made an Admiral and as the French would say we were 'arrivistes.' They wanted to know whether my husband would actually live in Round Wood. After his glorious victory of the Nile everything changed. In addition to my local friends Captain Boucher and his lady, the Miss Lloyds and dear old Admiral Samuel Reeve, the local gentry decided to call.

One of the most exciting events of my life at Round Wood occurred at the Victory Ball at the Assembly Rooms, Tower Street, Ipswich, on the 16 October 1798. I arrived at 8 p.m. to be greeted by the ringing of bells and repeated huzzas from a vast concourse of people in the streets. Admiral Sir Richard Hughes (Nelson's commanding officer in the West Indies) and Admiral Reeve introduced me into the Ball Room and conducted me to the top of the room, attended by our father and followed by the Boltons and the Matchams. Captain Boucher followed leading up Mrs. Berry (my friend Louisa) whilst the Regimental bands played 'Rule Britannia'. Dancing soon commenced and continued until midnight when the company of three hundred were regaled with an elegant supper and many appropriate toasts were drunk to me, my husband and his gallant officers. Dancing then continued until the early hours of the morning. The Ballroom was ornamented with wreaths of flowers. At the top was a whole length transparency of the 'Gallant Admiral' surrounded by naval trophies. I thought of my poor battered little husband limping into some foreign port with his sadly damaged ships, as his beloved East Anglian towns loaded him with honours.

Horatio had written to me from Naples (September '98) 'As to Round Wood if the place or neighbourhood is not to your satisfaction I hope the country will put me in a situation of choosing another, but my dear Fanny, unless you can *game*, and talk scandal that is *lies* most probably your company will never be coveted by country town tabbies. Young people have more goodness than old cats.' Rarely was my husband so outspoken and trenchant in his views.

The gentry who eventually called were the Trotmans, Lady Harland, and at the Ipswich balls, Lord and Lady Broom, Lord and Lady Rouse, Sir William and Lady Rowley, and Sir Harry and Lady Parker. Horatio always advised me never to force myself in any titled company that did not seek my acquaintance.

After the Nile General Manners, General Balfour, and Lord Chatham called to pay their respects to me and I met Sir William How on Westerfield Green. Mrs. Berners and Mrs. Middleton also paid me much attention. Josiah's aunt, Mrs. Mary Emilia Lockhart wrote (8 October 1798) from Camalthan House, near Glasgow with congratulations and sent two embroidered screens done upon white satin worked by her daughters Mary and Isabella for our Round Wood house.

Although the house was quite small, I found that I needed three women servants to help run it for me and my father-in-law. The Bolton family and their ill-washed girls were frequent visitors but I was reluctant to ask the Rector and his large family to stay, although our father wanted to see them.

The pattern of our life was that we spent our summer season at Round Wood and the winter season in Bath, since Suffolk was too cold and damp both for me and my elderly father-in-law.

From Round Wood in the summer and autumn of 1798 I wrote many letters to Horatio, mainly about Suffolk society, about his family and about his new estate. Even the domestic trivia about servants, plants, domestic expenses, would I was sure help give him peace of mind during his visit to Naples, his constant scouring of the Mediterranean to bring the enemy to battle, and the final crowning glory of the Nile.

The sad fact remains however that my husband never spent a night under the roof of Round Wood, and on 10 January 1801 we sold the house to Mr. Robert Fuller for £3,300.

During that summer whilst the Rev. Edmund and I were at Round Wood, my husband spent June and July scouring the Mediterranean seas for Bonaparte's fleet. We afterwards learned that thirteen French ships of the line and several hundred transport ships carrying his Army had sailed from Toulon for an unknown destination. Josiah in his ship the *Dolphin* (and then *La Bonne Citoyenne*) was one of my husband's command, looking for Admiral de Bruey's fleet. There was an acute shortage of frigates the eyes of the fleet – and my son was kept very busy. The responsibility on my husband of bringing the enemy fleet to battle was so great, that he lived in much nervous tension which he claimed took years off his life.

Much of my news that summer was about Round Wood, the first house that Horatio and I had ever owned. My father-in-law was probably even more enthusiastic than I! I sent Horatio a detailed description of the place, and particularly of the garden and trees. From our first five years of marriage 'on the beach' I knew how much that meant to him. I firmly expected to spend the rest of my life there.

The Boltons and the William Nelsons soon came over to inspect for themselves their famous brother's 'new' residence. Neither my father-in-law (charitable old person that he was) nor I liked the Bolton parents, and their young twin daughters are not much better! The Boltons seem to live from hand to mouth and are always in debt to me and their richer brother.

One of the nicest things that happened that summer was my meeting with the Berry family. Sir Edward (as he became a little later) was almost the most dashing Captain in the Royal Navy, and rivalled my husband in sheer audacity. His wife Louisa became my firm friend. We first met at the end of June, and I did not realise at the time that we were destined to know, like and respect each other for another quarter century!

Lemuel Abbot's painting of Horatio was delivered to me in July. It was commissioned especially for me and I have kept it near to me on all my travels. Daniel Orme painted me that summer [left] at the mature age of thirty seven.

After Horatio's glorious victory at the Nile, Cuthbert Collingwood wrote to him off Cadiz. 'Say to Lady Nelson when you write to her, how much I congratulate her on the safety, honour and services of her husband. Good God! What must be her feelings! How great her gratitude to Heaven for such mercies.' He was a true friend to both of us.

CHAPTER ELEVEN

BATH, THE SPA TOWN —
'COME LAUGHING BACK'

I had been to Bath once or twice during my first marriage to see the Pinneys, Webbes and Tobins, and other West Indian relations. Horatio and his father also knew this gay, sparkling town. The Reverend Edmund took his annual 'recruit' there from the time I was born. Horatio recuperated from his fevers gained in Nicaragua for a few months in the winter of 1780 and lodged with Mr. Spry, father of the Apothecary, at No.2 Pierrepont Street. He was attended by Dr. Woodward and Dr. Benjamin Moseley, and was pleasantly surprised at their modest charges. It is curious to think that I might have seen his poor limping figure taking the waters and the baths and failed to recognise my dearly beloved future husband. He wrote at the time of Captain Locker 'I have been so ill that I was obliged to be carried to and from bed. I drink the Waters three times a day and bathe every other night besides not drinking any wine, which I think the worst of all.' He spent nearly a year there before his recovered health and his good reputation secured him the command of the *Albemarle*, a converted French merchantman of 28 guns.

Since Bath figures so much in my life I must try to describe it. We and other visitors of slender means usually stayed at one of five boarding houses, all convenient for the Town centre. Mr. Burge at No.2 Pulteney Street, Mr. Ripley at No. 59 Pulteney St., Mr. Petrie at Nos.2/3 Pierrepont St., Mr. Oglethorpe at No. 4 Pierrepont St. and Mrs. Faulkner at No.16, Bond Street. Mr. Spry the Apothecary lived at No. 56 Gay Street and practiced at No.1 Argyle Buildings. Dr. Woodward also practised in Gay Street, a rather smarter address. Good sized lodgings for myself and our father and a maid and a cook (Dolly Jaccombe or Bett Thurlow) cost me £90 a year at Mrs. Searles, but up the hill on Gay Street would be as much as £160 a year.

The population of Bath was about 34,000 but there were 6,500 more ladies there than men – either wives of officers serving abroad or widows. The attractive Town centre was around Queens Square, the Royal Crescent, York and Paragon Buildings, St. James Square and Lansdowne Crescent. One could walk everywhere but chairmen's fares were reasonable for the many invalids who came to Bath.

Sydney Gardens at the end of Great Pulteney Street were designed by Mr. Harcourt Masters in 1795. The Kennet and Avon canal runs through the gardens with two elegant cast-iron bridges over it. There are swings, bowling greens and a Merlins swing in the labyrinth. In the summer on public nights there is music, fireworks and illuminations. One can ride on horseback around the garden and there is a special ride with most romantic views. Mr. Gale, who owns the Gardens, charges a subscription for visiting and walking of four shillings a month. The Sydney Hotel and Coffee Room are next door and are most popular as a social meeting place. There are two Gentlemen's clubs – the Subscription House in York Buildings (founded in 1790) and owned by Messrs Knubley and Oakes, and the other in York House, another Subscription Club owned by Messrs Lucas and Reilly. The London papers and gazettes are to be found in both, as well as a variety of card games.

Bath of course is famous for its Baths and Pump Rooms. The spa water helps cure gout, rheumatism and indigestion and causes a better appetite. The best time for bathing is in the morning when one is refreshed by sleep, from 6-9 a.m. The water can be drunk hot from the Pump but 1-2 pints are the maximum recommended. There are four main Baths: The Kings Bath is 150 feet away from the Abbey Church with two adjoining rooms, one for each sex, The New Private Baths erected in 1788 in Stall Street, the Cross Bath which has a cross in the centre erected by the Earl of Melfort, and is 100 yards Southwest of the Kings: and finally the Hot Bath, a building 500 feet square, 120 feet Southwest of the Cross Bath. It has the hottest spa water. The Sergeant in charge would demand not more than 3*d* for each bathing time and a cloth-woman's charges were also 3*d*.

There are three separate Pump Rooms with charges of 2*d* for each hundred strokes of the pump and 3*d* in the private baths. The New Pump Room built in September 1790 is the biggest and measures 60' x 40' x 34' high, with a music gallery open 1–3 p.m. each day. It is the general rendezvous for visitors and respectable inhabitants who are served with hot water. Near the Hot Bath Room is a small Pump room for wheeled or carried invalids, and finally Mr. Baldwin built a small Pump Room at the Cross Bath.

Mr. Francis John Guyenette is Master of Ceremonies at the Lower Assembly Rooms. Mr. Richard Tyson was elected Master of Ceremonies of the New Rooms, which is not so popular as Mr. James King's Upper Assembly. Each Master has a Ball in the winter and spring seasons. On Monday night there would be a Dress Ball, on Tuesday a Card Assembly, on Wednesday night a Concert and on Thursday night a Fancy Ball.

For the Dress Ball a subscription for the season of 14 shillings serves for 28 balls, or 26 shillings to include two tickets for ladies only. A charge of 6*d* is made for tea at each ball. Dancing starts at 8 p.m., although the Assembly Room opens at 7 p.m. The Fancy Ball on Thursday is the same, open from 7 p.m. to 11 p.m. exactly. Minuets alternate with country dances after allowing time for ladies of precedence to take their places. If ladies wear lappets for the minuets they must give notice the day before to the M.C. The three front ranks at the upper end of the room are reserved for ladies of precedence of the rank of Peeress. I little thought when I first went there in 1780 that twenty years later as a Peeress I would be able to sit in the reserved seats of precedence!

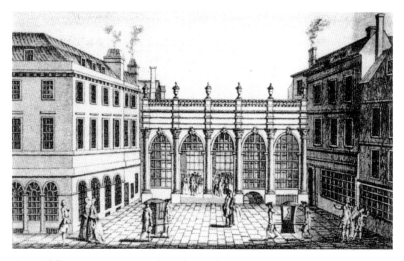

Top, Middle & Bottom:A view of North Parade, Bath, *c.* 1781; The Pump room and Colonnade, Bath *c.* 1829; Front of the Pump Room in the city of Bath *c.* 1756.

On 19 February 1796 I went to and much enjoyed Mrs. Western's Great Rout. Later that year I accompanied as usual the Rev. Edmund. I had a throat complaint at the time, was not well and was unable to attend many social events and thus wrote to a friend, 'we only hear of the Gaiety and luxury of this place now full of Royalty.'

Another rule is that Gentlemen must change partners every two dances so that ladies have an opportunity of meeting many partners. Gentlemen must not wear boots or half boots on ball or concert nights! Nor can they play hazard or unlawful games of cards (or play on Sundays) in the Assembly Rooms. Ladies can play cards at the Assembly on Tuesdays for a subscription of 5 shillings for the season.

The band of 12 performers included harp, tabor and pipes. Bath is a most musical town. Concerts are performed in the public rooms by Thomas Linley and family, by Mrs. Sheridan and by Mrs. Tickell. The great Signor Rauzzini, the violinist, lives there and gives frequent concerts. A subscription for 9 concerts, including 2 tickets for ladies only, costs five and a half guineas.

There are two Bath Harmonic Societies. The Rev. M. Bowen formed one in 1795 which meets at the White Hart on Stall Street every Friday evening at 7 p.m. from December to March. Glees and choruses are followed by cold supper and then by songs, duets and catches until midnight, when the President calls for 'God Save the King.' The members all wear garter blue ribbons with embroidered plumes.

The other Society has a thousand members with Mr. Robert Good as the Secretary. Twice during the season four hundred ladies are entertained with a superb concert, supper and ball at the Assembly Lower-Rooms. This is a grand affair for members only, proposed and balloted for! Finally there is the Bath Catch Club with 130 members backed by Mr. Rauzzini and Doctor Harington, with Friday evening meetings at York House (now the White Lion Inn), November to March. This club is for professional singers such as Mr. Braham, Signora Storace, Miss Parke and Mr. Incledon. For people who spend the season in Bath there is an excellent choice of musical occasions.

The Theatre Royal in Bath was managed by Mr. John Palmer. It was in Orchard Street, but moved to Beaufort Square in 1805. The entrance was by a private house, to 26 private boxes enclosed in gilt lattices. The length of the theatre was 125' x 69' x 70' high, coloured in deep rich red and gold ornamenté. The ceiling had paintings by M. Cassali. The performance days for serious works are on Tuesday, Thursday and Saturday, with actresses such as Mrs. Crawfurd, Abingdon and Siddons, and the Misses Brunton, Wallis and Smith. The actors include Mr. King, Henderson, Edwin, Murray, Incledon and Elliston. Mr. Charlton is the able stage manager. A company of Comedians plays in Bristol three times a week and comes to the Theatre Royal in Bath every Monday.

Other fine arts in Bath include a Painting Gallery in Union Street with exhibitions. Findlays Cabinet of Fine Gems at No.6 Union Street has cameos, intaglios and oil cabinet pictures of the old school. I am particularly interested in viewing these exhibitions, which put my own modest efforts to shame!

Although Bath is 13 miles from Bristol and 107 from London, there are thirteen coaches each day from 5 a.m. to 5.30 p.m. to London from the White Hart, White Lion, Christopher, Castle, Lamb, or the Greyhound Inns. On the way to Bristol past the tremendous St. Vincents Rocks there are near Clifton two Assembly Rooms near the Wells at Hotwell, already popular with my West Indian cousins.

Although London Newspapers are available in Bath, the three local papers are *The Journal*, published on Sunday evening by Mr. Keene of Kingsmead Street, *The Chronicle*, published on Wednesday evening by Mr. Crutwell of St. James' Church, and *The Herald* on Friday evening by Mr. Meyler at the Great Pump Room. The Bath Chronicle usually appears as a weekly paper.

There are good Public libraries on the Walks, at the Great Pump Room, Bond Street, Milsom Street the North Parade and Argyle Street.

A typical day would be spent visiting the Pump Room early in the day, walking in the Crescent, Parades, Orange Grove, Abbey Tower, and Sydney Gardens, visiting the shops and galleries, and thence to the Pump Room again, a fresh stroll until dinner, then to the Theatre or the Assembly Rooms for cards or dancing or to a Concert. It is a most civilised city. On Sundays we would go to the Cathedral church of St. Peter and St. Paul, called the 'Abbey'. Poor Ann Nelson, Horatio's young sister, lies buried in Bathford Churchyard. She died in November 1783.

Horatio and I made one first visit to Bath together on our honeymoon after we had packed poor little Josiah off to his new school in the spring of 1787. We spent two periods there each of two weeks, drinking the waters, meeting my West Indian relations and Horatio's 'pretty numerous sea-folks' – then went to Bristol Redlands to be with the Pinneys, Tobins and Webbes, with whom we could stay happily (and economically!)

My next visits to Bath were in 1793 and in 1794 when Horatio was at sea on the *Agamemnon* with midshipman Josiah. Each time I went with our father the Rev. Edmund, we stayed at Mr. Ripleys, No. 59 Great Pulteney Street.

The next year we had a family re-union at the George Tobins, where I met Mr. and Mrs. Lockhard and Miss Anne Nisbet (my two sisters-in-law by my first marriage). I also stayed with the John Pinneys in March at their house in George Street, and with Charles Pinney on Clifton Down. Mr. Robert Southey the poet was living at the time at No.8, Westgate Buildings.

During the first half of 1797, I wrote to Horatio from Bath usually once a week and often by courtesy of Admiral Young, who was able to make sure they reached their recipient swiftly and more reliably. My informant on naval business, Lord Hood, and his lady had deserted Bath and were installed at Greenwich. My 'Bath' Admirals during that period were Admiral Barrington, Young, and Admiral Dickson (who left the town in February). My brother-in-law Maurice at the Admiralty Office in London was also a reliable source of naval news.

My letters were full of family news (his family, rarely mine), of the Boltons, the Matchams and the Rectors.

Horatio was serving under Sir John Jervis in the *Captain* and took part in no less than two savage battles – one of them a fleet action. The first took place on 14 February when the English fleet of fifteen sail of the line engaged the Spanish fleet of double that number. Horatio disobeyed orders and, supported by our old friend Cuthbert Collingwood in the *Excellent* and Thomas Troubridge in the *Culloden*, won a glorious victory. The *Captain* was locked in combat with the two huge Spanish ships, the *San Nicolas* and the *San Josef* and the fleet christened the scene 'Nelson's Patent Bridge for boarding First-Rates.' Quite rightly my Commodore was given the Order of the Bath, and the *Gazette* of 22 February told me that he had become Rear Admiral of the Blue.

But the events of that summer will remain for ever in my memory. The desperate attack on Santa Cruz before which Horatio and Josiah burned many of my letters because they were convinced neither would survive. Poor Horatio was desperately wounded and gallantly rescued under fire by my son, Josiah. Finally my husband's return, his 'come laughing back' promise made to me and then fulfilled was one of the happiest events in my life.

I kept the following memorandum of the events of July 1797:

The night Sir Horatio Nelson lost his arm he called Lieut. Nisbet into his cabin whose watch it was, to assist him in sorting Lady N. letters in order to burn them saying they would not fall into the hands of anyone. After this business was done he said "what are you equipped for? the care of the ship falls to you."

"The ship, Sir, must take care of herself."

"You must not go, supposing your poor mother was to lose us both, what will she do?"

"I will go this night if I never go again."

In the action that followed Sir H., when putting his foot over the boat, was shot thro' the elbow. Lieut. N. who was close to him saw him turn his head from the flash of the guns, say to him "I am shot thro' the elbow." Upon which he seated him in the boat. The sight of the blood pouring from the arm affected him. Lieut. N. took off his hat in order to catch the blood and feeling where the bones were broken he grasped the arm with one hand which stopped the bleeding, the revolting of the blood was so great that Sir H. said he never could forget it and he tied up his arm and placed him as comfortably as he could with his two silk neckerchiefs from his throat, and then found one Lovel a seaman and 5 other sailors to assist in rowing him off. The tide had receded which caused great difficulty in getting the boat into the water. After 5 men had with difficulty got the boat into the water, Lieut. N. taking an oar, ordered the steersman to row under the batteries, upon which the sailor said "Sir, we will never get the Admiral on board." Sir H. called "Josiah lift me up", which he did by placing his back against one of the benches and from the very heavy fire of the battery he saw his perilous situation and said "Strike out to sea," upon which Lieut. N. said "No Sir, if we do that we never get you on board," he then said "Take you the tiller", and to the sailors "Obey Lieut. N." upon which they steered close under the batteries, thro' a heavy fire and tempestuous sea the spray from the shot coming and not long before they come to the ship and picked up 2 or 3 of the "Fox" cutter'smen. When the boat reached the side of the ship Nelson called out "Tell the surgeon the Admiral is wounded and he must prepare for amputation", upon which they offered to letdown the chair. Sir H. Nelson said "No I have yet my legs and one arm", and he walked up the side of the ship, Lieut. N. keeping so close that in case he had slipped he could have caught him.

On getting on the quarter deck the officers as usual saluted him by taking off their hats, which compliment Nelson returned with his left hand as if nothing had happened.

Lovel took off his shirt and gave him slips to tie the poor arm round his neck.

Lord Nelson often said to me "It was not so much Josiah's tying up my arm (Nisbet says a man in the boat, Lovel assisted him) the grasp he gave it stopped the blood immediately, but his judgement in getting me to the ship. By all account he, Josiah, rowed very, very hard that night and steered well too under the batteries for which I am thankful to Providence that I feel myself the humblest of Gods creatures – for my son went to sea to oblige me."

Josiah said "God knows I saved Lord Nelson's life at Tenerife. That's a pleasure no one can take from me."

During most of Horatio's long absence winning great victories and enhancing his fame, I spent part of each winter in Bath with our father, until after Santa Cruz on 3rd September 1797 – a warm Sunday morning – when my dearest husband came 'laughing back' to me, sorely battered and badly wounded, but alive, thank God.

The first I knew about the disaster was from Sir John Jervis who wrote to me on 10 August from the 'Ville de Paris.' 'Madam, Sir Horatio Nelson has added very considerably to the reputation he had won before the assault upon the town of Santa Cruz in the island of Tenerife. He is wounded but not dangerously and I hope your Ladyship will soon be made happy by his presence in England whither he will proceed the moment the *Theseus* joins. I have the honour to be with very great respect Your Ladyships most faithful and obedient servant J. Jervis.'

But the physical surprise of seeing my wounded husband again was great – white haired, a scar on his brow, haggard and feverish. His poor blind right eye and his empty right sleeve were further shocks to me. His unquenchable spirits and perpetual good humour more than compensated me for his battered body. His love for me shone brightly out of his good eye, but I had to be very careful how I touched him. His arm needed dressing twice a day and I summoned Mr. Nicholls, my own medical adviser, at once. Horatio persuaded me to acquire the medical skill to dress his wound. Doctor Cruikshank, the eminent surgeon, later praised my resolution to dress my husband's wound myself eventually, something which Horatio had earnestly desired. I wrote to his brother William on Wednesday 6 September

> My dear Sir, I beg you will accept the united thanks of my dear husband and myself for your kind enquiries and truly friendly invitation to your house which we would have accepted had it not been for the necessity of my husbands arm being dressed every day by a surgeon. We purpose being in London the middle of next week. I have written to Mr. M. Nelson to take us a lodging and as soon as my husband can do without a surgeon we shall spend some time with you. Earl Spencer has written a handsome letter and is to be in town next week. My husband's spirits are very good, although he suffers a good deal of pain – the arm is taken off very high, near the shoulder. Opium procures him rest, and last night he was pretty quiet. The Corporation have handsomely congratulated him on his safe arrival. Such a letter from Lord Hood! it does him honour, and I have forgot the ill treatment of former years which my good man received from him. Everything which concerns my husband I know you feel interested in therefore shall not make any excuses for what I have told you.

Meanwhile I wrote back to my friend Earl St. Vincent on 7 September.

> My Lord. The letter which your Lordship did me not only the honor but I must truly say the great kindness of writing by the *Flora* cutter, I received two days before the arrival of Admiral Nelson who gives me leave to say, speaks in such affectionate terms of you that I wish it was in my power to express my feelings and obligations to your Lordship. I am thankful that my husband is restored to me: his spirits are very good although of the suffering much pain owing to the want of indulgences he had left in your ship – no separate cabin from his brother sufferers, which occasioned his staying more on the deck than was proper. Rest and quietness I hope will soon restore him to good health. My husband desires his best respects and as soon as he has seen the first Lord of the Admiralty he will write you a long letter, giving all the particulars. My obligations are further increased to your Lordship from the pleasing news of your extraordinary favour to my son who I hope will exert himself and prove worthy of such marked goodness and attention. Believe me, your Lordships, Obliged, Frances H. Nelson.

The total bill for Horatio's medical attendance was as follows:

> Mr. Nicholls at Bath for dressing his arm, attendance 3-18 Sept. £12
> Mr. Spry for medicines provided at Bath £2
> Dr. Faulkner physician at Bath £1-1-0
> Mr. William Cruikshanks (surgeon) for 30 days attendance in London £31-10-0

The two surgeons on the *Theseus* were also paid for amputating and removing his arm, along with Ronicet of the *Agamemnon*. Thomas Estelby was paid £36 and Louis Remonier £25-4-0.

As soon as he felt recovered we set off for London, accompanied by the Rector (brother William), Mr. Nicholls, Horatio's servant and my woman. We broke our long journey at Newbury and arrived at Mr. Jones' lodging house at 141 Bond Street on the evening of Wednesday 13 September, ten days after Horatio's return to Bath. The wound was no better and Horatio was running a fever which laudanum kept down, and daily visits to the Admiralty made worse. Old friends appeared on our doorstep – Captain William Locker from Greenwich Hospital and many others. Horatio, brother William and our friend, Captain Edward Berry, attended a levée at St. James (25 September) where the King made a comment about the missing right arm and Horatio made a riposte about Captain Berry being his right hand.

In October we visited Greenwich where Horatio was painted by Lemuel Abbott of Bloomsbury and presented the finished work to me, which I always take with me when moving to my other home. On 5 October we dined with Lord Hood and Sir Gilbert Elliot now Lord Minto, at Greenwich. After the victory at Camperdown between Admiral Duncan and the Dutch fleet (at which Horatio stretched out his unwounded arm and said he would give up that limb too to have been present at the battle!) an unruly mob of roystering citizens passed down Bond Street celebrating noisily. They saw our unlit rooms and invaded Mr. Jones' house since illuminations were 'de rigeur' after a major battle. Mr. Jones and I told the noisy crowd that Admiral Nelson, still sore wounded, was asleep, and they quickly withdrew, mumbling apologies.

Every few days there was a meeting of the various doctors to consider Horatio's wounded arm – the stump being hot and swollen needed poultices – and they discussed whether the ligature applied originally to the wound to stop the heavy bleeding should, or should not, be removed. Like most medical experts they could not agree and the pain and the fever continued until on the 4 December the ligature gave way and brought instant and great relief to my brave, suffering husband.

Meanwhile Horatio was told by Lord Spencer that he would have the *Foudroyant* of 80 guns early in the New Year, and that on the 19 December there would be a Royal Pageant at St. Paul's to offer thanks for the naval victories of the war. Captain Berry, who was busy courting Louisa Forster, would attend him at the pageant.

On the 11 December Horatio and I visited Captain Ralph Willett Miller (and his wife Martha) who commanded the *Theseus* at Santa Cruz. Josiah was then his senior Lieutenant and we discussed the tragic action in which so many gallant sailors lost their lives.

That winter was probably the happiest of my life – nursing and loving my wounded husband, basking a little in the reflected glory and realising that after so long he was beside me at night, depending on my affection – it was Paradise regained again. Lady Spencer remarked upon our happiness and so did many others – Lord St. Vincent, the Mintos etc. We spent the Christmas season in London – levées, theatres, dinner-parties, and we were back in Bath in early January. We took Lord Lansdown's box at Palmers Theatre and Horatio wrote to a friend Thomas Lloyd afterwards 'Some of the handsomest ladies in Bath are partakers in the box and was I a bachelor, I would not answer for being tempted but as I am possessed of everything which is valuable in a wife, I have no occasion to think beyond a pretty face.' I could tell he was much better!

On 10 January (1798) Horatio wrote to Lord St. Vincent from Bath about his new ship the *Vanguard* now, not the *Foudroyant*, which would be ready for sailing in March, 'I have no wishes to convey but that my son-in-law Josiah may merit your good opinion and that health and every blessing may attend you in all of which Lady Nelson most cordially joins.'

By early February the *Vanguard* was at Spithead with Captain Berry preparing the ship. We were back in London this time at 96 Bond Street. The precious few days together soon came to an end. We attended a levée on 14 March. Later in March before my husband and son sailed away on the *Vanguard,* Earl Spencer (First Lord of the Admiralty) and Lady Spencer gave a dinner for all the Captains and their wives before they sailed to take up a new command. My husband told Lady Spencer that 'she must like Lady Nelson, who was beautiful, accomplished and above all, an angel, whose care had saved his life.' He handed me in to dinner and asked to be allowed to sit beside me as he had seen so little of me that he would not voluntarily lose an instant of my company. A truly loving scene. Shortly afterwards Horatio took the coach for Portsmouth and I back to Bath with my maid and niece Kate Bolton. I have never cared for the Bolton family but I was determined to be very kind to this little child. The trivia of the departure helped distract me from my sorrow – a missing watch and keys, black stock and buckle, lucky Portuguese gold coins, silk-stockings and huckaback towels. I wrote 'I wish very much it had been in my power to send your things more comfortably.'

Back in Bath again I watched the wind-vane on the top of Queen Square Chapel to see when the wind was favourable for my husband's ship to sail to war again.

I sent him a letter asking God to protect and bless him and my love as usual to Josiah. He wrote back at once 'Nothing in the world can exceed the pleasure I shall have in returning to you,' and 'I hope when you travel, you will not trust yourself in a stage[coach]'... at that time not particularly safe.

During Horatio's sick leave and convalescence in Bath and London my thoughts had often been with Josiah, Captain of his first ship, the old *Dolphin* of 24 guns, cruising with Lord St. Vincent's squadron off Lisbon and the Tagus. Horatio told me that he had been a midshipman, ill with fever, on the *Dolphin* returning from his East Indian tour of duties in 1776.

Horatio's new command of the 74 gun *Vanguard* sailed from Portsmouth in the spring of 1798 and I wrote letters to him, mainly from Bath, and then from the Suckling's house in Kentish Town. My husband insisted that his father and I should take up residence at Round Wood, Ipswich as soon as possible. My letters were not very inspiring, full of small-talk, of the Matchams, the Sucklings, our financial accounts and some naval gossip.

It was during our long sojourn in Norfolk in the early days of our marriage that I decided, not cold-bloodedly, but with love, that one of my roles in life (occasionally perhaps it was a duty) was that of looking after our father. Horatio's widowed father lived a lonely life in his large cold parsonage. He needed companionship and love whilst his favourite son was serving his country at sea. The Rev. Edmund cared little for his other sons and not much more for his daughters, but he was devoted to Horatio, and after initial reservations, I believe, to me too. So this indomitable righteous old man became a friend, and during the many occasions when we believed that my husband and son were lost at sea, we comforted each other. When we went to Bath – which was frequently – he took on a new lease of life and took part in many of the social activities at the Assembly Rooms and Theatre. This simple, uncomplicated, loving relationship continued until his death in Bath on 26 April 1802.

During my frequent visits to the Spa and seaside towns of Bath, Bristol, Salisbury and little sunny Exmouth, I could count on seeing and staying with my wealthy friends and relations from the West Indies. There were Nisbets and Lockharts, Webbes and Tobins, Herberts and Pinneys wherever I went. They were friends from my childhood days on Nevis, who had helped me and my two Josiahs in our sad and melancholy days in Salisbury when my first husband was dying. I could always rely on them to cheer me when my health and spirits were low.

My cousin Sally Morton, who had married Captain William Kelly (who later became Vice Admiral of the Blue) was a good friend, and I stayed with her from time to time in Plymouth and she with me in Exmouth. We reminisced about our many relations and friends on Nevis or in the West Country.

In my latter years another Nisbet cousin, Mrs. Fanny Francklyn, who was born a Webbe, stayed with me for many years as my companion in Exmouth, and in London at 26 Baker Street, Portman Square.

The Suckling family (Maurice and William were Horatio's uncles) were my favourites. When Captain Maurice died childless in July 1778 his brother William inherited his estate and entertained Horatio, myself, and Josiah on frequent occasions at his fine house in Kentish Town. William was attentive to me – on Horatio's 36th birthday he gave *me* a handsome present of £100. He was also a perceptive man who told me he could always tell the contents of Horatio's letters by the expression on my face as I read them. William Suckling was the only Nelson relative of substance, and Horatio on several occasions in his early impecunious days asked him for financial assistance. His second wife, a Miss Rumsey, was a younger, pretty and friendly woman. There were also various Suckling cousins – Elizabeth and young Maurice, who served with Josiah in the *Agamemnon*. I certainly counted the Sucklings as my good friends until Maurice's death in 1799.

Another naval family that we knew were the Lockers. Many years before I met Horatio, Captain William Locker was his 'old sea-daddy'. He was a cheerful looking man with rosy cheeks and a limp as a result of a battle with a French privateer off Alicante in 1757. Horatio was a second lieutenant under Captain Locker on the *Lowestoffe* on the West Indian station and he gave my husband his first command – a small schooner called *Little Lucy* after Locker's wife, heiress to Admiral William Parry. Until Locker's death in 1800, he and my husband kept up a correspondence – sometimes monthly, sometimes weekly. Eventually he became Commander in Chief, Nore, and then Lieutenant Governor of the Royal Naval Hospital in Greenwich. He collected portraits of all his many naval friends. I often visited the Locker family at Greenwich: his house faced that of Lord Hood who was the Governor. I became firm friends with his daughter Elizabeth Locker and when I was widowed after Trafalgar she would stay with me in Brighton or in Exmouth. She had lost her father and I had lost my husband and our warm companionship consoled us both.

Thomas Hardy was possibly Horatio's favourite amongst his many colleagues and was with him at the end on board the *Victory* at Trafalgar. The Hardy's family

Thomas Hardy first served under Nelson as a Lieutenant, being promoted to Captain after the Nile. He commanded Nelson's flagship the *Victory* until Trafalgar.

home was at Possum in Dorset, and he and his wife Louisa (eldest daughter of Sir George Cranfield Berkeley) were always kind and attentive to me. When Horatio was at the Court of Naples, Thomas, who had been relieved by Captain Edward Berry at Palermo, was on leave in London. He visited the coffee-house at Fladongs, much frequented by Naval Officers on leave, whilst he waited for news and interviews with Lord Spencer, the First Lord. He resumed his acquaintance with me and later became a firm ally in the troublesome times to come. My already warm regard for his character increased when he brought timely offerings of ducklings and sea-kale to my old father-in-law, who was much pleased.

Inevitably there were many other naval families that I met and occasionally stayed with. Poor old peg-legged Admiral Mark Robinson who lived in Bath; dear old Admiral Carpenter and his family who lived in retirement in Exmouth on the Beacon; Miss Ellis Cornelia Knight, the journalist-authoress, whose father was Admiral Sir Joseph Knight. She and her widowed mother were at the Court of Naples, and were part of the Queen of Naples' 'entourage' which included my husband, who made the long sad overland voyage to a stormy home-coming in 1800.

During my years in Norfolk, at Burnham Thorpe and later in Round Wood, I made few friends in Horatio's family, apart from Maurice Nelson and the grasping Rector's daughter, little Charlotte Nelson. That is until the time that I met Louisa Forster who was the daughter of a well-known Norwich doctor. She fell in love and married one of Horatio's most favourite and dashing young Captains, Edward Berry. I first met her when I was living at Round Wood with my father-in-law. She married Berry on 12 December 1797, a day or so before he sailed away as Flag Captain of the *Vanguard*. He had joined Horatio as First Lieutenant of the *Agamemnon* in June 1796, and stayed by his side in all the great battles still to come. He was described by Horatio to King George as his right hand man shortly after Horatio had lost his right arm at Tenerife. Josiah was entrusted to Captain Berry's charge so that he could gain more experience in a smaller ship under a different commander. Once (28 May 1797) Captain Berry came to visit me in Bath and dined with us. I told Horatio that I thought him 'one of the most grateful creatures I ever met, he ingratiated himself very much in our good opinion.' I showed him the miniature of Horatio that I always wore. Wherever there were battles at sea it was inevitable that young Sir Edward Berry would be in the forefront. Just before Trafalgar, Horatio said 'Here come Berry! Now we shall have a battle!' Like most of our naval friends Edward too became an Admiral. Soon afterwards I met other members of the Berry family. For the rest of my life Louisa remained my very good friend. I once wrote to Horatio 'Mrs. Berry's manners are very gentle and she is very good. I like her very much.' 'Oh this sad subject,' she said later, Lord Nelson always bore testimony to the merits of Lady Nelson, and declared in parting from her, that he had not one single complaint to make – that in temper, person and mind, she was everything he could wish. They never had a quarrel; but the Syren had sung, and cast her spell about him, and he was too guileless in his nature, and too unsuspecting, to be aware of his danger until it was too late. I am aware of your intention not to touch upon this delicate subject, and only allude to it in order to assure you, from my personal knowledge, in a long and intimate acquaintance, that Lady Nelson's conduct was not only affectionate, wise and prudent, but admirable throughout her married life, and that she had not a single reproach to make herself. The affections of her lord were alienated, not when they were together, but at a distance, and beyond the reach of her rare feminine virtues.

> I say this not to cast unnecessary blame upon *one* whose memory I delight to honour, but only in justice to that truly good and amiable woman, the residue of whose life was rendered so unhappy by circumstances over which she had no control. If mildness, forbearance, and indulgence to the weaknesses of human nature could have availed, her fate would have been very different. No reproach ever passed her lips; and when she parted from her lord, on his hoisting his flag again, it was without the most distant suspicion that he meant it to be final, and that in this life they were never to meet again. Excuse my troubling you with these observations, as I am desirous that you should know the worth of her who has often been misrepresented, from the wish of many to cast the blame anywhere but on him who was so deservedly dear to the Nation. There never was a kinder heart than Lord Nelson's; but he was in the hands of a very designing person, and few could have resisted the various artifices employed to enslave the mind of the Hero, when combined with great beauty, extraordinary talents, and the semblance of an enthusiastic attachment.

By a series of unusual co-incidences several families who had been at the Court of Naples during my husband's ensnarement returned later to London, and for one reason or another I became acquainted with them, and this matured into friendship. I have mentioned Lady Knight and her daughter already – in addition there were Gilbert and Anna Maria Elliot (née Amyard) who later became the Earl and Countess of Minto. They had considerable knowledge of the Hamiltons, disliked Lady Emma, and supported my unhappy position when my husband abandoned me in 1801. So too did the elegant Princess Castelcicala, who was born in Naples, and followed the Court in the retreat in my husband's *Vanguard* to Palermo in 1798. She and her husband became the representatives of the Neapolitan Court to England, and lived for a time in London, and then moved to Paris. Not only did I get to know them both very well, but they introduced me to Kitty, Duchess of Wellington, to the Princess de Joinville, and to my good friend, as she later became, the Duchesse de Berri.

It can be seen how fortunate I have been in my long life, to meet such a wide variety of people – the West Indian society of friends and relations – the Naval society (mainly, but not entirely, through Nelson's fame) and finally the High Society of the Court of London and Paris.

CHAPTER TWELVE

AT THE COURT OF NAPLES — JOSIAH'S ACCOUNT

In mid-September 1793 the *Agamemnon* had been ordered by Admiral Hood to sail from Toulon via Oneglia to Naples to supervise and protect a convoy of Neapolitan troops, 6,000 it was said, who were due to take part in the siege and taking of Toulon. We had been at sea since January and the crew and midshipmen looked forward to some leave on shore. After sailing past Mount Vesuvius at night the ship anchored in the Bay of Naples. We could see the thousands of twinkling lights and smell the usual port odours wafted out to the old *Eggs and Bacon*. My school days had taught me to 'see Naples and Die'. I little thought that this would be the prelude to other visits to this large and dangerous port.

Captain Nelson took me ashore and I carried the despatches for him to the Court and the Palazzo Sessa, where the Ambassador lived. He told me that the Kingdom of the Two Sicilies had a Spanish King called Ferdinand IV and an Austrian Queen called Maria Caroline, sister to Marie Antoinette, Queen of France. It was very complicated but my step-father explained that the Queen of Naples was strongly hostile to the new French revolutionary Convention and that she ruled the roost in Naples. We initially met the elderly Ambassador, Sir William Hamilton, who had been there for many years, and his beautiful young wife Lady Emma. Later I discovered she was about twenty eight (and thus double my age). We also met a very strange man who was the Prime Minister. His name was Sir John Acton, then approaching sixty, whose main task was to command the Neapolitan navy. My step-father thought that Acton was an honest and capable man, 'I can perceive him to be still an Englishman at heart'. Acton had served several European countries in his unusual career.

Once we explained our mission Captain Nelson was greeted like a hero at the Queen's orders. (We did not see her because she was pregnant with her 16th child). To some extent, as Nelson's 'son-in-law' this attention also came to me – a snotty, uncouth midshipman of nearly 14. Sir William was a charming, urbane, civilised diplomat, but Lady Emma for some reason almost adopted me at sight. I thought she was beautiful and fell in love with her immediately! If I had not been so young and innocent and naive I would have noticed that my step-father was receiving, and was responding warmly to, Lady Hamilton's attentions. These were markedly more than that of Ambassadress and a visiting Navy Captain! He stayed several nights on shore at the Palazzo Sessa – Sir William's large classic mansion. This was a strange event because the *Agamemnon* was ready to sail at short notice. French ships were known to be at sea and the ships' captains would normally have stayed on board at night.

We were the first English naval ship to visit the Court as an ally against France, and the town went wild with excitement. Lord Hood's 'most glorious and great success' at Toulon had been greeted with enthusiasm and we were England's representatives. Nelson was entertained and feted during our five day stay. Sir William acted as interpreter and his wife made a great fuss about both of us. Nelson wrote to my mother 'Lady Hamilton has been wonderfully kind and good to Josiah. She is a young woman of amiable manners who does honour to the station to which she is raised.'

On Sunday the 15th there was to have been a ceremonial Royal visit to the *Agamemnon*, but a heavy sea in the bay was too rough for the King and Queen. So Nelson and I and the officers dined at the Royal Palace, the Palazzo Reale, and he, my stepfather sat on King Ferdinand's right hand – the seat of honour.

The next morning the Neapolitan troops were due to embark for Toulon, and Nelson gave a breakfast party on board ship for the British bigwigs of Naples: the Hamiltons, the Bishop of Winchester, Lord Grandison and his daughter, and Lord and Lady Plymouth. At noon Sir John Acton, who was supervising the loading of the Neapolitan army, sent us a message to say that three French ships had been seen off Sardinia. Within the hour we had sailed to intercept them. Thus ended my first exciting visit to Naples. It was nearly four years before Nelson and I visited Naples again – by then I was an adult.

My second visit to Naples was very short. Lord St. Vincent did not know where the French Fleet was. All we knew was that it was out and somewhere in the Mediterranean, and my step-father and his fleet were desperately seeking out the enemy. It was June 1798 and I was commanding the sloop *La Bonne Citoyenne*, and in company with Captain Hope of the *Alcemone*, 32 guns, and the *Emerald*, we called in at Naples for news of the French under Admiral De Brueys. We carried despatches for Admiral Nelson, and in Naples collected messages from Lord and Lady Hamilton for him. I think she wanted to make sure that the Navy would come to their rescue if Boney's troops over-ran the Neapolitan Kingdom.

We finally found Nelson's main fleet at Aboukir Bay on the 12 August – two weeks after the Glorious Victory of the Nile. We fired our salute to the Admiral and his battered fleet guarding the many sunken French ships, some still on fire. There is no place for a small sloop in major battles between first rate ships of the line, but I wished with all my heart I had been on board the *Vanguard* with my step-father during that epic struggle. Predictably he was in the midst of the action and had been badly wounded with considerable loss of blood. Poor unlucky Troubridge had been a spectator at the battle, as the *Culloden* had run aground on a sandbank before the general action started. Not only did I deliver Lord St. Vincent's despatches to Admiral Nelson, which ironically contained orders for our fleet to sail west for Minorca on the assumption that De Brueys' found and sunk, but also a report on my activities. He complained of me that I was young for my age, 'very active, certainly ungracious in the extreme' and 'may have lain too long at Lisbon' [with the *Dolphin*]. The fleshpots of Lisbon and the good red wines of Extramadura may not have helped my career, but I certainly enjoyed myself there! However worse was to come. 'It would be a breach of friendship to conceal from you that he loves drink and low company, is thoroughly ignorant of all forms of service, inattentive, obstinate and wrong-headed beyond measure and had he not been your son-in-law must have been annihilated months ago. With all this, he is honest and truth telling and, I dare say, will, if you ask him, subscribe to every word I have written.' Nelson read me this dreadful report and I had to agree with it, despite the fact that Lord St. Vincent was an old stickler for rigid, unthinking discipline and was notorious throughout the Navy for it. I could think of a dozen young commanders whose activities were no better than mine. Nelson defended me against Lord St. Vincent's charges but in his heart of hearts he could not forgive me and probably through me, my mother. Nelson chose to forget his own frivolous moments in Quebec and New York when he was aged 24. He also forgot that at my age – then 18 – he was a midshipman in the Far East with no prospects, whereas I had seen action on a dozen desperate occasions and had had my own command for six months! The trouble was that Lord St. Vincent and Nelson wanted frigate captains to show initiative, act on their own without support, and to be paragons of private behaviour. I made him promises for the future, but the events that took place in Naples were too much for me.

On the slow voyage north-west-wards, Nelson wrote to Lord St. Vincent 'I am glad to think you are a little mistaken in Nisbet. He is young but I find a great knowledge of the service in him, and none that I see, as so good a Seaman in any ship. He may have lived too long in Lisbon.' Unbeknownst to me Nelson was pressing Lord Spencer at the Admiralty and St. Vincent at Gibraltar for me to be made Post-Captain. He sent me ahead to Naples with a despatch for Sir William Hamilton, 'I beg my best regards to Lady Hamilton. Captain Nisbet who you remember as a boy is the bearer of this letter, ever yours, Horatio Nelson'. He expected to stay in Naples for not more than four or five days for refitting and re-victualling 'for these times are not for idleness'. Most of the English ships with their French prizes sailed westwards to Gibraltar, whilst *La Bonne Citoyenne* accompanied the *Vanguard* 74 guns (Captain Hardy), the *Culloden* (Captain Troubridge) and the *Alexander* (Captain Ball) to Naples Bay. The *Vanguard* was in terrible shape under jury rig, and our voyage for urgent repairs took a month. My third visit to Naples was on the 16 September.

To celebrate my step-father's glorious victory in Aboukir Bay, I wrote a poem to him which was circulated amongst the squadron's officers and men. I wrote it before the temptations at the Court of Naples became obvious to me, to Captain Foot, and many others.

On the Arrival of Admiral Nelson.

He's come the British hero see advance
His country's glory and the dread of France
Each patriot's bosom glows with warm desire
To view the hero they unknown admire
Each in idea would a portrait frame
A portrait such as suits with Nelson's fame
By most (as judging by the action wrought)
Of age advanced he's painted in their thought
While Nelson yet but in the prime of life
With aged veterans vies with noblest strife.
Their warlike virtues in his bosom dwell
Not' rash, but brave, 'tis prudence guides his helm
With generous zeal inflamed to serve the state
Brave Nelson fought and scorned the frowns of fate
His tranquil bosom fearless of surprise
From innate virtue felt its courage rise.
In combat terrible but victory won
He shewed the Christian and the hero one
Humanity again resumed its place
And Nelson's bent before the throne of grace
No vain presumption filled the hero's breast
He felt that heaven the enterprise had blest
And deaf awhile to every vain applause
With bended knee adored the Great first cause
In whose blest aid depends all human force
Who crowns at will, or stops the victors course.
by Josiah Nisbet

My step-father kindly continued to try to advance my career and wrote to Earl Spencer on 16 September (1798) on the *Vanguard* off Stromboli 'I am looking for the *Foudroyant* and also for your Lordships goodness to my son-in-law. I of course wish he had a good Frigate ...'

Lord Nelson also wrote to Earl St. Vincent on 14 September 1798 'I hope you will not think me too presuming in expressing my wishes for Captain Nisbet's being put in a good frigate. As [Capt] Hope refuses *Thalia* and has I hear asked for *Majestic* if Josiah could replace him I should be gratified for putting him into either *Terpsichore* or *Aurora* who must go home would be sad news to me. Depend on it he is very active, knows his business but is ungracious in the extreme'... Earl St. Vincent then wrote to Lord George Spencer, First Lord of the Admiralty two weeks later, 'Your Lordship will observe that Sir Horatio Nelson is very desirous to have his son-in-law Captain Nisbet made post [captain] into a good frigate which is certainly due to the Admiral's unexampled services. If therefore you are not able to send a frigate out under a commander who may on joining the *Bonne Citoyenne* take command of her, I will provide for him in the first frigate which becomes vacant ...' And on the same date I wrote to my mother 'Dear Mother, I am now Captain of *La Bonne Citoyenne* and expect to go off to Malta very soon with the Admiral. Malta is expected will be given up to the English directly they appear off there. Believe me, your affectionate J. Nisbet'.

To and fro we went carrying messages between the King and Queen of Naples again, followed by the frigate *Thalia* towing the crippled *Vanguard* and the *Minotaur* and *Audacious*.

The reception of Nelson and his small battered squadron was extraordinary. The King of the Two Sicilies arrived alongside the *Vanguard* in his gilded state galley having come three leagues to meet us. There were salutes, parades, banquets, speeches – days of triumph in the hot Italian sun. My poor wounded step-father was now ill of a fever and had a perpetual cough, so he was given a large room at the British Embassy in which to recuperate. It was on the upper floor with a semicircular window overlooking the bay, where our small squadron could be kept under His Lordship's keen one-eyed gaze. He celebrated his 40th birthday in Naples on the 29 September, by which time we had been there a week. He was not attending to his duties. Captains Troubridge and Hardy *wrote* to him from their ships in the bay about their urgent need for 'slops and bedding.' After this he despatched one frigate to see what was happening at Malta, but the refitting of the two damaged ships of the line predictably took far, far longer than the four or five days the Admiral had originally anticipated. He wrote to my mother about the Court and the political situation, and about Sir William Hamilton. He also wrote about the Ambassador's wife who bathed his head and gave him asses' milk and many other favours.

> She is one of the very best women in this world. How few could have made the turn she has (i.e., from her very humble background). She is an honour to her sex and a proof that even reputations may be regained, but I own it requires a great soul. Her kindness with Sir William to me is more than I can express. *Her Ladyship if Josiah was to stay would make something of him and with all his bluntness I am sure he likes Lady Hamilton more than any female. She would fashion him in 6 months in spite of himself, which indeed he wants.*

We were all under Lady Hamilton's spell, except for Captain Troubridge, recently widowed, and my friend Captain Foot. She rivalled Medusa in her seductive charms and her famous 'Attitudes'. Her husband was a captive, so was I, and much more to the point, so was my gallant step-father. I had not seen my mother for six years and my step-father had only seen his wife on brief occasions in that time, and now he was lavishing his praise and; it seemed to me, his admiration and love, on another man's wife.

Lady Hamilton's fête for Nelson's birthday was attended by 80 officers of the squadron, by the English residents in Naples, and after the banquet, 1,700 Neapolitan guests came for a grand ball. By midnight I was as drunk as the proverbial Lord. In my cups I made it quite clear that my step-father, the Victor of the Nile, was pressing his amatory attentions on the British Ambassadress, although they were only due to my poor mother, now back in Norfolk. Captain Troubridge and other officers then removed me, but only after I had said out loud what was plainly evident to the whole squadron and to the complaisant Ambassador.

Early in October I was still in disgrace with Nelson. He now realised that the large, handsome, bosomy woman had, like Circe, cast her spell over him – despite her cast eye and large feet and provincial dialect. I can remember to this day her fiery eyes and magnificent dark auburn hair, because the spell was on me too.

I was sent off from Naples by Nelson to get me out of the way out of *his* way. My task was to recruit and press by any means sailors from the African ports to replace our inevitable casualties, deriving more from sickness than from wounds. It proved to be more hazardous than either he or I had contemplated.

Major Perkins Magia, British Consul at Tunis, wrote to Admiral Nelson on 18 October 1798 'I beg to acquaint you that Captain Nisbet with part of the crew of *L'Aigle* sailed hence in a neutral vessel the beginning of last month in quest of you since which no accounts have been received of him though it was expected the vessel would have returned here before this'. He wrote the following day to the Admiralty in London 'I have hired the use of a vessel for Captain Nisbet who is going in search of Admiral Nelson's fleet with one hundred men'. I had sailed with Captain Charles Tyler on the frigate *L'Aigle* which was totally wrecked on Plane Island near Tunis. There was no salvage possible and the ship's crew rowed to Tunis, where the Consul chartered a vessel for me, in which I eventually rejoined the squadron at Naples with the much needed replacement crews. It was reported

The British fleet at anchor in the bay of Naples.

to my mother that I had been lost at sea, which dismayed me. My friend Captain Sir James Saumarez of HMS *Orion* was convinced that I would always turn up. Although he put this in rather more nautical phraseology!

Eventually in mid October Nelson tore himself away from the siren's songs and we sailed for Malta, where Captain Ball and the *Alexander* had been despatched a week before to meet a Portuguese Squadron. The French garrison of 5,000 troops occupied the main island of Malta, chiefly around the citadel of Valetta, the capital, and the little island of Gozo in the north, which we soon captured. Nelson was immediately bombarded with passionate letters from the Ambassadress at Naples, and on the 30 October he returned to her clutches leaving Captain Ball and five sail of the line to continue the blockade of Malta. He ordered *La Bonne Citoyenne* back with the *Vanguard* to Naples. During the three weeks there the fascinating young siren turned her attentions to me when His Lordship was elsewhere attending to his duties. She knew that I was not yet nineteen and obviously torn apart by calf love for her. Perhaps I was jealous of my step-father and certainly I felt much pity for my absent mother. Lady Emma taught me how to dance and made much of me. At one moment I loved her and the next I hated her. She wore thin muslin dresses over a voluptuous, very womanly body – with nothing underneath – that was quite evident. She liked to touch people; her husband, Nelson of course, and frequently, to my surprise, me!

Three weeks after our arrival we sailed 300 miles north to Leghorn, arriving there on the 28 November. Nelson landed 5,000 Neapolitan troops and the town Governor surrendered at once. It was rumoured that the Admiral had a whore there in the town – many of the officers talked of it. [Adelaide Correglia, an opera singer from Leghorn.]

By early December Nelson was back in Naples, leaving Captain Troubridge in command at Leghorn. On one voyage north to Leghorn my ship ran into a violent storm and the Portuguese ships in the squadron were blown off course. *La Bonne Citoyenne* was blown back in the gales and I returned alone to Naples. Lady Hamilton wrote to Nelson, 'How unhappy we are at the bad weather how are you toss'd about why did you not come back? Pray keep your self well for our sakes and *do not go on shore at Leghorn there is no comfort their for you. We have got Josiah how glad I was to see him.*' I returned to Leghorn eventually to hand this missive over to Nelson. *La Bonne Citoyenne* stayed on with Captain Troubridge to take possession of twenty French privateers and no less than seventy Genoese merchant ships in the harbour. Of course I was in trouble very soon. On patrol I took a French ship out of a neutral port and, when ordered to return my prize, refused to give it up. Soon I was back in Naples listening to the siren song again – step-father and 'son-in-law' – both almost equally love struck. Lady Hamilton gave me a daily lesson in manners, deportment and dancing. 'The improvement made in Josiah by Lady Hamilton' Nelson wrote to my mother 'is wonderful. *She seems the only person he minds and his faults are not omitted to be told him but in such a way as pleases him,* and his, your and my obligations are infinite on that score. Not but dear Josiah's heart is as good and as humane as ever was covered by human breast, but his manners are so rough, but God bless him I love him dearly with all his roughness.' My step-father had a kind, charitable heart and he had nearly forgiven me for the drunken scene at his 40th birthday ball. However several officers, including my friend Captain Edward James Foote commanding the *Seahorse* frigate, disapproved strongly of Nelson's private conduct.

By mid-December the French army was threatening to take Naples. The French General Championnet, although outnumbered six to one, was more than a match for the wretched General Mack and the miserable, cowardly Neapolitan army. On the 6 December the French army took Rome and a week later the fugitive King Ferdinand arrived back in Naples.

Nelson wrote on the 10 December to Captain Edward Berry, now safely back in London after adventures with the French following the battle of the Nile 'Josiah is not made Post-Captain nor do I see any probability of that event ...' and the next week to his Excellency the Grand Vizier 'I send my dear son-in-law Captain Nisbet to carry Kelim Effendi to Constantinople ...'.

The evacuation of the Court of Naples and the English merchants and residents took place on the night of 21 December. The Royal Family, their many attendants, their 700 casks of silver and gold coins, and two thousand subjects left Naples in a well planned naval manoeuver. Twenty merchants vessels and three British transport took the British subjects and Court, the *Vanguard* took the Royal Family and the Hamiltons. English crews were put aboard the two Neapolitan warships – the *Archimedes*, 74 guns, and the *Sannita* corvette – the rest were towed out to sea and Nelson ordered Commander Campbell i/c the Portuguese squadron to burn them when the French entered Naples. The convoy sailed on the 23 December to Palermo, the second Kingdom, in a vicious tempest. The squalor aboard the ships laden with the refugees was unbelievable. Palermo in the new year of 1799 was under snow. The Royal Family, the Hamiltons, and of course the Admiral, took up residence in the villa of Montalbo near the Flora Rele. Later the Hamiltons and Nelson removed to the huge Palazzo Palagonia near the harbour Mole.

Retribution caught up with me. I had deeply offended Captain Thomas Troubridge off Leghorn and he complained twice to Nelson at Palermo.

My Lord, I wish to withdraw my [first] letter respecting Captain Nisbet: but after pointing out to him his ingratitude to you and strange and insulting conduct to me and that so publickly I could obtain no promise of any change. The only answer I could procure was that he knew it would happen, that you had no business to bring him to Sea, that he had told you so often and that it was all your fault. I again pointed out to him in the strongest language his black ingratitude to you by making use of such speeches: no arguments I could make use of would induce him to alter his language, I therefore have no alternative as your Lordship will see. I am convinced he has a bad set about him. I therefore again take the liberty of intreating your Lordship not to permit him to take any followers from the sloop ...

Much to my surprise I was gazetted Post-Captain in December 1798 despite Troubridge and others!

Troubridge and I left Palermo on 7 January– he for Alexandria to destroy the French ships there and I – more or less in disgrace – to take *La Bonne Citoyenne* to Constantinople with the Turkish Ambassador to the Court of Naples, little old Kelim Effendi, and his staff under Mr. Pisani.

To Captain Nisbet HM Sloop *Bonne Citoyenne* – Order Book.
Vanguard, Palermo, 7 Jan. 1799.

> You are hereby required and directed to receive on board his Majestys sloop La Bonne Citoyenne, under your command, the Turkish Ambassador Kelim Effendi, with his dragoman and servants and proceed without a moments loss of time, to Constantinople, showing him every attention and civility in your power during his stay on board and on your arrival there you will deliver the despatches you will receive herewith, to his Excellency Spencer Smith Esq. his Majesty's Minister and return immediately and join me at this place. Should Mr. Smith wish to introduce you to the Grand Signior or the Vizir on your arrival you will comply with his request and you are to be particularly careful not to permit any irregularities to be committed by any person who may go ashore, but to do the utmost in your power to cause the dignity and discipline of the British Navy to be respected and you are to bring any despatches which the Grand Vizir or Mr. Smith may have for me in return. And I desire you will acquaint all Captains which you may fall in with in your route, senior to you, that it is my desire that they permit you to proceed on your voyage and not by any other orders to prolong your passage to join me which you are to do with all possible expedition. The letters for Smyrna you will leave with Mr. Smith. Nelson.

My step-father wrote to my mother on the 17 January 'I wish I could say much to your and my satisfaction about Josiah but I am sorry to say and with real grief that he has nothing good about him he must sooner or later be broke, but I am sure neither you or I can help it. I have done with the subject it is an ungrateful one.' He wrote the same week to Earl St. Vincent from Palermo 'Let me thank you for your goodness to Captain Nisbet and wish he may deserve it: the thought half kills me ...'

Despite the winter gales I enjoyed our voyage to Constantinople. *La Bonne Citoyenne* was on its own: no Admirals or indignant senior Captains looking over my shoulder. Our brief stay in Turkey was pleasant. In my absence my step-father wrote to my mother on 2 February 'Josiah has got a commission for *Thalia* I wish he may deserve it. However he has had more done for him than any young man in the Service and made I fear the worst use of his advantages'.

Admiral Nelson wrote to Constantino Ypsolant from Palermo on 8 March 1799 'Sir, Your very elegant and friendly letter was delivered to me yesterday by Captain

Nisbet: and I return him to Constantinople to assure the Sublime Porte, that whilst I have the honour of commanding the detached squadron of his Britannic Majesty's Fleet in the Levant Seas and Coast of Italy, whatever the Sublime Porte wish me to do, it is my duty and indeed it is my inclination: for I shall if it is necessary go myself to serve the Grand Signior ... I have directed Captain Nisbet who is acquainted with my sentiments to express them to your Excellency ...'

The previous day Nelson had ordered me to convey the Maltese deputies back to Malta, but he then cancelled that task and I was sent back to Constantinople. I was partly aware of the problems the Admiral was having with Captain Sir Sidney Smith of the *Tigre*. He was claiming political responsibilities, to which he was not entitled, and was also usurping Nelson's own command in the Levant.

On my return from the East, the Admiral packed me off to join Captain Alexander Ball's squadron blockading Malta. Nelson stayed closely attached to Lady Hamilton and deemed it his duty to protect the Hamiltons and the Royal Family in Palermo. I am sure my step-father had made love to Lady Hamilton in the Palazzo Palagonia. The gossip on board was fast and furious and the whole fleet seemed to think so. Eventually on 19 May Nelson left Palermo after living in the greatest friendship and intimacy with the Hamilton menage. I know my mother got wind of the situation and wanted to take ship to Sicily to protect her marriage. The London papers were by now full of the scandal.

I know the world subsequently criticised my behaviour towards my dear step-father and perhaps with reason. But what both I and Lady Hamilton knew was that during the period of the winter of '94 throughout the spring, summer and autumn of the following year whilst the "Agamemnon" was refitting at Leghorn, a handsome Greek/Italian woman who answered to the absurd name of 'Dolly' was aboard ship in the Admiral's quarters. Much of the time I was at sea but quite often put into Leghorn. My friend Captain Thomas Fremantle, who later on married Betsy Wynne in Naples, and was then commanding the frigate *Inconstant* often reported to me about the Admiral's affaire 'he makes himself ridiculous', he wrote. The wretched woman was once ill with an abcess in her side and was treated by the ship's doctor. Can you wonder that I was so unhappy and so angry at his behaviour? Even Lady Hamilton had cause to warn him to keep away from his slut in Leghorn.

CHAPTER THIRTEEN

MY FRIENDS THE NAVAL SEA LORDS – AND AT COURT

The Hoods were and are one of the great naval families of England, and it has been my privilege to know three generations of them.

Before I ever knew him, Horatio as the young Captain of the *Albemarle* frigate had served under Admiral Samuel Hood on the North American station in 1782. He had a fine reputation and beat the French fleet at Basseterre. The great Admiral was then 58 and Nelson was only 24. The next year back in London the Admiral took Nelson to a levée at St. James to meet the Royal Family. He wrote that the Admiral 'treats me as if I was his son and will I am convinced give me anything I can ask of him.' In turn he regarded the Admiral "as the greatest sea-officer I ever knew." Unfortunately this relationship was rudely disturbed by King George's displeasure with Nelson over Prince William's activities on the West India station, which meant that Lord Hood whatever his private feelings – was unable to help his protégé with a new command. Samuel Hood had been made a Baronet in 1753 and became one of the two Naval Sea Lords in 1789 and I met him and Lady Hood frequently at Bath Spa and occasionally in London, when he was on leave. He always had a paternal twinkle in his eye for me and 'was as affectionate as if I had been his child.' He referred to Josiah as 'one of the finest colts I ever saw in my life'. After the battle of the Nile we corresponded on the subject of Horatio's new title. I preferred Alexandria and Baron Nelson as titles. From Round Wood I sent him a brace of pheasants and a hare to his noble house in Wimpole Street.

Due to disagreements with Lord Spencer (who succeeded Lord Chatham as First Sea Lord) in 1795, Admiral Hood was forced to resign. Horatio wrote at the time

> Oh miserable Board of Admiralty. They have forced the first officer in the Service away from his command. His zeal, his activity for the honour and benefit of his King and Country are not abated. Upward of 70, he possesses the mind of 40...

So Nelson's greatest patron – that tall, handsome, hawk-faced commander – became Governor of Greenwich Hospital, a post which he held for twenty years more until his death in 1816. I visited him and his lady (and the Lockers) there on frequent occasions. In 1800 I went with Lady Hood to the Court of St. James, and remained friends with her until she died in 1806.

Lord Hood's son Samuel was Horatio's contemporary and served alongside him in the Mediterranean, at the attack on Santa Cruz, at the Nile commanding the *Zealous*, and became a Vice-Admiral and a Baronet. In due course he too became Baron and Viscount Hood. Alexander Hood, young Sam's uncle, became Viscount Bridport, and on his death in 1814 his son Henry succeeded to the title.

Lady Hood's brother was Rear Admiral Robert Linzee, under whom Horatio briefly served in the Mediterranean in the negotiations with the Bey of Tunis in November.

I was delighted when Lord Hood's second grandson Samuel married Lady Charlotte Nelson, (the Rector's daughter) on 29 August 1810, and I wrote to Sir Samuel to say how pleased I was. It was a wonderful romantic link between our two families. If Horatio had still been alive he would surely have approved – his niece marrying into the greatest naval family of the time.

The Countess Spencer, mother of Georgiana, Duchess of Devonshire, used to visit her brother Canon Poyntz of North Creake. The Poyntz were Norfolk cousins of the Nelsons, and our father of course knew Canon Charles Poyntz well.

George Spencer, the second Earl, who had married the beautiful Lavinia Bingham, became First Lord of the Admiralty in 1794, succeeding Lord Chatham. Despite the distant relationship Horatio mistrusted Lord Spencer. His wife had ambitious ideas, and meeting serving sea-officers and their wives was not one of them. Nevertheless, before Horatio's Nile victory, we dined with the Spencers. Our hostess took one look at my badly wounded husband (this was just after the loss of his arm at Santa Cruz and he looked desperately ill and tired) and she refrained from looking at him again. But she was usually very kind to me. She was a curious woman – a snob, frequently a gossip – but she occasionally showed a glimpse of tenderness. She presented Horatio with a special gold plated combined knife and fork for a one-handed person!

By this time Lord Spencer had a very high regard for Horatio's talents. It was reported that on hearing of the victory at Aboukir Bay, achieved without the loss of a single British ship, he fainted in his office! Nevertheless he recovered and when Horatio was dillydallying at the Court of Naples he administered a sharp rebuke. 'He would best be advised to come home *at once* rather than remain inactive at a foreign Court while on active service.' On his return, after being snubbed by the King at St. James Palace, we dined (November 1800) with the Spencers on the evening when Horatio behaved so rudely to me in public. In February of the following year Lord St. Vincent succeeded Lord Spencer and our old friend Admiral Sir Thomas Troubridge became a Lord of the Admiralty.

All the great Sea Lords and most of Society strongly disapproved of Horatio's activities at the Court of Naples. Lord and Lady Keith recoiled in horror at the relationship with the Hamiltons. Thomas Troubridge most actively disapproved of Lady Hamilton as a person, and the Mintos were angry that her behaviour caused the breakup of our marriage.

At the time Lord Minto had written to his wife 'Lady Hamilton looks ultimately to the chance of marriage as Sir William will not be long in her way and she probably indulges a hope that she may survive Lady Nelson. She is in high looks but more immense than ever. The love she makes to Nelson is not only ridiculous but disgusting ...' The Mintos were my good friends and made their views plain to all.

Horatio first met Sir John Jervis when he was a very young Captain. Sir John was sixty three when he became Commander in Chief of the Mediterranean fleet when Horatio was commanding the *Agamemnon*. He had had a most distinguished record in the Seven Years War, in the War of American Independence, and then in the West Indies. His reputation was therefore excellent, but he was also known for his high temper, grim humour, and as an inflexible disciplinarian. He at once recognised Horatio's talents and swiftly had him promoted to be Commodore with the Broad Pendant flag. Sir John was made Earl St. Vincent after the victory of that name when my husband, who largely contributed to the success of the battle, was given the Order of the Bath. Sir John resigned due to ill-health in 1799, much to the dismay of my husband, who implored him. 'For the sake of our Country do not quit us at this serious moment ... we look up to you as we have always found you, as to our Father under whose fostering care we have been led to Fame.' On the Earl's return to London he became First Sea Lord, and had a house in Mortimer Street.

Lord St. Vincent wrote to Lady Hamilton in Naples 'Pray do not let your fascinating Neapolitan dames approach too near him: for he is made of flesh and blood and cannot resist their temptation.' His words of warning were not heeded and the temptation of the siren's song was not resisted. He wrote to the Secretary of the Admiralty 'It is evident from Lord Nelson's letter to you on his landing that he is doubtful of the propriety of his conduct. I have no doubt he is pledged to getting Lady H. received at St. James and everywhere and that he will get into much brouillerie about it ...' He referred to my husband and Lady Hamilton as 'a pair of sentimental fools.' Later on Lord St. Vincent refused to go to Merton to see Nelson and the Hamiltons. Unfortunately in 1801 he and my husband were engaged in litigation about prize money gained in the Mediterranean campaign.

Lord St. Vincent wrote frequently to his sister Mrs. Ricketts. In 1806 off Ushant in the *Hibernia* he wrote

The executors of the late Lord Nelson will receive a good sum from the money granted by Parliament to the persons engaged in the battle of Trafalgar. Give my love to Lady Nelson and inform her ladyship that the Solicitor-General is the ablest and one of the most honest men that ever appeared in the Chancery Bar. I love Lady Nelson dearly and admire her delightful pride and spirit. Any assistance I can give her she may command. I shall be in town the latter end of the month (January), for six days, of which I will thank you to acquaint her ladyship. Your truly affectionate St. Vincent.

Lord St. Vincent – that great old man of the sea died in 1823 aged 90 years – Nelson's friend and always one of my admirers.

Sir Peter Parker and Lady Margaret Parker (she was a Nugent before her marriage) had known Horatio since 1778 when he was serving on the New York station as third lieutenant on the former's flagship the *Bristol*. He was rapidly promoted to First lieutenant. Lady Parker, a most formidable lady, approved of the young Nelson then aged twenty one, and nursed him at Port Royal when he had fever and was invalided back to England and Bath. The Parkers earned a great deal of prize money on the West Indian station and built a new house in Essex with the proceeds. He then was given command at Portsmouth.

The Parkers were another distinguished naval family. At Copenhagen Horatio served under Sir Peter's brother, Admiral Sir Hyde Parker, although Horatio had command of the fleet in the actual battle. I wrote to Horatio at the end of '99 from Alexander Davison's house in St. James Square 'Sir Peter and Lady Parker called yesterday. We have agreed to go and see the famous French Milliner. Lady P. declares they will put me in a sack (sac) and send me to Bonaparté. Her spirits are good indeed. She sends Sir Peter to the Admiralty to hear when you are expected home. I have ordered a suit of clothes for her Majesty's birthday ...'

Although the Parkers (and the Hoods) wanted Horatio to return home from Naples where he was inactive, they too made a token visit to Merton when he eventually returned with the Hamiltons. Still the Parkers visited my father-in-law and I on many occassions in the period 1798-1805.

After Trafalgar Sir Peter Parker, then aged 85 years, was chief mourner and followed Horatio's coffin to its last resting place in St. Pauls Cathedral – near where his friend – our friend from Nevis days, Cuthbert Collingwood – was to be buried five years later.

I met many Admirals in London and Bath – Young, Nugent, Dickson, Joseph Bullen, Carpenter, Mason, Hotham, Pole, Lord Howe, Lord Keith, Sir Frank Laforey, Samuel Barrington – a very gallant company. Of them all the Hoods, the St. Vincents and the Parkers were the kindest, the most steadfast and the most influential. Admiral Sir Thomas Troubridge, who deeply admired Nelson, always supported me in the difficult years before and after Trafalgar.

For a period of about ten years from 1797 I attended the Court Levées at St. James Palace, occasionally with my husband, but usually without. I would meet the rosy cheeked old sovereign with his bright clear blue eyes, occasionally the Duke of York, and more frequently our old friend the Duke of Clarence. The Levées usually took place on Thursdays a little after noon in the long gallery of the old blackened red-brick palace. Famous people of the day were allowed to present their young protégées. Usually it was an occasion for medals, decorations or the Order of the Bath to be presented by the King. On 22 November 1798 I attended the Drawing Room (as the ceremony was called) and was presented to the Queen by the Countess of Chatham. *The Times* noted that I was 'among the principal female nobility and gentry.' That was the era when 'Lady Nelson's Fancy' was the popular dance in the English towns.

On 4 June 1799 I went to the King's Birthday Levée with Lord and Lady Walpole (Horatio's cousins) and the *Morning Herald* reported 'Lady Nelson was most magnificently attired in a robe embroidered with silver, ornamented to correspond and a beautiful head-dress with an elegant plumage of ostrich feathers.'

The following spring (March 1800) at a Drawing Room I conversed with the King without embarrassment and wrote to Horatio 'Our gracious King thought it was a long time since I heared from you and told me the wind was changed therefore he hoped I should hear from you very soon. The Queen always speaks to me with so much condescension that I like her very much.'

On the 14 November Horatio and I and the Nile captains were presented to the Queen at St. James Palace. After the victory at Copenhagen in the spring of 1801 I attended a Drawing Room with the Spencers, travelling up to Town from Bath to do so.

After Horatio's final rebuff to my letter of 18 December 1801 offering him a warm house with me in Somerset Street, I put on my bravest face and went to the Queen's Birthday Drawing Room (17 January 1802). I dressed in the most simple but elegant style. A white satin robe and petticoat orinmented with gold fringe and tassels. A head-dress of plain white and gold colour with a beautiful plume of Paradise and ostrich feathers.

I was still a proud, dignified good looking woman with means of my own and the entrée to the grand houses of London, and was determined to appear before the world (discreetly of course – that is my nature) as Nelson's well-dressed wife.

From 1803 onwards from my town house at 54 Welbeck Street I often went to the Drawing Room occasions under my new title of the Duchess of Nelson and Bronte. Naturally it was Court etiquette that Lady Hamilton, even when her husband was alive, was not invited to Court by either sovereign.

Apart from a Dance being named after me, the Admiralty did me the great honour of launching a ship with my name. A brig was named *Lady Nelson* and went on exploration voyages to Australia in 1802, the Barrier Reef and Torres Strait under the command of Lieutenant James Murray. The victors of Waterloo assembled in London during the summer of 1814. Alexander, the Czar of all the Russias, old Field Marshall von Blucher, Prince Metternich of Austria, and the King of Prussia all came to England for the peace celebrations and were met by my friend the Duke of Clarence on HMS *Impregnable*. King George III was ill – some said mad – and was unable to greet these distinguished visitors. The Prince Regent, 'Prinny', received them in. his palace.

On the 1 August, as part of the ceremonies, a representation of the Battle of the Nile was made on the Serpentine in Hyde Park, and as Nelson's widow, my Admiralty friends persuaded me to see this spectacle. The European visitors also visited the Greenwich Hospital for Naval Pensioners, where my old friend Admiral Lord Hood was Governor two years before he died.

The tragedy was that a few months later Napoleon escaped from Elba and all was in the melting pot again.

Frances Nelson, 1st Vicountess Nelson, a portrait by Sir William Beechey, 1801.

Lord Nelson by Simon de Koster, 1801.

CHAPTER FOURTEEN

'NAPLES IS A DANGEROUS PLACE'

My husband's first mention of Lady Hamilton – 'that woman' – who subsequently became his mistress, took him away from me, and conceived his only child – was in mid September 1793 when he and Josiah in the *Agamemnon* arrived in Naples. They stayed for five days and he wrote and told me why he was there – to give support to the King and Queen of Naples against possible French influence or even attack. There he met the King, Ferdinand, but not the Queen, Maria Caroline, who was pregnant, and Sir John Acton who, although an English baronet, was in charge of the Neapolitan navy, such as it was. He also met the British Ambassador and his wife, who invited him to stay with them ashore.

About that time Horatio wrote to Lord St. Vincent 'Naples is a dangerous place, we must keep clear of it.' I wish that he had taken his own advice.

My husband slept therefore not on the *Agamemnon*, but in Prince Augustus Fredrick's room at the Embassy. King George III's sixth son, who had been on an Italian tour, was then on his way back to England. The Palazzo Sessa was described to me as a large private mansion halfway up the hillside of the Pizzofalcone quarter, with a beautiful view over the Bay of Naples. The Ambassador, Sir William Hamilton, had furnished the inside with his exquisite collection of antique furniture and paintings. My husband was royally entertained and thoroughly enjoyed himself. He reported that the Ambassador's wife, Lady Hamilton, had been kind to Josiah and that she was a great friend of the Queen, Maria Caroline, who was sister to Louis XVI's Queen, Marie Antoinette. After the short visit to Naples my husband wrote to Sir William on naval supply matters and also to Lady Hamilton from Calvi. He also wrote later to them from the Nile in 1798, a month or two before his great victory at Aboukir Bay.

After the battle in poor health, wounded in the head, sick with a fever and a hacking cough, my husband and his battered ships limped into Naples for a few days in which to recover and to refit. He was greeted as a Conquering Hero and he stayed there for four months! He wrote glowing reports to me of the great kindness shown him by both the Hamiltons, 'She is one of the very best women in the world. How few could have made the turn she has. She is an honour to her sex.' Never in our eleven years of happy marriage had he written so enthusiastically and so lovingly of *another woman*.

Lady Emma Hamilton.

It was reported to me that the reason why my son Josiah behaved himself so badly at the great banquet and ball given in honour of my husband's fortieth birthday, was that he was ashamed and angry at the attentions being paid to Lady Hamilton which were *my* due!

The news of the great battle of the Nile duly arrived in England on 2 October and the whole country went into a state of extreme enthusiasm and joy. I was overjoyed that my Horatio was created Baron Nelson of the Nile and of Burnham Thorpe in the County of Norfolk. At the time the news was brought I was sitting opposite my Admiral's portrait at Round Wood House in Norfolk. The likeness of his is great and I am well satisfied with Lemuel Abbott, the

Sir William Hamilton.

painter-artist. I was not however satisfied that Mr. William Pitt had been fair to Horatio. Lord Hood had told me that Mr. Pitt was disposed to grant him an Earldom – perhaps of Alexandria. Admiral Jervis received one after the victory of St. Vincent, and Duncan a viscountcy after Camperdown. The Nile was a far greater victory.

On 1 October Horatio's letter said to me 'The continued kind attention of Sir William and Lady Hamilton must ever make you and I love them and they are deserving of the love and admiration of all the world ... *My pride is being your husband,* the son of my dear father and in having Sir William and Lady Hamilton for my friends.' I received strange enthusiastic letters from Lady Hamilton who sent me poems she had composed in Horatio's honour and some decorated fan-mounts.

On the 11 December he was writing 'what can I say of her and Sir William's goodness to me. They are in fact with the *exception of you* and my dear father the dearest friends I have in the world. I live as Sir William's son in the house and my glory is as dear to them as their own'. That letter and its sentiments about 'glory' caused me to re-read it and ponder. I knew my husband very well. He was a vain man. He liked to write glorious prose, to act glorious deeds and to win glorious battles. The result was fame – beautiful medals, beautiful titles, and now perhaps the adulation and praise in a beautiful woman's arms.

Because she *was* beautiful. My friends in London had described to me. The artist George Romney was besotted with her and painted her two dozen times. At this time she was thirty three, seven years younger than Horatio and thirty five years younger than her husband. She was christened Amy Lyon and born in the Wirral, Cheshire. She posed as the 'Goddess of Health' at the Adelphi and was kept by various young men about Town, until as Emma 'Hart' she was taken up by Charles Greville, Sir William Hamilton's nephew. She arrived in Naples on her twenty-first birthday, and was transferred by nephew to uncle – from being a Paddington Green kept mistress to being the vulgar Lady Hamilton, confidante of the Queen of Naples.

She sang well and stridently. She acted in strange clothes in her peculiar 'Attitudes'. Her long rambling, enthusiastic, illspelt letters summed up her character. And she lavished many presents on my husband.

I could not yet see her as a rival. I was genuinely glad that she *and* Sir William were looking so well, so warmly and so attentively after *my* Horatio: he needed all the nursing and care they could give him.

But I underestimated the amazing flattery that she was lavishing hour by hour, day after day in warm exotic surroundings on my vulnerable, badly-battered little Admiral. Blind unthinking flattery, of which my nature has never been capable – praise, yes of course – when it was due...

Even his friends at home were dropping heavy handed hints that he ought to be back at sea again. Lord St. Vincent, Lord Keith and Lord Spencer were worried about 'the fascinating Neapolitan Dames approaching too near him for he is made of flesh and blood and cannot resist their temptations'. Visions of Glory at Sea seemed to have faded away – at least for the time being.

When we heard in London about the evacuation of the Royal Family and Court from Naples to Palermo in Sicily, I was indeed sorry for them. But I was glad that my Horatio would be at sea again, which occurred a few days before Christmas 1798. He wrote to me to buy a 'neat house in London near Hyde Park but on no account on the other side of Portman Square. I detest Baker Street'. In the early days of our marriage when we counted every penny we were not so fussy about our lodgings in London. But wealth, fame and titles do, I suppose, alter all of us. Certainly Horatio was now very conscious of his new role in society.

I now expected almost daily to hear directly either from Horatio or from my Admiral friends and their ladies that he was on his way home. He had done everything possible to guard the Kingdom of Two Sicilies. Now that Naples had fallen he must surely deserve some home-leave.

By early spring, with no news of a homecoming, I wrote to Horatio to say that I would like to leave London and sail to join him if he felt that he had to stay in Sicily. He answered 'Good Sir William, Lady Hamilton and myself are the mainsprings of the machine which manages what is going on in this country. We are all bound to England *when* we can quit our posts with propriety.'

A phrase which apparently they used to describe their situation was 'tria juncta in uno' which worried me considerably. I felt that I was losing Horatio.

British 'Society' of taste has always travelled widely, particularly to the Continent of Europe. There are dozens of English families resident in Naples and many more passing through on their worldly explorations. 'Le milord anglais' of noble birth or not, was to be found in the most obscure of towns, even villages in France (even in times of war), in Austria, and certainly in the Italian Kingdoms. Reports, letters and of course gossip of affairs overseas were being received with great regularity in London. I could mention several worldly travellers from whom perhaps at first, or second, even third hand, rumours and stories came back to me. Lord and Lady Minto, Lord Montgomery and his companion Major Pryse Lockhard Gordon, Lord Bristol, Prince Augustus, Lord and Lady Elgin, Lord and Lady Holland, Miss Cornelia Knight, Charles Lock, the Consul-General, the Wynne family, Mr. John Rushout and others. Young officers sent letters home frequently with the doings of the Fleet: Mr. William Hoste, Mr. George Parsons and many others. Indeed Horatio would often write a dozen letters in a day.

I know that after meeting Alexander Davison one day in London – before setting off for Bath with the old Rector – I told him and his wife that I would sail for Sicily to join Horatio. I asked him to write and let Horatio know that unless he returned home *soon* I would join the *Standard* at Naples – or later Palermo.

When the Royal Family were finally returned to Naples in June – my husband and his fleet of 18 ships escorting them home safely. The consequential riots, anarchy and distressing reprisals resulted in many atrocities and deaths. The trials and executions were heavily criticized in the London papers and by implication the Hamiltons and Horatio were associated with the deplorable situation. Even the news received in August that my husband had been created Duke of Bronte (a totally insignificant little estate near Mount Etna) did not ease my anxiety. I could not believe nor could my friends, the great Admirals and their ladies at the Admiralty – that his presence at the Royal Court was *now* really necessary. He was a skilled and very brave sailor, not a politician. He was still there in the autumn at a grand Fête Champêtre held on the 3. September. It was the Court's tribute to the Hamiltons and Horatio, and created despondency in London in my small household. Miss Cordelia Knight's description of the tributes and adulation and flattery were, to me, quite nauseating. My husband wrote to me gloomily that he hoped 'to rub through the winter in Naples'. Lord Elgin wrote (not to me of course) 'He looks very old, has lost his upper teeth, sees ill of one eye and has a film coming over both of them. He has pains pretty constantly from his late wound in the head. His figure is mean and in general his countenance is without animation.' And Lady Elgin (Mary Nisbet that was) wrote 'They say there was never a man turned so vainglorious (that's the phrase) in the world as Lord Nelson. He is now completely managed by Lady Hamilton ... you never saw anything equal the fuss the Queen made with Lady Hamilton and Lord Nelson wherever she moved was always by her side ... I never saw three people made such thorough dupes of as Lady Hamilton, Sir William and Lord Nelson.' Later at Palermo, Nelson went to sea 'At the Queens Ball I heard people laying bets he would not go to sea.'

Gilbert Elliot, who was Viceroy of Corsica and became Lord Minto, reported that Horatio said to him in October 'We are the real tria juncta in uno.' It was also reported to me that the 'tria juncta' were gambling and spending huge sums of money on entertainment and banquets.

Now that Horatio was acting as commander in chief in the Mediterranean (he was not of course *the* Commander in chief) he had great responsibilities: the blockage of the French garrison in Valletta, keeping the French army in Egypt, the blockade of Geneva, and the defence of Minorca – all this still did not justify gambling and high expenses at Court. Details of the scandalous life that the Hamiltons and my Horatio were now leading were now being published in London. Even *The Times* on 14 November took them to task. Lord Keith is going out immediately to take the command in the Mediterranean.

Upon his Lordships arrival, Lord Nelson will return to England.

Perfidium ridens Venus & Cupido!

These perfidious Gods have in all time spread their smiling snares for the first of mankind. Heroes and Conquerors are subdued in their turn. Mark Anthony followed Cleopatra *into the Nile,* when he should have fought with Octavius! and laid down his laurels and his power, to sail down the Cydnus with her in the dress, the character and the *attitudes* of Venus. What will not the eye effect in the bosom of a Hero?

And on 28 November 'By a false point in one of the morning Papers, the admirable attitudes of Lady HAM-T-N are called Admiral-attitudes,' and so on.

I was so mortified – not for myself – because I think I can withstand innuendo, even attack, well enough, but for Horatio and his reputation. In my heart of hearts I was sure that he and Lady Hamilton were lovers, but for the Great British Public to be told so with malicious authority by our London papers was galling and humiliating to me and my friends. I wrote 'I am fully persuaded many are jealous of your character.'

His letters were sweet and sometimes tender and affectionate. He described the celebrations for the anniversary of the Battle of the Nile when the horrible King Ferdinand IV dined on board the *Foudroyant*.

> When His Majesty drank my health, a Royal salute of 21 guns was fired from all his Sicilian Majesty's Ships of War and from all the Castles. In the evening there was a general illumination ... in short, my dear Fanny, the beauty of the whole is beyond my powers of description. More than 2,000 variegated lamps were suspended round the vessel. An orchestra was fitted up and filled with the very best musicians and singers. The piece of music was in a great measure to celebrate my praise, describing their previous distress. But Nelson came, the invincible Nelson, and they were preserved and again made happy. This must not make you think me vain; no, very far from it. I relate it more from gratitude than vanity; I return to Palermo with the King. May God bless you all – [but no protestations of love.]

Lady Elgin had described Lady Hamilton as pleasant, saying she sang remarkably well and looked very handsome in undress at dinner: 'My Father would say "There is a fine Woman for you good flesh and blood. She is indeed a Whopper" Lord Nelson whenever she moved was always by her side he seems quite dying, and yet as if he had no other thought than her.' Some of these comments came home to me, sometimes relayed with sympathy, sometimes with amusement, occasionally with malice, but outwardly I remained unmoved. I wrote to Horatio every two weeks as usual and sent him new publications and papers from London, and behaved *exactly* as I had done in the last happy dozen years. He now wrote that he was bringing Queen Maria Caroline and her royal entourage of fifty, including three unmarried daughters, from Palermo to Leghorn – this was mid May. The Queen then planned to go overland to Vienna (where her mother, the Austrian Empress Maria Theresa, lived) to visit her daughter and son-in-law at Court. The Hamiltons were then to retire to London. He had been succeeded by Mr. (later Sir) Arthur Paget. I was overjoyed at this news, although I had wanted to go to Lisbon to meet Horatio there. One letter to me ended 'Lady Hamilton has never received from you the scrap of a pen or any prints.'

The curious thing is that Lady Hamilton felt compelled to write to me several times from the Court of Naples. One such letter was on 2 October 1798.

> I hope your Ladyship received my former letter with an account of Lord Nelson's arrival, and his reception by their Sicilian Majesties; and also (sic) the congratulations and compliments from this amiable Queen to your Ladyship which I was charged with and wrote a month back, but as the posts were very uncertain, you may not have received that letter. Lord Nelson is gone to Leghorn with the troops of the King of Naples, and we expect him soon Back, as the King is gone to Rome with his army; and he beg'd of my Lord Nelson to be as much in and about Naples as he cou'd, not

The only known painting from life of Admiral Nelson and Lady Hamilton together in Naples.

only to advise and consult with her Majesty, who is Regent for the good of the common cause, but, in case of accident, to take care of her and of her family.

Lord Nelson is adored here, and looked on as the deliverer of this country. He was not well when first he arrived, but by nursing and asse's milk he went from Naples quite recovered.

The King and Queen adore him, and if he had been their Brother, they cou'd not have shown him more respect and attentions. I need not tell your Ladyship how happy Sir William and myself are at having an opportunity of seeing our dear, respectable brave friend return here with so much honour to himself, and glory for his country. We only wanted *you* to be completely happy. Lord Nelson's wound is quite well. Josiah is so much improv'd in every respect, we are all delighted with him. He is an excellent officer and very steady, and one of the best hearts in the world. *I Love him much, and although we quarrel sometimes, he loves me and does as I wou'd have him.* He is in the way of being rich, for he has taken many prizes. He is indefatiguable in his line, never sleeps out of his ship [the frigate *Thalia*] and I am sure will make a very great officer. Lady Knight and her amiable daughter desire to be remembered to your Ladyship. I hope you received the ode I sent; it is very well written, but Miss Knight is very clever in everything she undertakes.

Sir William desires his kind compliments to your Ladyship and to Lord Nelson's respected father.

The King is having his picture set with dymonds for his Lordship, and the Queen has ordered a fine set of china with all the battles he *has* been engaged in, and his picture painted on china. Josiah desired his duty to your Ladyship, and says he will write as soon as he has time, but he has been very busy for some time past.

God bless you and yours, my dear Madam, and believe me your Ladyship's very sincere friend, Emma Hamilton.

Sir William is in a rage with (the) Ministry for not having made Lord Nelson a Viscount, for, sure, this great and glorious action greater than any other – ought to have been recognised more. Hang them, I say.

On 10 June 1800 the 'tria juncta in uno', as they so fatuously described themselves, finally left the Kingdom of the Two Sicilies – for good. My husband had been at the service of the Kingdom and I fear of the Hamiltons for almost exactly two years. My spirits were still hopeful and optimistic although my health was giving me problems – rheumatism and so on – although insignificant in comparison to my poor mutilated Admiral.

Ten days later Horatio wrote to me from Leghorn – a very strange and disquieting missive: 'We are detained by the situation of the armies but a few days will I hope enable Her Majesty to prosecute her intended journey to Vienna when Lord Keith I think must allow the *Foudroyant* to carry me and my party to England for she cannot be refitted in the Mediterranean. My health at times is better but a quiet mind and to live content is necessary for me. A very difficult thing for me to enjoy I could say much but it would only distress me and be useless.' No message of hope and not the faintest particle of his love for me.

General Sir John Moore arrived at Leghorn with his expeditionary force on 1 July. Total confusion reigned because Queen Maria Caroline did not know what to do or where to go. Lady Hamilton and Sir William were there attending the Queen. According to Sir John Moore 'Lord Nelson was there attending upon Lady Hamilton. He is covered with stars, ribbons and medals more like the Prince of an Opera than the Conqueror of the Nile. It is really melancholy to see a brave and good man who has deserved well of his Country cutting so pitiful a figure.' Eventually the whole comic opera set off overland to Florence, Arezzo and Ancona, where they sailed to Trieste. Horatio and the Hamiltons sailed in a Russian frigate. Eventually during late August they reached Vienna. My naval husband – victor of a dozen sea battles was travelling meekly by coach across Europe. I was desolate.

Lord Fitzharris described Lady Hamilton as 'without exception the most coarse, ill-mannered disagreeable woman I ever met with.' Lady Holland described the Hamiltons as 'tiresome as ever he as amorous, she as vulgar.'

It was difficult for me to disagree with those comments.

Nelson by Sir William Beechey *c.* 1800, covered 'with stars, ribbons and medals'.

CHAPTER FIFTEEN

LETTERS TO MY DEAREST HUSBAND
1799-1800

Whilst my husband was at Naples with the *Vanguard* and later the *Foudroyant* in the last six months of the century, I wrote frequently to him. I missed him very much. Much of the time I was at Round Wood, occasionally in London for the Drawing Room and to visit my old Admirals – Barrington, Pole, Thomas Pringle of Nevis days, Nugent, Dickson, Young, Lord Hood, Earl St. Vincent and Lord Spencer.

My father-in-law was seriously ill that winter. Fortunately we were at the time staying in London where the quality of the surgeons (notably Mr. Younge, Mr. Hawkins and Dr. Baille) probably saved his life with their experienced treatment.

My letters were full, as usual, of family news. Little Susanna Bolton was fond of me and stayed with us frequently and I took her to concerts. So too did young Charlotte Nelson, still a schoolgirl at Whitelands in Chelsea, but growing up fast. When Captain Hardy was on leave we took her to a grand ball and supper, and I lent her a pair of pearl ear-rings and a wreath of flowers to wear on her head and a pair of white kid gloves. She looked a very chic little girl and enjoyed that evening. I took great pleasure in looking after my husband's nieces.

Financial matters took up some of my time: we lived modestly but everything seems to cost more month by month. Mr. Marsh, Horatio's agent, was very active, and with prize money had purchased £10,000 of East India stock for me to distribute to his brothers and sisters.

I was not well that cold and chilly winter and my doctor recommended a visit to the warmer climates of Lisbon or Naples, but Horatio was reluctant to let me come to see him. I sent Lady Hamilton various presents at his request – prints, a cap and kerchief – but I received no acknowledgement or thanks. Here are a few examples of my letters to Horatio:

Round Wood, October 14, 1799

My Dearest Husband,

The public news you have by the papers, and truly my chit chat is hardly worth your reading, but such as it is you must accept.

Major Dundas Saunders is quartered at Ipswich. Mrs. Godfrey requested me to visit his wife, which I did and conclude it was acceptable from

Mrs. D's returning the visit the next day. Our good father is pretty well, the garden affords him great amusement and now and then some of our acquaintances give him a nosegay.

Lady St. Vincent writes me her Lord recovers very fast. Sir J. Orde has again made himself the subject of conversation. Matters are very properly set to rights by binding him over 'to keep the peace'. Every man who refuses a challenge exalts himself in my opinion. From all this you may suppose the Earl is a first rate favourite. I long to hear from you. My latest date was August 4th. I wonder Lady Hamilton never acknowledged all the prints I requested Mr. Davison to send her. I packed them up myself and Mr. D told me he would send them by the first good opportunity. This is 10 or 11 months back. Make my best regards to her and ask if they are received.

Mr. W. Bolton come bowing to congratulate me on your being created Duke de Bronte and was surprised I had not heard it. It seems all the papers have mentioned it, excepting the *Sun* and *Star*. I hope this news is true if you have money given to support the rank. I assure you I am frightened at the money I spend, every article of life is so dear. Beef 9/4 a stone. Coals very dear. Since Sir E. Berry and his wife dined with us, I have never had any dinner company.

My love to my Josiah God bless you both believe me my dearest husband your affectionate wife, Frances H. Nelson.

Our father's love and blessing attend you.

Right Honourable Lord Nelson, *Foudroyant*, Mediterranean.

Round Wood, 21 October

My Dearest Husband,

Lieutenant Edward Parker called last night at ten o'clock just to tell me you were well on the 8 September. Thank God for it and may you enjoy health and every other blessing this world affords.

The young man's extreme gratitude and modesty will never be obliterated from your good father's and my memory. He stayed a very few minutes as the express from Vienna was in the chaise at the door. I was so glad to see anyone who could give me such late accounts of my dear husband and my son, that it had such an effect on me that I could not hear or see and was obliged to call in our good father, who made many enquiries and amongst the rest, if you were Duke de Bronte, not but we were well satisfied you were from a letter I received from my Josiah who gave us a very good account where the place was situated and from whence you took your title. Sicily may be a desirable island to have property in probably better than near Naples...

Captain James Oswald called last week, he came from Yarmouth and returned immediately as he was going to the Texel. I long to hear of the arrival of Sir William and Lady Hamilton. The carriage the coachmaker let me have during the building of yours is just worn out, at least the coachman says the wheels will not last long, therefore I intend to deliver the old carriage and take the new one down, and any little alterations can be made immediately. Besides all this I should have such a good opportunity of acknowledging and thanking Sir W. and Lady Hamilton of their attention and kindness to you and my son.

Our good father stays at home and Miss S. Bolton is to accompany me. What a sad thing it is those girls cannot or will not conceal these unpleasant tempers. They are, I tell our father, very young, he says 'True Boltons, I pity the men that marry them but no man will venture.' You will find George Bolton a very affectionate temper. He speaks of Lady Nelson as a very superior creature only six weeks attention to him. The dampness occasioned by the constant rain is beyond description – However we stand high, therefore under no fear of suffering from it, which is no bad thing I assure you.

Mr. and Mrs. Hamilton are arrived in England from Nevis. I congratulated her on the occasion and received a letter of thanks and full handsome expressions of you and speaks highly of your goodness to my Josiah. She concludes by saying with economy and good crops she hopes to remain in England.

I shall send this letter to Admiral Young. Our good father sends his love and blessing to you. Believe me my dear husband your affectionate wife, Frances H. Nelson.

George Tobin and his little dasher are home. Mr. T. wishes as well as G. T. he could be sent to you, if I could give him any information of your movements which I could not.

Right Honourable Lord Nelson, *Foudroyant*, Mediterranean.

Round Wood, 27 October

My Dearest Husband,

Our good father and myself were highly gratified at the perusal of the King of Naples' letter and grant of the territory attached to the Dukedom of Bronte. God bless you and grant you health and long life to enjoy all this well earned honour.

Mr. Marsh has been successful in getting the East India Company to pay the £10,000. He writes me [he] has bought £2,000 in the India stock and wishes I would say what was to be done with the £8,000 or should he purchase more

in the East India stock. Upon the receipt of this intelligence from Mr. Marsh
our father the following day asked me what I intended doing in regard to the
sum you had desired me to give to your family out of the donation from E.I.C.
I said I would write to Marsh to distribute the money you had mentioned if
he pleased, but candidly I did not intend noticing your letter 14 of July which
contained your desire till I had wrote to you upon this subject. However our
father gave me his opinion in these words 'If his brothers and sisters ever hear
that you have a letter desiring a portion of the E.I.C. gift to be given to them
and you withhold it, I think it will make an irreparable breach between you
and them and Horace may say "I knew very well what I was about." Therefore
after this conversation I wrote to Mr. Marsh that you had desired me to give
£2500 to your father, brothers and sisters and the remainder I was certain he
would take care of. I was no judge nor did I wish to interfere in money matters.
Our father intends giving the family notice of your donation but wishes me to
shew Mr. Marsh your letter of the 14th of July and not send it, particularly as
I am partly obliged to go to London. The carriage Mr. Lukin lent me while he
was building yours is so very old and crazy that your father thinks I had better
take it up myself. The charges of the waggon is pretty high and the coachman
wants to change horses. All these considerations makes it necessary for me to
go. He remains at home and Miss S. Bolton is to go with me.

I hope Sir E. Berry has seen you long before this time, as Lady Berry had
a letter a week back dated Gibraltar 2nd of October.

I had a letter from my dear Josiah, he was the first that told us of Bronte.
He has had a fever. I have since heard that he was better. I hope it is true. My
anxiety for my dear son is great. He thinks you will soon be in England.

Our father will write to you very soon. Believe me my dear husband,
Frances H. Nelson.

Mr. Berners has been at Bronte. He gives so delightful an account of it,
that with great difficulty I refrain from making you a visit, therefore I hope
you will consent to my going out, particularly as my health is really very
indifferent. I think our father would go with me. Patty Berry says she would
go out with me as femme de chambre.

Right Honourable Lord Nelson, *Foudroyant*, Mediterranean.
Post paid 1/8*d*.

54 St. James' Street, 26 December, 1799

....Captain [Thomas] Hardy has made us all happy by the flattering accounts
he gave us of your health. I mentioned your letters were written quite out
of spirits. He assures me that is owing to the tiresome people you have to
deal with. It is impossible to tell you how much pleasure the arrival of Capt.
Hardy has given to all our acquaintance. When I enquired after poor George

Bolton, Capt. Hardy did not seem to know anything of him. Susanna was surprised, the conversation dropped and Maurice informed me the next morning that the little boy died on his passage from Gibraltar to Minorca. I own at first I was afraid he had fell overboard. Mrs. Bolton and Kitty have been absent from home some weeks, which frets our good father. Your sister assured us Mr. Bolton was quite easy and happy in his cirumstances. I repeat all these things as I find one half of my letters never reach you.

Everything you desired to be sent you will receive by the first frigate. Capt. Hardy told me you would be gratified if I sent Lady Hamilton anything, therefore I shall send her ladyship a cap and kerchief such as are worn in the cold weather. I have ordered a suit of clothes for Her Majesty's birthday [on 19 Jan.] I am frightened to tell you the expense of your new chariot, nothing fine about it. Only fashionable, £352 harness etc. for one pair of horses.

Colonel Suckling has called several times, and seems highly gratified by my civility. Good Capt. Locker desires I would give his love to you, in short I was to say everything that was kind and affectionate for him, and at the same time I was to tell you he is grown quite old; one of his hands are stiff which prevents him from writing.

Lord Hood is still at Bath. I must write to him. I have seen Capt. Hardy for he is wonderfully anxious for your coming home. The Parkers are in town. Lady P. was kind and attentive to me. Unfortunately Sir Peter in going upstairs with a candlestick in his hand fell backwards, very much bruised and one of his legs cut in several places. No danger is apprehended from the fall, but although this accident happened upwards of a fortnight he is not out of his room. Admiral Pole looks well, desires to be kindly remembered to you.

I am clothed in two suits of flannel and I hope I shall be the better for it. My health is much mended within this month. And Admiral Pringle desires me to tell you that he longs to see you. He has been very ill with a complaint in his head. He is better and they give him hopes of getting quite well. He has bought a house and land on the borders of England, 7 miles from a town, which he finds very inconvenient. I am now going to take this letter to Mr. A. Stanhope who sends all your letters, for I cannot bear the idea of your not receiving them when truly I write once a week.

God bless my dearest husband. Our father's blessing attend you…

St. James's Street, March 15, 1800. No.11.

My Dear Husband,

Admiral Young has called to tell me of this conveyance and have just time to say our good father continues to mend, and he sometimes talks of returning to Round Wood when I return from the hot sea bathing which I sometimes flatter myself will be of service to me.

I shall make you smile at my economy. My birthday suit could not be worn after Easter therefore I took the first tolerable Thursday to pay my respects at St. James's which was last Thursday, March 13th. Our gracious King thought it was a long time since I heard from you, and told me the wind was changed therefore he hoped I should hear from you very soon. The Queen always talks to me, with so much condescension that I like her very much. And Lady Harrington endeavoured to persuade me to make you a visit. Spoke of the climate how necessary it was to me who had so bad a cough. She little knew how much virtue I had in not going out.

Is my dear son with you? I hope he is. The neutral vessels that were taken by Captain Foley and himself are to be considered as prizes, therefore tell him how to send his money home. Mr. Marsh tells me private bills are dangerous. With your affectionate advice he will do things right. A little independence he will find a great comfort.

Aunt Mary is very ill. Mr Nelson from the letters from Hilbro' does not think she [can] last long. To give you an idea of the extreme danger our father was in, when he was able to sit up the physician called to see him, and when he found him in the parlour, he told me he had seen a prodigy. Mr Nelson in the parlour. Our good father wrote to you during his illness. His love and best love attend you.

God bless you is the sincere wish of your affectionate wife, Frances H. Nelson.

My love to my dear Josiah. The Berrys, the world says, are grown very great indeed. How could they give out Lady B. was with child?

Right Honourable Lord Nelson, *Foudroyant*, Mediterranean.

Nelson's ships, from left to right; *Agamemnon, Captain, Vanguard, Elephant* and *Victory.* Fanny wrote to Nelson while he was serving aboard each of these ships.

CHAPTER SIXTEEN

THE KEEPER AND THE BEAR

The return of the Comic Opera Party to England was eventually achieved on 6 November 1800, via Vienna, Eisenstadt, Prague, Dresden and Hamburg. Five months the cavalcade had taken to wend their way through the flesh-pots of Europe. The Queen of Naples leading the Hamiltons, and Lady Hamilton leading my poor husband. Both men had been ill on the way.

Reports on their extraordinary activities had reached London through a variety of sources and the London papers made the most of the scandals – gossipy little Miss Cordelia Knight, Sir Arthur Paget, gallant Sir John Moore, my friends Lord and Lady Minto, Lord Fitzharris, Hugh Elliot (Lord Minto's handsome brother), a young Irish widow Mrs. Melesina St. George and others sent their impressions to friends and relations and sometimes to the journals in London.

Lady Anna Minto wrote that 'Nelson is devoted to Emma, thinks her quite an angel and talks of her as such to her face and behind her back and she leads him about a *keeper* with a bear. She must sit by him at dinner to cut his meat and he carries her pocket handkerchief.'

Mrs. St. George noted

October 3rd. Dined at Mr. Elliots in Dresden with only the Nelson party. It is plain that Lord Nelson thinks of nothing but Lady Hamilton who is totally occupied by the same object. She is bold, forward, coarse, assuming and vain. Her figure is colossal but excepting her feet which are hideous, well shaped. Her bones are large and she is exceedingly embonpoint. She resembles the bust of Ariadne; the shape of all her features is fine as is the form of her head and particularly her ears: her teeth are a little irregular but tolerably white: her eyes light blue with a brown spot in one, which, though a defect, takes nothing away from her beauty of expression. Her eyebrows and hair are dark and her complexion coarse. Her expression is strongly marked, variable and interesting: her movements in common life ungraceful: her voice loud, yet not disagreeable. Her ruling passions seem to me vanity, avarice and love for the pleasure of the table.

Lord Minto described Lady Hamilton in 1796

> She is all Nature and yet all Art that is to say, her manners are perfectly
> unpolished, of course very easy though not with the ease of good breeding
> *but of a barmaid*: excessively good humoured and wishing to please and
> be admired by all ages and sorts of persons that come in her way; but
> besides considerably natural understanding, she has acquired, since her
> marriage some knowledge of history and of the arts and one wonders at the
> application and pains she has taken to make herself what she is.

Gilbert Elliot (Lord Minto) and his wife were good friends of mine and they
supported me in the course of the next four difficult years.

I had heard about Lady Hamilton's acting background and her extraordinary
Attitudes, which (some) sophisticated witnesses regarded as sublime. So I made it
my business to find out more about the 'Keeper' of my 'Bear'.

Mrs. Melesina St. Georges description was shown to me.

> Breakfasted with Lady Hamilton and saw her represent in succession the
> best statues and paintings extant. She assumes their attitude, expression and
> drapery with great facility swiftness and accuracy. Several Indian shawls, a
> chair, some antique vases, a wreath of roses, a tambourine and a few children
> are her whole apparatus. She stands at one end of the room with a strong light
> to her left, and every other window closed. Her hair (which by the bye is never
> clean) is short, dressed like an antique and her gown a simple calico chemise,
> very easy, with loose sleeves to the wrist. She disposes the shawls so as to
> form Grecian, Turkish and other drapery, as well as a variety of turbans. Her
> arrangement of the turbans is absolutely sleight of hand, she does it so quickly,
> so easily and so well. It is a beautiful performance *amusing to the ignorant* and
> highly interesting to the lovers of art. The chief of her imitations are from the
> antique. Each representation lasts about ten minutes. It is remarkable that,
> though coarse and ungraceful in common life, she becomes highly graceful
> and even beautiful, during this performance. It is also singular that in spite of
> the accuracy of her imitation of the finest ancient draperies, her usual dress
> is tasteless, vulgar, loaded and unbecoming. She has borrowed several of my
> gowns and much admires my dress: which cannot flatter as her own is so
> frightful. Her waist is absolutely between her shoulders! ... Her voice is good
> and very strong but she is frequently out of tune... I think her bold, daring,
> vain even to folly and stamped with the manners of her first situation much
> more strongly than one would suppose after having represented Majesty and
> lived in good company fifteen years.

Lady Holland who in 1794 had described the Hamiltons as tiresome as ever
('he as amorous, she as vulgar') went on to describe the 'Attitudes' – 'She had

The 'Tria Juncta in Uno': Sir William, Nelson, and Emma all portrayed by the same artist, Charles Grignon, in Palermo in 1799. The portrait of Nelson is one of the few informal studies of him to have survived. The portrait of Emma shows her performing one of her famous 'attitudes'.

worked ones imagination up to a pitch of enthusiasm in her successive imitations of Niobe, Magdalen and Cleopatra. Just as she was lying down and her head reclined upon an Etruscan vase to represent a water nymph, she exclaimed in her provincial dialect 'Doun't be afeard Sir William, I'll not crack your joug.' I turned away disgusted and I believe all present shared the sentiment.'

I believe that Sir William Hamilton directed the lighting effects for her posing, usually in dumb-show with the adjuncts of shawls and tambourine. Once, I was told, during a dinner for several distinguished guests in Palermo, she appeared to have fainted and several male guests went to her rescue to help her revive, only to find that she was in the midst of 'An Attitude'. I shudder to think of *my* Horatio enjoying such a curious and unedifying charade.

I knew what and who was now my enemy but worse was to come. 'Lord Nelson is a little man without any dignity. Lady Hamilton takes possession of him and he is a willing captive, the most submissive and devoted I have seen.' I think I started to lose hope when I read that statement written by Mrs. St. George.

In the winter of 1799 I had taken a house in London, No.54, St. James Street – a good address upon which Horatio now insisted. We paid the considerable sum of seven guineas a week, but the Victor of the Nile (although long absent) and his Lady, now Duchess of Bronte – endowed with the handsome annual pension of £2,000 per annum from the Government – could afford that rent. The old Rector, always with me, slept in the back drawing room and I promised Horatio 'a light closet, on a floor, quite large enough for you and my Josiah should you think it right for him to come home.' On 20 September 1800 from Vienna Horatio wrote to me 'Sir William Hamilton being recovered we set out tomorrow and shall be in London the 2nd week in October. I have written to Davison to take a house or good lodgings for the very short time I shall be in London, to which I shall instantly proceed and hope to meet you in the house. You must expect to find me a worn out old man. Make my kindest love to my father who I shall see the moment I have been with the King.' Again no loving warmth or sentiments to which I had been accustomed for so long.

I was looking after his father for him. I liked the dear old man but it was not my role in life to act as guardian and nurse to my sweet righteous old father-in-law. I wrote 'Rest assured, my dear, no one thing that can be done for our good father shall be omitted … I can safely put my hand on my heart and say it has been my study to please and make you happy.'

Eventually my husband sent a letter from Yarmouth on 6 November to me addressed to Round Wood, Ipswich, Suffolk.

My dear Fanny, We are this moment arriv'd and the post only allows me to say that we shall set off tomorrow noon and be with you on Saturday, to dinner. I have only had time to open one of your letters, my visits are so numerous. May God bless you and my Dear Father, and believe me ever, your affectionate Bronte Nelson of the Nile.

Sir and Lady Hamilton beg their best regards and will accept your offer of a bed. Mrs. Cadogan [Lady H.'s mother] and Miss Knight with all the servants will proceed to Colchester. I beg my Dear Father to be assured of my Duty and every tender feeling of a son.

In due course this letter was re-forwarded to me at No.64, Upper Seymour Street, Portman Square. My father-in-law and I had vacated Round Wood months ago – a cold, damp, forlorn and unhappy house.

The cavalcade made their way there and found an empty, closed house.

A crowd greets Nelson during his tour with the Hamiltons in 1801 – a holiday that became a triumphal progress.

CHAPTER SEVENTEEN

THE FATAL HOME COMING

Everything went wrong from the moment the 'Tria juncta in uno' arrived on the King George packet at Yarmouth in a storm, on Thursday 6 November.

All Yarmouth greeted the Victor of the Nile and a tall thin elderly diplomat and a large vulgar lady who stood between them. The Victor promptly wrote me a note addressed to Round Wood. They arrived at the empty house on the following day and, obviously mortified at what they took to be a deliberate snub (for I was in London on Horatio's instructions from Vienna), drove on to Colchester. They stayed the night and arrived in London early on Saturday morning in a freak whirlwind storm (which I thought was significant). I had written however to Yarmouth inviting the Hamiltons to stay with Horatio and myself at Round Wood.

The *Morning Post* reported

His Lordship – Lord Nelson of the Nile – arrived yesterday afternoon at three o'clock at Nerots Hotel King Street, St. James, in the German travelling carriage of Sir William Hamilton. In the coach came with his Lordship, Sir William and Lady Hamilton and a black female attendant. The noble Admiral who was dressed in full uniform, with three stars on his breast and two gold medals, was welcomed by repeated huzzas from the crowd which the illustrious tar returned with a low bow. Lord Nelson looked extremely well, but in person is very thin: so is Sir William Hamilton but Lady Hamilton looks charmingly, and is a very fine woman.

The first interview between the Admiral and his father and myself took place in the hall of Nerot's Hotel at 3 o'clock on the afternoon of Sunday, 9 November – in a thunderstorm.

My first glimpse of my husband showed the ravages of the last two years abroad. I described it as 'the wonderful change, past belief' but I did not mean a change for the better. His hair was pure white, he was thinner and altogether smaller, his eyes looked dim, and it appeared to me that it was only his uniform covered in stars and medals that held him together. My feelings were of tenderness and love, but more than that – overwhelming pity. His letters – far fewer after his stay at the Court of Naples than ever before – had not really prepared me for the dreadful shock of seeing him in such a state. I suspended my judgement and opinion on That Woman until I knew her a little better.

That same evening at five o'clock Horatio and I dined at the Hotel with the Hamiltons. A difficult few hours for all of us. Horatio said little. I was polite and fairly forthcoming and Lady Hamilton, with many small gestures, made it clear that she regarded Horatio as her property. Sir William, who looked tired and frail, did not say much. At half past seven my husband left to see Lord Spencer by carriage and a little later I followed to meet my good friend Lady Lavinia Spencer, where we both passed an uncomfortable evening.

Neither that night or any other night did we ever sleep together in our warm matrimonial bed the way we always used to. Horatio's seduction by Lady Hamilton was now complete. Try as I could with charm, love, kindness and everlasting politeness I could make no impression on him. Most evenings he dined out without me. The Hamiltons stayed at William Beckford's house at No.22 Grosvenor Square, with the funny little Mrs. 'Cadogan' and Miss Cornelia Knight and her mother.

At the Lord Mayor's Feast on the Monday following the arrival in Town of the 'Tria Juncta', Horatio was presented with the Sword voted him by the City. He visited the Admiralty several times, as he was anxious for command again. I went to Somerset House with the Neapolitan Princess Castelcicala to watch the Lord Mayor's procession going by water to the City. Horatio and Sir William joined the parade at the Tower of London.

On Tuesday Horatio spent much time with the Duke of Clarence, who was proud of his friendship with Nelson and the fact that he had acted as Best Man at our wedding on Nevis. On Wednesday Horatio and Sir William, both in full uniform, went to the levée at St. James but the King's reception was curiously remote – very nearly disapproving. It was two years since the Battle of the Nile and the Admiral had been resting too long on his laurels in Naples and Palermo. This snub – and snub it was – was remarked by Admiral Collingwood and others and came as yet another shock to my husband. The same evening we dined with Lord and Lady Spencer inside the Admiralty buildings. Two years previously in the spring of 1798 my husband had told Lady Spencer how beautiful and accomplished I was and that I had saved his life – an angel no less – by my care and love and attention. I remember well his devoted attentions to me and how he refused to be parted from me. Now he behaved like a complete stranger.

The Countess afterwards remarked to her friend that Horatio treated me with every mark of dislike and even of contempt. During dinner I had carefully peeled some walnuts and put them in a glass for him to eat. He pushed the glass aside, overturned and broke it scattering the walnuts. Normally he had impeccable polished manners both in private and on public occasions. He had been totally corrupted by that woman in every single way. Never at any time had I given him cause for these alien emotions. After dinner I wept, broke down, and told the Countess of the dreadful situation I was in.

Lady Hamilton then wrote to me

> I would have done myself the honour of calling on you and Lord Nelson this
> day but I am not well nor in spirits – Sir William and self feel the loss of our
> good friend the good Lord Nelson. Permit me in the morning to have the
> pleasure of seeing you and hoping my dear Lady Nelson the continuance
> of your friendship which will be in Sir William and myself for ever lasting
> to you and your family. Sir William begs to say as an old and true friend
> of Lord Nelson if he can be of any use to you in his Lordship's absence, he
> shall be very happy and will call to pay his respects to you and Mr. Nelson to
> whom I beg my compliments and to Capt. Nesbit.

The Queen's Drawing Room reception was held on Thursdays. My husband and
I were invited of course. Sir William was there *without* my husband's mistress.
Most of the veteran captains of the Nile battle were there – all of them most polite
and considerate to me.

The following day, 14 November, the London papers discussed Lady Hamilton.
The *Morning Herald* wrote this unflattering editorial on my rival

> Her Ladyship is in her 49th year, rather taller than the *common* height, still
> displaying a superior graceful animation of figure, now a little on the wane,
> from too great a propensity to the en bon point. Her attitudinarian graces,
> so varying in their style and captivating in their effect, are declining also,
> *under this unfortunate personal extension.* Her teeth are lovely and her hair
> is of the darkest brown, immensely thick and trails to the ground. Her eyes
> are black and possess the most fascinating attraction but her nose is rather
> too short for the Grecian contour of her face which notwithstanding is
> singularly expressive – and her conversazione if not solid and argumentative
> are at least sprightly and unceasing. Such after ransacking Herculaneum
> and Pompeia for thirty-eight years is the chief curiosity with which that
> celebrated antiquarian Sir William Hamilton, has returned to his native
> country.

The most disturbing thing to me about the Herald article was the unforgettable
phrase 'unfortunate personal extension.' I had expected to meet a large (common)
and buxom lady, and that is exactly what she was. I do not have a suspicious mind
at all. It never occurred to me that she could be pregnant, for that is what the
Morning Herald was saying. Moreover in ten years of marriage to Sir William no
child had been conceived and in any case she certainly was not the advanced age
that the *Herald* made her out to be. It seemed that they were no longer lovers, so
there was little doubt now in my mind *who* the father was. It was hateful to be so
suspicious of the man I knew so well – had known so well – but who alas was a
complete stranger.

Moreover the *Herald* wrote a second article 'Lady Hamilton has been a very fine woman but she has acquired so much "en bon point" and her figure is *so swoln* [sic] that her features and form have lost almost all their original beauty.' On the 1 December the *Morning Post* wrote 'Lady Hamilton has arrived *in the very nick of time in this country*. It was owing to her Ladyship's activity that Lord Nelson's fleet was so soon *victualled* at Syracuse'. There could no longer be any doubt that she was heavily pregnant.

I had tried so hard to give Horatio a child – we both had tried. It was clear that having conceived my large obstreperous Josiah, I was not born barren, and the thought had crossed my mind that perhaps Horatio was infertile. In any case I could not, must not, tax him with my suspicions. My marriage looked lost, but such charges, however well founded, would be the truly bitter end.

The next few days were frenetic. I seldom saw my husband. He was obviously genuinely busy – visiting India House, the Admiralty again, the Royal Exchange, the Turkey company where he was given yet another trophy – this time a silver bowl. Nevertheless it was also quite clear to me and clear no doubt to the watching society that he was ignoring me. In the evenings we went to the theatre, never alone, always in parties. Much of the charm of the theatre was off-stage: the celebrities coming and going, the audience always noisy – either in favour of the performance or the contrary – leaving little doubt to the acting company of their views. The Victor of the Nile and his Lady and his Mistress provided a theatre within a theatre. One went either to Drury Lane or to Covent Garden, and the London newspapers would usually anticipate which performance their Hero and his Womenfolk would visit. Every visit we made was greeted with incredible applause with Horatio taking many, many bows to the clapping, hatwaving, huzzas and general rather hysterical noise that he was met with. He loved every moment of it – his stars twinkled on his chest and his eyes sparkled at the noisy adulation.

The theatre entrepreneurs knew their business. The cast often sang 'Rule Britannia' and at Covent Garden there was a new spectacle entitled 'The Mouth of the Nile', a representation of the battle there on the Glorious First of August. Our father, old Reverend Edmund, was quite easily persuaded by me to come to the theatre (usually he associated the Theatre with Original Sin) but if his son Hor was being honoured – well that was something altogether different and Heavenly dispensation was granted. He usually burst into tears at the end of each performance – overcome with all sorts of emotions. He was intelligent and perceptive enough, even at his age, even with his unworldly life, to realise that Hor was the centre of a savage dispute between his wife and mistress.

On the 18 November the *Morning Herald* described our dresses.

Lady Nelson appeared in white with a violet satin head-dress and small white feather. Her ladyship's person is of a very pleasing description, her features are handsome and exceedingly interesting and her general appearance is at once prepossessing and elegant. Lady H. is rather "en bon point" but her person is nevertheless highly graceful and her face extremely pretty. She wore a blue satin gown and head-dress with a fine plume of feathers. Sir William H., Nelson's father and Capt. Hardy sat behind. The comedy went off with a bang. Then Munden came forward and sang a song by young Dibdin

> "May Peace came forward and be the end of the strife we maintain
>   For our Freedom, our King, and our right to the main!
>   We're content to shake hands: if they won't, why, what then!
>   We must send our brave Nelson to thresh 'em again."

Then "Rule Britannia" – "The Mouth of the Nile" again cheers and huzzah, followed the party out into the Garden. A great evening – on to Lady Elcho's where Lady Hamilton sang and the Nelsons listened – one intently – one distractedly.

The next week we all went to Drury Lane – on the 24 November – myself and the Tria Juncta with our Reverend Edmund and the Princess Castelcicala who was becoming a good friend of mine. We were in a box together, six of us. As usual the house was full for *Pizarro and* Admiral Nelson's attendance, and although Mrs. Powell was standing in for the famous Mrs. Siddons in the role of Elvira, we all thought it was a good exciting performance. At the end of Act Three Elvira made a long tragic speech which ended with the words 'Come fearless man! now meet the last and fellest peril of thy life: meet and survive – an injured woman's fury, if thou canst.' At which pinnacle of despair, I uttered a wild cry – and fainted (probably the first and only time in my life). It was too much. After a few moments I recovered. Horatio sat like a statue – cold and totally remote – and to my chagrin I was helped up and out of the theatre by my little old father-in-law ... and by the tall buxom 'femme fatale' Lady Hamilton. We left the theatre but my husband sat impassively until the end. We retreated in some disorder to the house at No. 17 Dover Street where we had moved after the stay in the Hotel Nerot. By Horatio's standards it was a 'good' address, but we did not live there as a good married couple. He was obviously desperately unhappy and was anxious to go to sea again, not only to escape the problem of making decisions about our marriage, and his ménage, but also because his career was still in the making. Admiral Sir Thomas Troubridge, until recently Horatio's subordinate, was now effectively his superior officer. The year or more at the Court of Naples had not helped my husband's naval career – despite his plethora of beautiful (foreign) stars and glamorous (foreign) titles. He needed another major victory to counter the criticism, however oblique, from the Spencers, Hoods, and St. Vincent.

Unbeknownst to me he had been spending large sums of money on subsidising the Hamilton establishments and on the long expensive journey home through half the Courts of Europe. Our relationship was now so strained, so fragile, that I dared not ask him questions, even about the £4,000 in his care which had been left me by Uncle Herbert.

In November Horatio sat to Lemuel Abbott, the artist, who was adorning the 1798 portrait with the new stars and medals. He also sat to a Mrs. Damer, who was making a bust of him for the Guildhall. He went to Court and to the House of Lords. He dined out frequently with the Hamilton's relations, with Alexander Davison, at the Scottish Corporation, and at the East India Company. Horatio could reasonably claim that he was not avoiding me with all these social activities, but nevertheless he contrived that we rarely met, and certainly not in any intimate way.

All the papers – *The Times*, the *Morning Post*, the *Morning Herald* and the *Morning Chronicle* – carried stories in doubtful taste on the subject of Lady Hamilton. Her pregnant figure, (though the word pregnant was carefully not used) and whether she would be received at Court, were the two main topics.

The 'tria juncta in uno' were united at Christmas. Our father and I spent a lonely Christmas in Dover Street. My husband went to William Beckford's estate near Salisbury. It was interesting to see how Nelson's own family behaved to me in the altered situation. The William Nelsons were now openly siding with the Tria Juncta. I wrote on the 22 January to Mrs. William Nelson to persuade her to accompany me to Brighton 'I need not repeat my constant desire to do anything in my power to serve or accommodate my dear Lord's family.' She declined – rudely. The others were not indifferent to me. Maurice I knew would remain my friend. I was not too sure about the Boltons and the Matchams.

Early in the New Year of 1801 Horatio was promoted to Vice Admiral of the Blue on the huge captured *San Josef* refitting at Plymouth – almost immediately dear Captain William Locker died. He had always been a great friend of Horatio's and his daughter Elizabeth always a good friend to me.

The third event in the New Year was a final, perhaps inevitable, certainly irrevocable quarrel between my husband and myself. Mr. William Haslewood, who was the family solicitor, a partner with Messrs. Booth and Haslewood of Craven Street, arrived to have breakfast with us just before my husband was due to go to Portsmouth. He brought Lady Hamilton into the conversation. He obviously wanted to make some financial provisions for her which as far as I was concerned was the most terrifying insult. Financial commitments to 'That Woman' and the unspoken illegitimate child! The combination was too much for me and my iron self-control snapped. Angrily I said 'I am sick of hearing of dear Lady Hamilton and am resolved that you shall give up either her or me!' Horatio had not been behaving as a 'married' husband to me for some time (in fact for several years): he had made it abundantly clear in the last two months that he was besotted and thoroughly seduced by Lady Hamilton – and now preferred her to me as a friend and lover. Perhaps he hoped that I would be as complaisant as Sir William Hamilton undoubtedly was! He answered with calmness

'Take care, Fanny, what you say. I love you sincerely, but I cannot forget my obligations to Lady Hamilton, or speak of her otherwise than with affection and admiration.'

I thought for a moment. His behaviour certainly did not suggest that he could love *me* sincerely and he certainly could *not* forget the wretched Lady Hamilton. So I looked at him, sadly, walked out, and shortly afterwards drove by carriage from the house.

On the 13 January he came to say a formal farewell before he sailed with the Fleet to the Baltic. We made little reference to the previous painful episode. He said to me 'I call God to witness there is nothing in you, or your conduct, I wish otherwise' and left. The same night he wrote to me from Southampton 'My dear Fanny. We are arrived and heartily tired; and with kindest regards to my father and all the family, believe me, your affectionate Nelson.' He left me the Dover Street house rented for a year and his Agents paid me £400 on account. I wrote to him at once

> My dearest Husband, Your generosity and tenderness were never more strongly shewn than your writing to Marsh yesterday morning for the payment of your very handsome quarterly allowance, which far exceeded my expectations. Knowing your income, and had you left it to me, I cou'd not in conscience have said so much. Accept my warmest, my most affectionate and grateful thanks. I could say more, but my heart is too full. Be assured every wish, every desire of mine is to please the man whose affection constitutes my happiness. God bless my dear husband ...

Round Wood, where Nelson had never spent a night, was to be sold to Mr. Robert Fuller. Our father expected to go to Bath with me, and I planned to give up the Dover Street house, which was too big for the two of us. My husband was away, possibly for ever, and young Josiah's plans were most uncertain. He was still a stranger to me after 7 years at sea. I went to Brighton with my friend Miss Elizabeth Locker.

Nelson wrote mundane, pathetic little epistles to me. 'All my things are now breaking open for only one key can be found.' Half his wardrobe had been left behind – all the wrong things ordered not enough supplies of tea. 'In short I find myself without any thing comfortable or convenient.' He might have been writing to a housekeeper, not to a loving but absent wife. 'It is now too late to send my half wardrobe as I know not what is to become of me, nor do I care.' The following week I reminded him that the bad packing was not my fault and back came a petulant tirade about nails driven into his mahogany table and decanter stands without decanters to fit them. Pathetic domestic trivia omitting the fundamentals between us.

The fundamentals however soon came back into focus. During February and early March Nelson had decided to make a definite and final break with me and our marriage. After consultation with his Agent Mr. William Marsh, with his solicitor Mr. William Haslewood and Alexander Davison his banker, he made me a settlement. The latter was an admirer of Lady Hamilton's but the first two I counted on as friends.

The arrangement was that he would allow me £2,000 a year, subject to the Income Tax, to be paid quarterly in advance on the 1 January, 1801, 1 April, 1 July, 1 October, by Messrs. Marsh, Page, Creed at the net rate of £400 per quarter. My capital of £4,000 from Uncle Herbert would be returned to me, which would produce additional income of £200 a year, giving me altogether £1,800 a year clear of tax. All bills and expenses incurred up to the day Nelson left London would also be paid.

So there it was. A final settlement leaving me on my own. No husband and a recalcitrant son about to leave the Navy. Outside events were not conducive to bringing me relief. King George was ill and the Prime Minister Mr. Pitt resigned. After eight years of war with France the Treaty of Luneville between France and Austria left England alone.

Curiously enough Nelson still wrote me letters 'As I am sent for to town on very particular business for a day or two I would not on any account have you come to London but rest quiet where you are. Nor would I have you come to Portsmouth for I never come on shore.' That was dated the 24 February from Lothians Hotel in London.

The last letter I received from him was dated the 4 March. Almost my last letter to him was written in July just after the victory at Copenhagen.

My dear Husband, I cannot be silent in the general joy; throughout the Kingdom, I must express my thankfulness and happiness it hath pleased God to spare your life. All greet you with every testimony of gratitude and praise. This victory is said to surpass Aboukir. What my feelings are your own good heart will tell you. Let me beg you, nay intreat you, to believe no wife ever felt greater affection for her husband than I do. And to the best of my knowledge I have invariably done everything you desired. If I have omitted anything I am sorry for it. On receiving a letter from our Father written in a melancholy and distressing manner I offered to go to him if I could in the least contribute to ease his mind. By return of post he desired to see me immediately but I was to stop a few days in town to see for a host. I will do everything in my power to alleviate the many infirmities which bear him down. What more can I do to convince you that I am truly your affectionate wife?

Having no answer I went to show myself at Court!

To my surprise my sister-in-law Susanna Bolton wrote to me when I was at Brighton with Elisabeth Locker (8 March)

Will you excuse what I am going to say? I wish you had continued in town a little longer as I have heard my brother regretted he had not a house he could call his own when he returned. Do, whenever you hear he is likely to return, have a house to receive him. If you absent yourself entirely from him there can never be a reconciliation. Such attention must please him and I am sure will do in the end. Your conduct as he justly says is exemplary in regard to him and he has not an unfeeling heart. I most sincerely love my brother and did quite as much before he was Lord Nelson and I hope my conduct was ever the same towards you as Mrs. Nelson as ever it was as Lady Nelson. I hope in God one day I shall have the pleasure of seeing you together as happy as ever he certainly as far as I hear is not a happy man.

She undoubtedly meant well but her kind letter came too late – much too late. Nelson's love-child had been born to him and reconciliation was impossible. After the Battle of Copenhagen she wrote to me again (14 May 1801), addressing me for the first time as Viscountess

I suppose by this time, my dear Lady Nelson, you are returned to Bath after your appearance in the Drawing Room which I hope you found as pleasant as you expected. I thought perhaps you would have stayed in town until my brother arrived, but you and my father are better judges than I am, what is proper and you are with his father. Keep up your spirits my dear Madam and all will come right again for tho' he is warm, he has a truly affectionate mind.

I had returned to my Somerset Street house from a visit to Lord Walpole's house in Norfolk in early November and our father expressed a wish to visit his son and concubine at their new expensive residence in Merton, Surrey. He went there for two weeks and admitted to me that his son seemed well and happy there living with the Hamiltons. He and I then went together to Bath, but I determined on our return to London to make one last final effort with Horatio, although I feared that Merton was a commitment he could not now lightly shake off. Rumour had it that Lady Hamilton's new offspring had now been duly born. So I had no high hopes, but one of the few things I have learned in this life is that one must continue to try and never give up a cause one believes in.

So on 18 December 1801 I wrote a letter to my husband from Somerset Street which was my final vain effort.

My dear Husband, It is some time since I have written to you. The silence you have imposed is more than my affections will allow me and in this instance I hope you will forgive me in not obeying you. One thing I omitted in my letter of July which I now have to offer for your accommodation, a comfortable warm house (This was his sister Susanna Bolton's advice to me). Do, my dear husband, let us live together. I can never be happy till such an event takes place. I assure you again I have but one wish in the

View of Marlborough House, Brighton, (after refronting by Robert Adam) and Mrs Fitzherbert's House. Aquatint *c.* 1805.

world, to please you. Let everything be buried in oblivion, it will pass away like a dream. I can now only intreat you to believe I am most sincerely and affectionately your wife, Frances H. Nelson.

The letter was later returned to me with a cruel little note on it 'Opened by mistake by Lord Nelson but not read. A. Davison.' Not a word of commiseration or sympathy from either husband or his banker.

The Reverend Edmund wrote from Bath to my husband 'Yesterday I received your joyous news (of the victory of Copenhagen) but all things have their alloy. Lady Nelson was heavily affected with her personal feelings at not receiving a line from your own hand.' The sweet old man of 80 was reproving his much beloved son on my behalf, so at the end of October I wrote to him 'The impression your situation has left on my mind is so strong that I cannot delay any longer offering my opinion on the subject of your living with me: the deprivation of seeing your children is so cruel I told Mrs. [Catherine] Matcham at Bath that Lord Nelson would not like your living with me.' The old man continued to live with me – where else could he go? When he died I was with him. Horatio refused to attend his dearly beloved father's funeral. I refuse to believe that he was unable to spare the time to make his last farewell. It is conceivable that he was reluctant to see me again.

CHAPTER EIGHTEEN

THE LOG OF THE SS *THALIA* – JOSIAH'S ACCOUNT

On 1 April 1799 I took command of the *Thalia* off Malta. Lord St. Vincent gave me Lieutenant Colquit as my First and Lieutenant Quarell came from the *Alexander*. Captain Alexander Ball wrote to Nelson 'I shall endeavour to make him feel his very fortunate situation'. I know that these two excellent officers had been planted on me to keep me in order and on the straight and narrow path.

On 4 May in the *Thalia* off Malta I wrote to the Admiral

Dear Father, I am sorry to find from Mr. Tyson's [Nelson's secretary] letter that you thought I was very imprudent in messing in the Gunroom which I had not the least idea of doing only until I got to Palermo where I could fit myself out. I have now determined to do everything in my power to deserve the unmerited promotion which you have given me and hope my endeavour for the future will always meet with your approbation as you are the only person on earth who has my interest truly at heart and I trust and hope my future conduct will effectually do away my former folly. I have been off Linosa [between Malta and Africa] and have taken two vessels by one of which I shall send this letter tomorrow. Captain Ball has given me another cruise off Linosa and I hope we shall take something more and Believe me, Dear Father, Your affectionate Son J. Nisbet.

Indeed I meant every word. Command of the *Thalia* was a wonderful opportunity. My step-father then wrote to my mother 'He has sent to say that he is sensible of his youthful follies and that he shall alter his whole conduct. I sincerely wish he may both for his and your sake.' He also wrote to Captain Ball on HMS *Alexander* from Palermo on 25 March 1799

Now my dear Friend, Captain Nisbet is appointed to the *Thalia*, a very fine frigate and I wish he may do credit to himself and in her. Will you do me the favour of keeping her and sending me the Minerve for I want Cockburn for service of head. I send you Captain [Richard] Dunne with the Thalia for Captain Nisbet in which ship Captain [Thomas] Maling takes his passage to supersede Captain Nisbet in the Bonne Citoyenne ... enclosed is the commission for Captain Nisbet for the *Thalia* ...

The next month he wrote to Captain Ball 'I hope Captain Nisbet behaves properly: he is now on his own bottom and by his conduct must stand or fall.'

On the 25 May off Maritimo, west of Sicily, my step-father made a new will – he knew there was another great battle in the offing. Despite his now evident love for Lady Hamilton he left everything to my Mother, and if she died before him or intestate, the huge sum of £10,000 to me (not of course that I knew about it at the time). He proposed to leave a diamond box from Turkey to Lady Hamilton and 50 guineas to her husband to buy a mourning ring.

In mid June Nelson left Palermo for Naples and arrived there with a fleet of 18 vessels on the 24th. and re-captured the city without immediate bloodshed. He had 1,700 troops with him, and Lady Hamilton, who naturally accompanied him on HMS *Foudroyant* (80 guns). On his arrival he wrote a happy and evocative letter to my mother describing the Royal return to Naples!

My *Thalia* arrived in Naples, again, on 5 July and anchored alongside the *Foudroyant*. Five days later Nelson sent me off to Leghorn, recently occupied by the Russians along with Captain Foote of the *Seahorse* frigate of 38 guns. On the way there we suffered a sprung mainmast and ended up off Civita Vecchia, 30 miles north west of Rome. Trying to make the best of a bad job I attacked the French garrison there but was rebuffed without loss (apart from pride and dignity). My step-father read my report and wrote 'I am persuaded it was done for the best.'

On 23 July the *Thalia* anchored off Civita Vecchia again and I decided to persuade the local town governor to surrender to me, and sent him this despatch by boat.

By the enclosed you will positively learn that the French are drawn out of Tuscany and the Austrians in possession of Leghorn. And expecting as you must daily to be attacked by a considerable body of troops now on their march for Civita Vecchia, I from a certain knowledge of your preparations to evacuate the same by sea which will now be effectively prevented by a close blockade. I leave you, Sir, to judge of the advantage you will derive by acceding to the terms you may at this moment receive rather than by being under necessity of complying with the demands of an enraged and victorious enemy. I therefore recommend you to surrender to the Arms of His Britannic Majesty the Town Fortifications, etc. etc. under your command. I am, Sir, with consideration, J. Nisbet Captain of His Britannic Majestys Ship *Thalia*.

Four days later I sent a despatch to Admiral Nelson.

Off Civita Vecchia. My Lord, Having in Persuance of your Lordships Orders sailed from Naples Bay on the 11 July I was unfortunate enough on the 18 to find my Mainmast badly sprung and was oblig'd to go into St. Stephans

Bay to fish it, with orders from Capt. Foote to proceed from thence to join him at Longona, Leghorn or Genoa. I remained in the Bay part of the 18th, 19th, 20th, 21st, part of the 22nd during which Period I had frequent Communications with the Governor of Orbiterlo who daily receiv'd good News from Tuscany and the Roman States. He informed me he had certain Information that the French were preparing to evacuate Civita Vecchia and that they had embarked all their property on Board armed vessels then ready to sail for Corsica – that 2,000 Tuscan Troops were on their March to attack Civita Vecchia and that it was his Opinion they were in that desperate State that they would surrender the Town upon its being summon'd. I therefore (as I supposed Capt. Foote would have been on his Return, 'ere I could have join'd him) thought it for the Good of His Majesty's Service to proceed to this place which appeared before and summon'd on the 23rd. A Copy of which Summons and the Answer of the Commandant I herewith transmit you. I have since had frequent Intercourse with the People from the Shore who seem so eager to shake off the Tyranny of the French that I have no doubt but that they will act with Vigour whenever Opportunity occurs. It is my intention to remain here waiting your further Order and with Hopes that the Measures I have adopted will meet with your Approbation. I am, My Lord, Your Lordship's most obedient servant, J. Nisbet.

The following month my step-father wrote me a formal letter dated 3rd. August from the *Foudroyant*, Naples Bay

My dear Sir, I herewith enclose you a letter received some days ago and on receipt of this you will keep a good look-out for the *Northumberland* who is coming your way and join her as soon as you can, Captain (George) Martin having letters for you. I am sorry to find you have been cruizing off Civita Vecchia. I was in hopes of your being on the North Coast of Italy but I am persuaded it was done for the best. I here enclose you the copy of a letter sent open to me from Mr. Smith at Constantinople respecting some supplies furnished the *Bonne Citoyenne* at the Dardanelles and request that you will give the necessary directions to have it settled or explain it to me that it maybe settled. Mr. Tyson has written the Purser, Mr. Isaacson to desire he will draw out bills for the amount and fresh vouchers for your signature and the settlement of his account. I am, wishing you every success, yours very affectionately, Nelson.

The new Commander in Chief for the Mediterranean was Lord Keith, who was at Gibraltar on 6 December 1799, where he found me and the *Thalia* still under Admiral Duckworth's command in the western Mediterranean. Duckworth had sent me to Minorca for the court-martial to be conducted by Admiral Sir Thomas Louis. The rest of the squadron had been ordered to watch the enemy off Ferrol.

My mother wanted to come and be a wife once again to her husband, by taking sail for Lisbon, but was sadly discouraged by Nelson. The Commissioner at Gibraltar and, to my surprise, Admiral Duckworth, had sent my step-father encouraging reports about me and the *Thalia*. Nelson wrote to my mother 'I hope he will yet make a good man, his abilities are equal to anything, he was too much spoilt by me in his younger days'. I was sent packing and I was back in Leghorn with the *Thalia*. Having entered the port without having observed the formalities of the quarantine regulations (rarely done) I was in trouble again. Lord Keith wrote about me to Nelson 'Now my good Lord, for God's sake let the young man write a letter of apology to the Grand Duke (His Senate) because you know if it comes to me in form what must be done and it may end ill for him.' Needless to say nothing came of this pettifogging mistake!

Nelson then captured almost by himself one of the two survivors of the Battle of the Nile. He took *Le Generoux* of 74 guns and a large storeship west of Palermo on the way to Malta. Lord Keith on the *Queen Charlotte* was chagrined by this success, achieved without *his* orders! A few months later Nelson captured the last French ship from the Nile – *Le Guillaume Tell*, the 80 gun flagship of Admiral Villeneuve's fleet at Aboukir Bay. As Lord Keith's own flagship, the poor *Queen Charlotte* had caught fire and blown up at harbour in Leghorn two weeks earlier, Nelson's personal triumphs were now total.

On the 13 August my step-father was created Duke of Bronte, and of course my mother Duchess of Bronte. None of us aboard the *Thalia* knew where Bronte was. Apparently it was a modest estate at the foot of Mount Etna in Sicily with a yearly income, possibly theoretical, of 18,000 ducats. As soon as I heard I wrote to my mother with the news. I was in Leghorn with the *Thalia* at the time.

To celebrate Nelson's award we attacked and seized an Austrian privateer. She caught fire and we broke her up and sold her for firewood! The Austrian General was of course duly upset and complained to Captain Troubridge, who predictably complained to Admiral Nelson 'better to get Captain Nisbet to make some slight apology and some recompense. Complaints of this sort does a young Officer harm at the Admiralty' he wrote. I was ashore sick, at Leghorn, and ordered the *Thalia* back to Genoa without me. I went to the Theatre there and got involved in a brawl with some Neapolitans, and my officers lodged a complaint against me.

Troubridge at the end of August had been made a Baronet – he still went on persecuting me for the most trifling affairs. He then proceeded to capture Rome, an event unique in British naval history!

To anyone who enters the Royal Navy, to have independent command of a 36 gun frigate in the central Mediterranean must be to reach the height of one's ambition (apart from commanding a squadron or even a fleet). Aged but nineteen, in charge of two hundred men and officers with apparent freedom to roam the seas, was an idyllic situation. I kept of course the Captain's log, which usually occupied 3 or 4 lines. On one page was the ship's sailing course at the start and the end of the day. The daily comments were written by me opposite. There were certain indispensable occurrences which had to be logged. The day's weather and activities, any disciplinary floggings or other punishments, the monthly reading of the Ship's Articles, the sighting of any craft friend or foe. And any interesting events of the day – at the Captain's discretion.

The *Thalia's* task was to help blockade Malta and keep an eye on the many small islands such as Gozo, Lampedusa, Linosa, Pantelleria and others off the coast of Sicily, including Ustica and three small ones off Marsala, west of Palermo. We also sailed North to Elba and Leghorn. We saw our own *Alexander*, the *Penelope*, the *Goliath* and my old command *La Bonne Citoyenne* off Valetta, and occasionally sailed with Captain Foote of the *Seahorse* (who, like me, was in disgrace for criticising the Admiral).

The *Thalia* was a lovely sailing ship and could catch anything on the high seas. We captured several small ships – *Ragaseas*, *Cartils*, sloops and small schooners. We met so many nationalities: an Algerine Corsair which we nearly brought to battle, Neapolitan frigates escorting convoys to Naples, and we chased one ship from Messina to Palermo and saw Mount Stromboli. We boarded a Neapolitan Row Galley, a Portuguese brig, a Neapolitans loop of war, and a Leghorn Privateer. Once we chased a Spanish brig from Messina bound for Gothenburg, and a Danish brig on its way to Altona. We boarded and took prize a Spanish vessel laden with barley and a Danish brig sailing from Ireland to Barcelona. Once we boarded an American brig bound from Philadelphia for Leghorn. We boarded every ship we met to ensure that they really were neutrals or had friendly ownership. If not I put a petty officer and crew of seven ratings aboard, and made them sail in company until we could hand the prize over. Twice we raided hostile harbours and towns. Twice we took aboard Neapolitan or Imperial troops to be conveyed several hundred miles to their destination. Each day we wore ship, made and shortened sail and carried out essential tasks or training: painting the ship, mending the rigging, exercising our great guns. We employed the carpenters in scarfing the top gallant masters or fishing the main-mast, scrubbed hammocks, washed between decks, blacked the bends etc. We took aboard cattle '833 lbs. of fresh beef and 3 oxen and 8 pipes of wine'. Off Marsala we took in 12 ½ pipes of red wine! Once we collected 100 shells and 150 fuzes. Often we went ashore for wood to burn in the galley and to refill empty water casks.

The ship's company was mustered regularly and read the Articles of War. Discipline had to be maintained, and during our year at sea Roger Phillips, John Carson, Andrew Lace, John Theulders, Patryk King, William Ford, Wm. Harris, John Knowles, Joseph King, John Williams, Wm. Cogan, Dan Hartand George Ashwell were some of the seamen or marines flogged for crimes such as drink, theft, insolence or disobedience. The maximum sentence was 72 lashes and the minimum 12. One fell overboard and was lost. Mark Summers, a boy of 3rd Class died on board.

In storms we often suffered heavy damage – a mizzen topmast being carried away or the main-mast being sprung – but usually our carpenters were able to deal with any mishaps. Twice we cannonaded the towns of Ricks and Espezia and once lost a seaman killed and four wounded. On the King's birthday we fired a salute of 21 guns.

Only twice in that command of 20 months did I ever meet my step-father.

Once was in the middle of October when he was in the *Foudroyant* off Port Mahon, Minorca and I was on the *Thalia*. Disaster again. He wrote to Admiral Sir John Duckworth about my ship

> I wish I could say anything in her praise inside or out. You will receive an order for holding a Court Martial on the Lieutenant of Marines, perhaps you will be able to make something of Capt. Nisbet he has by his conduct almost broke my heart. There are two women in the *Thalia's* Gun-Room who do no good and I wish were out of her, excuse my plaguing you with this, but I cannot help being interested for this young man and my wish is only that he would let me be kind to him.

On a small ship the Captain's lot is lonelier than most and I had fallen into the (bad) habit of messing in the Gun-Room with the other officers.

Early in the New Year of 1800 I had been having problems with my officers on the *Thalia*. Alternatively they had been having problems with me. Lieutenant Colquit had been behaving to me, in my opinion, very badly: I had placed our surgeon under arrest for indiscipline and he had demanded a Court-Martial and finally the Master was complaining over my head to the Navy Board that in a moment of ill-temper I had told him to jump overboard. Lieutenant Quarell, despite his unfortunate name, was serving me and the ship most competently. On any Royal Naval ship the Captain – right or wrong – is right. He is all-powerful and the mutinies at the Nore and Spithead were occasioned mainly by Captains who abused this power. I know I was impulsive, hot headed, intemperate or hot-tempered, but I was never a tyrant. I was much the same age as my own lieutenants – none of us more than twenty except the surgeon. Possibly because of my connections with my illustrious step-father (and his patronage) I presumed a great deal. Keith got to hear of the *Thalia's* problems and packed us off to Madeira to protect the merchant trade from privateers (and perhaps to decide who was to be Court-Martialled). Meanwhile I heard that my step-father, still consorting with Lady Emma Hamilton, was not only ill but gambling at Faro and other games of Hazard.

Nevertheless one favourable report on my activities went to the Admiralty. James Murdoch, Agent at Madeira, wrote to Lord Keith on May 24th 1800

> My Lord, I have already had the honour of writing you Lordship by the *Thalia*, Captain Nisbet who after a three weeks cruise has returned here for some necessary articles he found himself deficient in. Meantime we stand indebted to him for having kept us so free of the enemy's cruisers that a variety of arrivals have brought us seasonable supplies and relieved a threatened

scarcity. He now further obliges the trade by seeing clear of the island all the vessels in readiness to sail and they are forward in expressing their wishes that your Lordship may allow of Capt. Nisbet's return to take care of us.

On the *Thalia* I gave passage to a Mr. Heron with his wife Lady Elizabeth and their daughter and a wounded Colonel Lumsden.

But Nemesis was looming on the horizon.

Mr. Arthur Briarly, the *Thalia's* Master, Mr. Pughe the Purser, and Mr. Colquit, the First Lieutenant collectively lodged complaints about my activities aboard and in Leghorn to the Admiralty. As a result Admiral Sir John Duckworth wrote to my step-father in June.

> The near connection Capt. Nisbet bears to your Lordship must ever make me interested that no disgrace should attach itself to him. I therefore felt great concern to find on his arrival at Leghorn that he and his officers were at daggers drawn. The surgeon above three months under an arrest waiting for a court-martial on his captain, the First Lieutenant with a string of complaints which he signified his intention of sending to your Lordship, that must, to say the least of them quite destroy Capt. Nisbet's reputation: though on my honour I view much of them as invidious and watching every indiscretion of a young man of his years when summed up in the aggregate few of us could bear, and his being in disrepute has encouraged those around him to take liberties they would not dared to have done with others, which being naturally resented but with an ill regulated warmth, has produced this dilemma, to which your Lordship's kind intentions may have a little aided, by authorising the First Lieutenant to give him advice, which probably from his youth (for he otherwise seems a very good young man) may have been so dictatorial as for his Captain to spurn at a kind of pride I cannot condemn entirely and true it is there is much of human nature in it. In consequence from viewing the errors on both sides I thought a publick investigation best avoided and after some labour brought it to a compromise and all is buried in oblivion and the surgeon cleared; but there can't be a second opinion of the necessity of the parties being divided and if I might suggest, I think (as the state of the ship must cause her to be paid off) a few months with Lady Nelson would *now* correct his foibles.

Lord Keith kept the *Thalia* under his command until he discovered that I had broken the accepted rule of the Service and was acting as my own prize agent, instead of appointing a proper agent, if not the Commander in Chief's Secretary. Lord Keith felt himself insulted of course and sent the *Thalia* home. We arrived in October and I reported our arrival to Sir Evan Napean at the Admiralty. We sailed from Plymouth to the Nore and finally to Deptford where we paid off the crew.

That effectively ended my career at sea at the ripe old age of twenty – a veteran of a score or more of battles and skirmishes and half a dozen commands.

CHAPTER NINETEEN

NELSON'S LAST BATTLE, HIS FUNERAL, HIS WILL

'The death of Nelson was felt in England as something more than a public calamity: men started at the intelligence, and turned pale, as if they had heard of the loss of a dear friend' wrote Robert Southey after the Battle of Trafalgar and the death of my husband in action. I had known that he would eventually chase and destroy the French fleet under Admiral Villeneuve and the action might result in his death.

I was in Bath at the time and the *Bath Journal* of 4 November had noted my arrival there. Lord Barham wrote to me two days later from the Admiralty, a formal letter advising me of Horatio's gallant death in action. The next day Lady Katherine Walpole, Horatio's rather grand cousin in Norfolk, wrote from Wolterton to 'Captain Josiah' a warm kind letter of sympathy for me, and said 'Lady Berry is here and will go directly to Lady Nelson to give her comfort.' I was desolate and wept bitterly. Not even Josiah nor Louise Berry nor Elizabeth Locker could console me.

Immediately after Trafalgar was won and lost the Theatre in Bath produced a new musical piece in one act called 'Nelson's Glory', written in celebration of the victory. I think he would have approved of it. I did not see it of course in the midst of my mourning, but my friends and relations who did see it felt it not inappropriate.

The battered *Victory* with Nelson's flag at half mast had anchored at Spithead on the 5 December, and England discussed nothing else except the glorious victory and his death.

Nelson's body, in a coffin fashioned from the wood of the French ship *L'Orient*, arrived in the *Victory*, which anchored near Greenwich on 23 December. It lay in state in the Painted Chamber in the Hospital from 5-8 January, attended by Doctor Alexander Scott. Then it was taken on the river to the Admiralty.

Of course I was invited to the Funeral at St. Paul's on Thursday 9 January. I felt that I had a duty to go and see my husband to his last resting place under the Cupola of the great Cathedral. On the other hand all the world and the Nelson family knew that he had abandoned me five years earlier. There was a risk that his mistress might have been present, which would have embarassed, not only me but the nation as well. So I stayed away, and relied on Josiah and my many naval friends to tell me of the grand occasion. The official *Gazette* decreed 'On

Thursday the 9th day of January at Nine o'clock in the Morning, the Nobility and Gentry in Mourning without Weepers and with Mourning Swords: the Knights of the several Orders wearing their respective Collars, the Naval Officers (who have no particular Duties assigned them in the Solemnity) and the Military Officers, in their full Uniforms, with Crape round their Arms and Hats will pass through the Gates at Constitution Hill and Stable Yard into St. James Park where they will be duly marshalled in a line of Procession.' No less than thirty-one Admirals, a hundred Captains, and most of the Royal Family attended the Parade. It was a beautiful sunny day, unusual for mid-winter, and Horatio's coffin was borne on a funeral car meant to represent the *Victory*. When it reached St. Paul's at two o'clock the coffin was taken by twelve men of his flagship and was greeted by six Admirals bearing a canopy. The service lasted four hours and the whole ceremony

Nelson's tomb in the crypt of St Paul's Cathedral.

was probably the greatest, the most solemn, and the saddest that London had ever seen. But I could not have borne to be present. My Horatio had prophesied so many times that he would end his days on earth in Westminster Abbey – but he would have been well content with St. Paul's.

The *London Gazette* announced the Trafalgar honours. Admiral Collingwood fully earned his Barony, he 'fought that day like an Angel', but to everyone's surprise Horatio's clerical brother, the Rev.

Lady Fanny Nelson, *c.* 1804.

William Nelson, a most indifferent brother-in-law to me, was created an Earl. Parliament voted the new Earl a pension of £5,000 per annum, £10,000 (later increased to £99,000) for him to buy an estate, and also £10,000 later £15,000 to his sisters Susanna Bolton and Catherine Matcham.

Unbeknownst to me Lord Barham wrote to Mr. Pitt (9 November 1805) 'A ribbon to Lord Northesk compared with an English peerage is trifling. Have you ever thought of one for Lady Nelson during her life? She is as far as I have heard a valuable woman and irreproachable in her conduct. Such instances seldom occur and it does not add to the Peerage.'

A pension of £2,000 per annum was granted to me in February 1806, which was ample for my modest needs, but modest in relation to the sums granted to Horatio's brother and sisters. The Rev. William was a mean man and behaved as such to me (and to Lady Hamilton) in relation to Nelson's last Will and Testament, and I had recourse to litigation. This I regretted but my legal advisers told me that there was no alternative. The new Earl (the Rector) immediately wrote to me 'If I could find pleasure amidst so many mournful reflections as press upon my mind it would be in the opportunity afforded me of renewing with your Ladyship that intercourse of kind offices which I once hoped would have always marked our lives – which untoward circumstances have occasioned some interruption of, but which I trust will never again be suspended.' William was no friend of mine and never had been. Now like Manna from Heaven he – at a stroke – had received as a result of *his brother's bravery in battle* – the glorious title and a very large sum of money. He was in the process of abandoning the large 'untoward circumstances' residing at Merton, which he and his wife had courted so assiduously for the last five years (whilst throwing me into outer darkness).

The *Morning Chronicle* of the 11 November stated 'The greatest part of his [Admiral Nelson's] fortune is to be sold to constitute a fund to provide £1,000 a year for Lady Nelson. The house and part of the land left to the person of all others he most perfectly esteemed.' The new Earl was so mean that he refused to pay 'That Woman' income from the Duchy of Bronte, and in 1814 she had to threaten to sue him for it.

William Nelson was self-importantly busy. He retrieved the aigrette, the Nile sword, the diamond sword and the collar of the Bath from Lady Hamilton at Merton. He tried to take from me Horatio's gold box (that he had in his possession all the time). I went to law with him over the interpretation of the Admiral's will. I wanted my pension from my husband to be continued, and as his *wife* I wanted one third of his personal fortune at his death.

Finally, after litigation, in May 1806 I continued to receive my pension, but failed to secure even a modest share of my husband's estate. I was then living in Cheltenham and was still distant with the Nelson family, even my erstwhile friend Susanna Bolton regarded me as a 'Vindictive Woman going to law to enrich her son ...'

James Western, my able Solicitor, of No.11 Grays Inn Square, wrote to me (4th February 1806) about a financial meeting to be held between Earl Nelson and Mr. William Haslewood, my husband's solicitor. Then Sir Robert Burton on the 17 May took out a writ on the Nelson executors. The ensuing Chancery suit was settled on the 17 October, when the Executors purchased £33,333. 6. 8*d* of 3 per cent Consols to provide my annuity. William Marsh was in the invidious position of acting both for me and for many years as Horatio's prize agent. He it was who was responsible a few years later for sending me the Patriotic Fund's 'Nelson Vase' made by Messrs. Rundle and Bridges, from Lloyds. It was a wonderful silver-gilt vase to commemorate Trafalgar and cost £650. It is shaped like an urn: on one side in relief is an emblem of merit and an inscription on the other 'As a lasting memorial of the transcendent and heroic achievements of the ever-to-be-lamented Warrior, Horatio, Viscount Nelson, Baron of the Nile, who while the British Fleet under his command conquered or destroyed the united Fleets of France and Spain off Cape Trafalgar on 21 October 1805 gloriously fell in the moment of victory. This vase is presented to his relict, Viscountess Nelson by the Committee of the Patriotic Fund.' A glorious memento treasured ever since.

For my pension and annuity I was asked to apply in appropriate fashion. So I wrote on 6 February 1806 from No.36 Weymouth Street, Portland Place

Gentlemen, My late husband Vice Admiral Lord Nelson, Duke of Bronte having been kill'd in Battle with the Enemy on the 21st of Octr last while serving as Commr in Chief of His Majestys Fleet off Cadiz I beg leave to request that you will be pleas'd to order me to be paid the usual Gratuity of one Years pay. I am Gentlemen, Your very obedt Servant, Frances H. Nelson & Bronte. To the Honble Commrs of His Majesty's Navy.

I also sent the Admiralty a true copy of our marriage certificate. By return of post a Bill of Exchange was made out to me 6 February 1806. 'Vice Admiral Lord

Nelson, Duke of Bronte, etc.
Slain in fight 21 October 1805.

One year full Pay is	£912. 10s. 0d.
Geo. Daysh	6 Febry 1806.

In the year after Trafalgar I needed many and varied Mourning clothes. My dressmakers E. Franks, Milliners and Dress Maker to their Royal Highness the Prince of Wales and the Duke of York of St. James Street sent me their Account.

17 Jan. A rich black silk gown made up compl. with body lining persian sleeve lining fine muslin weepers etc.	7. 17. 6d
1 May. A black crape bonnet	1. 16. 0d
A rich black twill sarsnet dress made up complete with body lining bound with crape	6. 16. 6d
A black crape full dress gown made up complete with rope and tassel for the waist	5. 15. 6d
Jet ornaments	2. 12. 6d
A black sarsnet slip made up complete with body lining	4. 4. 6d
A fine muslin turban	1. 16. 0d
A black crape turban with Bugle, Bandeau	2. 12. 0d
A fine muslin Hadn'f with frills	1. 11. 6d
A fine muslin Hadn'f with frills	1. 11. 6d
A black sarsnet Spanish cloak trimmed round with back crape	4. 4. 0d
A black twill sarnet spencer lined and made up complete	3. 10. 0d
A black crape hat and flowers	2. 2.0d
A black crape veil	14. 0d
Boxes	8. 6d
To Bill delivered 13 Dec.	1. 5. 0d
	£48. 17. 0d

It was a substantial amount but I like to think that poor Horatio would have approved. He always took a considerable interest in my clothes, frequently of his own initiative purchasing items for my wardrobe on his Mediterranean voyages, even on his return with the Hamiltons. He wrote (24 May 1797) from the *Theseus*, 'I have some Naples sashes to send you and a gown also five elegant drawings of the action when opportunity offers.'

An early biography of my husband was produced by James Harrison in 1806, editor of the *British Classics*. He was much helped by Lady Hamilton, and his *The life of Lord Nelson* was first in the field. It was biased and I wrote at the time 'I think without exception Mr. Harrison's *Life of Lord Nelson* is the basest production that ever was offered to the public. It is replete with untruths.'

Nelson's dying moments. Fanny never stopped loving him, and mourned his loss 'till her dying day.

The Reverend J. S. Clarke and Doctor John M'Arthur (lately secretary to Lord Hood and purser of the *Victory*), had combined to produce the first complete biography of my late husband. They asked me for the loan of all my correspondence to and from Lord Nelson. To a great extent I co-operated with them, only refraining from sending them (via Mrs. Ross) some of the more intimate correspondence. Subsequently in 1810 I purchased one copy.

By that time I was aged 49. I was a middle aged titled widow lady. I had many friends, some affluence, an excellent and occasionally difficult son, but above all I still had my memories of fifteen happy years with Horatio, now buried gloriously with eternal fame whenever his name was mentioned in his country. I had his portrait, his name and title, the Nelson Urn and his 'son-in-law' to keep me company.

CHAPTER TWENTY

THAT WOMAN ABANDONED

Lady Hamilton not only had succeeded in seducing my husband, but had caused a temporary alienation between my son Josiah and myself. As if this was not enough, she set out systematically to seduce Horatio's own family away from my affection (and in the case of his father, my care) into her clutches.

My favourite in the Nelson family was Maurice, theoretically a bachelor, but through his common law wife, blind Mrs. Sarah Ford, a parent. Poor Maurice, a clerk in the Admiralty, was promoted and died almost immediately. That was in April 1803 and Horatio, to his credit, paid to his 'widow' at Laleham a pension of £200 per annum. I like to think that Maurice would have stayed with me, unlike the others, who deserted me so cruelly.

From their country house at Merton in Surrey, Lady Hamilton spun her cruel web. The Reverend William with his rough manners – who was always asking Horatio for favours – and his wife Sarah, were the first to scuttle into her arms. I wrote of him once to my husband as 'the greatest enemy I ever had'.

Lady Hamilton sent the Nelson family many long rambling letters which (I was soon told) contained diatribes against me and Josiah. The Boltons and the Matchams soon followed into her camp, seduced by my husband's new fame and title, and her blandishments.

Even dear old, Reverend Edmund succumbed despite initial protests. 'If Lady Nelson is in a hired house, and by herself, gratitude requires I should sometimes be with her, if it is likely to be of any comfort to her', and to Kitty Bolton he wrote of me 'No prospect of better times for her, nay I think worse.' But like the others, seduced by gifts and flattery, they all landed up on her doorstep, To the old man she sent a handsome plaid, to the Matchams a set of porcelain.

Sir William Hamilton died on 6 April 1803 in his wife's and Nelson's arms. She proceeded to spend money in a profligate way, even when my husband sailed that summer on the *Victory* on his last great Mediterranean command and vain chase to the West Indies after Villeneuve.

Lady Emma was now great friends with the William Nelsons and visited the Nelson family in Norfolk where she was made welcome. She even, when sent a begging letter from his eldest sister for school and doctor's bills, sent them £100 to tide them over. The Boltons were always in debt, and once or twice I had helped them out in the old days.

Horatio returned to England for a month in the late summer of '05. He refused to see me, and the Boltons and Matchams hastened to Merton Place to pay their respects. Lady Hamilton kept on a house in London at No.11 Clarges Street, but my husband usually stayed at Gordons Hotel in Albemarle Street. A few days later he was at sea again on his final voyage to victory and death.

Lady Hamilton was now nearly forty and had put on a lot of weight, particularly after the births of her two children. (The second died in infancy). After Nelson's death she had started to drink heavily – then became ill – and drank even more. Her debts piled up partly through the meanness of the new Earl and Countess of Nelson. Merton Place had to be sold and she went to live at lodgings at No.136 Bond Street, where even wilder extravagances took place. She went to the theatre frequently and was reputed to gamble. She suffered an attack of jaundice and was so heavily in debt that she placed herself within the rules of the Kings Bench. Her applications to the Government for recognition of her services at the Court of Naples came to naught. The Bronte estate legacy was not paid by the new Earl until litigation compelled him to do so.

The fickle Boltons and Matchams quite quickly abandoned her to her sad fate. Soon after she was re-arrested for debt and spent nine months in detention until she obtained her release and fled to France with little Horatia, where she died in January 1815. Fortunately the Matchams had a belated fit of conscience and gave Horatia a home until her marriage in 1822 to the Rev. Philip Ward.

There can be little doubt in my mind and I believe in most people's that she gave my husband much happiness in their limited time together. She also gave him a child, which I could not, although I believe that Horatio regarded my *Josiah in every way as his son* from the age of five until he was twenty.

I think that the Nelson family – the William Nelsons, the Thomas Boltons and the George Matchams were false and fickle friends of mine and then equally false and fickle to the wretched Emma – who died unwanted, unloved, in a pauper's grave in Calais.

Lady Hamilton gave birth to Nelson's daughter at the end of January 1801. After much initial subterfuge, Horatia was brought up as his adopted daughter by Lady Hamilton at Merton.

CHAPTER TWENTY ONE

LIFE IN EXMOUTH AND LITTLEHAM

It was on our honeymoon in 1788 that Horatio and I discovered the charms of little Exmouth on the south Devon coast. It was pretty, the oldest seaside town in Devon 'frequented for diversion and bathing in the sea' and comprised mostly of cot-houses, neat and clean and often whitewashed, consisting of four or five rooms, often let at a guinea a week. The Littleham and Withycombe Raleigh parishes were part of Exmouth. I doubt whether there were more than a thousand souls there altogether, although by 1800 there were 2,000 and by 1821 a population of 3,000. It was well-known for its 'Honiton Lace' works and its healthy bracing sea air. Josiah kept his boat and then his yacht in the harbour, convenient for the other Devon ports and for a long sail over to Brittany. When the tide is in, the view is superb across the estuary from the houses on the Beacon of Powderham Castle – ancient home of the De Force and Courtenay families – and of Mamhead on the opposite shore. When the tide is out the wide bed of mud is less pleasant. Fishing is important to the community and crab pots are set out every day beyond Exmouth Bar. Fresh salmon is another popular delicacy. The long sandy beaches are particularly interesting for me. I used to walk a lot on Nevis and I still like to walk now, along the Devon coastline.

During the month Horatio and I spent at Exmouth I met the celebrated Mrs. Piozzi (the Mrs. Thrale mentioned by Boswell in his life of Johnson). She wrote a Prologue for the newly formed Exmouth Theatre. Lord and Lady Rolle, Edward Iliff, Samuel Eyre, Charles Baring and Gerard Gustavus Ducarel were the principal gentry of the town. I little thought at the time how well I was going to know Exmouth in due course.

When Horatio was serving in the Mediterranean, I returned to Exmouth for short visits as its fame as a Watering Place grew. My cousins Mr. and Mrs. Harry Tobin had a house there in the period 1790-5 and I remember invitations to tea and cards with them. Our friends the apothecary Sprys of Bath leased a house there, and when Mrs. Sarah Spry died in 1791, she became a beneficiary to the Town Charities.

My cousin Sally Morton, who married Captain Kelly, also rented a house in Exmouth in March 1794, so the resort was becoming known to West Indian Society! The New Assembly Room was in the Globe Hotel on Chapel Hill and Mr. William Pomeroy was the landlord. He had been butler to the Ducarel family, and later became a highway robber! One could see every vessel passing to Torbay, Brixham, Teignmouth, Dawlish, Topsham and Exeter. We never tired of the lovely views.

The card assembly was on Monday evenings from 5.30 – 10.30 p.m. with play at shilling whist or twopenny quadrille. The cynics said 'no belles dames amusing to the unmarried but some belldames unamusing to the married'! The walks and the wonderful views 'seabathing and a look at the fishing catch' visits to neighbouring towns and tea drinking society in the evening all made Exmouth a gay little town. Josiah and I would go on Sundays to services at SS Margaret and Andrew in Littleham, a picturesque church and churchyard, the oldest parish church of Exmouth. The Rev. William Sykes was the Curate then.

A little over a year after Trafalgar, I decided to make Exmouth my home and visited it in February 1807. Later that year I wrote to my friend Lady Stewart, wife of Lieutenant General the Hon. William Stewart (who fought with Horatio at Copenhagen)

> I had never seen Weymouth and truly it is soon seen: a few days leave it for Exmouth where I propose staying a few months if I can get a comfortable house. If I do not succeed I shall return to Bath till the spring. I would have got a cottage a mile and half out of Dawlish but they had the conscience to ask six guineas a week and then it was a sort of favour which I declined. I have fortunately met some of my old friends here, the Pinneys which makes it very gay. The weather is very warm. I am sitting with the windows open (8 Oct.) and without a fire. I hope you and all your children are well remember me to them particularly my God daughter. My son Josiah's compliments ...

The handsome new houses on the Beacon had been built in 1792 and I decided to take No.6 on lease for Josiah and myself, three maids and a coachman, and Sam Norman, who was my well-tried and trusty servant. He came from a farm in Holcombe Rogus and had been a footman to Horatio and myself when we lived briefly in London at the turn of the century.

Exmouth was full of interesting people. The poet George Crabbe made visits there; Mr. Mead the painter lived there and I asked him to show his portraits to some of my friends; my friend Admiral Carpenter and his family lived at No. 23, the Beacon. Many of them were members of the excellent Society of Exmouth which held a whist club and gave dances, to which we went in sedan chairs. The elegant little theatre in Exmouth was on the site of the Brethren's Room run by Mr. Samuel Fisher (brother to the Bishop of Bristol) where Edmund Kean in his early days played and gave readings from John Milton three times a week. A New ballroom at Ewens was the scene of twice-weekly dances.

Mundane affairs obtruded – the cost of my coach repairs (1807) – a bill in favour of John Brock for £66 for wine was protested to my chagrin (1810). The wine was for Josiah, who had gone to Dartmouth by sea 'his return uncertain'. Our wine bill was always heavy. Josiah and his friends were fond of Madeira and French white wine, which I ordered by the Hogshead from Mr. Thomas Forster (Louisa's brother) of Portsmouth Dock Yard. Mr. Wright the Taylor produced suits of livery for my man-servants (1808), Thomas Barnes my coachman was unsatisfactory and had to be discharged (1807).

Although my finances seemed secure enough – I gave subscriptions to the Devon and Exeter female Penitentiary of two guineas (1821) and the Naval Asylum for Girls four guiness (1807), to Mrs. Anne Hawkins £200 (1818), and to my erstwhile sister-in-law Anne Nisbet in Edinburgh an average of £50 per annum – I had my anxious moments. In November 1812 the Exmouth Bank failed (luckily my losses were small), but in 1824 I had an unpleasant experience with my (and Horatio's) bankers Marsh, Creed and Co. Their partner Henry Fauntleroy was tried for forgery on 30 October. He had forged powers of Attorney for me of £11,995 Consols, for which he was executed on 30 November. Meanwhile the firm paid out to me 20 shillings in the 20 shillings on 28 September. Nevertheless there were moments when I felt that all was lost and I would be penniless.

In 1810 the legal case about my share of Josiah's estate continued, with Mr. John Baillie trying to achieve a settlement for me. Exmouth was perhaps not the most exciting of towns but our life here has always been full of surprises. During 1812 there was great rejoicing for Wellington's victories and an immense dinner was given at the Globe and London Inn. In 1817 and 1824 there were great storms – in the first, five acres of the Warren were washed away, and in the latter, many houses in the Beacon were damaged and unroofed, two thirds of the town was under water, and the river *Exe* overflowed its embankments. The first Fire engines appeared in 1819, followed by a series of two-day wrestling matches, and Josiah watched Abraham Cann, the champion wrestler of England.

Mrs Mary Ann Clarke was one of the interesting inhabitants who lived at Manchester House in Exmouth, and she made a considerable stir in St. Stephen's Chapel. As early as 1804 she had become notorious in connection with the Duke of York and the famous motion made against him in the House of Commons by Colonel Wardle in 1809. At first I regarded her with suspicion, but she was such a generous, kindhearted creature that I soon changed my mind. We went for walks together on the Warren. She was pretty but her face wanted expression, although she had a lively sense of humour. She lived a very private life but received an immense quantity of letters, many franked from the London Court. It turned out that we had many friends in common amongst the Royal Family and at Court – although she tried to keep her connection with royalty unknown.

My reconciliation with the Nelson family – who had all basely deserted me for 'that woman' in Merton, dated from the time when I was presented with the celebrated 'Nelson Vase' by the Patriotic Fund. Lady Charlotte Nelson persuaded her parents, the new Earl and Countess, to meet me. The meeting took place at No.8 Russel Street in Bath on 29 January 1810. I had regarded William Nelson as no

Lord Hood was the commander-in-chief who gave Nelson crucial opportunities in the Mediterranean.

friend of mine for the last decade, and I believed that he had behaved most unkindly to me. Nevertheless I was pleased that little Charlotte had taken this initiative. The final reconciliation with the Nelson family was made later in Paris with the George Matchams.

That same summer, on 29 August, Lord Hood's second grandson Samuel married Lady Charlotte, Horatio's niece, and I wrote to Sir Samuel Hood 'I have had the pleasure of receiving my new relation Mr Samuel Hood and his wife Lady Charlotte who I hope you will like very much. This marriage has made me very happy. A Union of Names that will not easily be forgotten.'

Subscription Balls were started in Exmouth late in 1819. *Trewmans Exeter Flying Post* reported of one that 'it was more numerously and fashionably attended than any for some time remembered. The dresses of the ladies were unusually elegant, whilst not one animal of the Dandy kind appeared. The dancing was kept up with spirit until a late hour. Miss Ewen gave a Twelfth cake [13 Jan. 1820] with the characters placed on it which being an old custom diverted the company and added to the jovial scene.'

The death of the Duke of Kent in nearby Sidmouth caused the postponement of the next Ball two weeks later. At these Balls, Lady Young was usually the Patroness. Mr. William Webber was the Steward and dancing at the New Rooms on the Hill started at 9 o'clock.

After I had been living in Exmouth on and off for over ten years, with frequent visits to Paris, London and Bath, I decided that I should return some hospitality to my friends in Exmouth. The *Trewmans Exeter Flying Post* reported

On Wednesday last [31 Jan. 1821] Lady Nelson gave a most splendid Ball and Supper at the London Hotel Exmouth to the nobility and gentry of that place and its environs. Among the Company were Sir Sidney and Lady Young, Admiral and Mrs. Carpenter, W. T. Hull, T. Simpson and J. Sweetland Esq., the Misses Roberts of Courtlands and many other distinguished personages. After supper the health of Lady Nelson and Captain Nisbet and family were drunk with enthusiastic applause and the merry dance was kept up with great glee until a late hour.

Exmouth church of St Margaret and St Andrew.

Exmouth – the Beacon where Fanny & Josiah lived

Mrs Sarah Gifford was the owner of the London Hotel. She was rightly proud of her selection of fine wines and spirits, excellent stalled stabling, and lock-up coach houses, neat Post Chaise and Dickey Chariots with able horses and careful drivers.

That summer Exmouth celebrated the Royal Coronation. It was reported 'the morning was ushered in [24 July] with the animating sound of cannon fired from a well-constructed battery under the direction of Mr. Turner RN. At 12 o'clock 700 families sat down to a plentiful supply of roast beef and plum pudding with an ample supply of good ale and cyder, provided by a subscription of the inhabitants. At the end of the repast the health of the King was drank with 9 x 9 when a Royal Salute was again fired which was succeeded by loud and re-itterated huzzas, this was answered by a most numerous assemblage of the gentry of the place who were ranged on a. more elevated situation near the spot from whence they enjoyed the pleasant sight. The vessels laying off the port were decked with colours, which added much to the beauty of the scene. In the evening there was a brilliant display of fireworks. The gentlemen retired to the Globe Tavern where they were entertained to a sumptious dinner. Sir Digory Forrest in the chair and John Sweetland Esq. vice president. After the dinner the president gave 'The King God Bless Him, long may he reign', which was drank with enthusiasm and was replied to by a roaring of cannon and the shouts of the populace without. Other loyal and patriotic toasts followed and many appropriate songs were sung.

My friend Prince William Henry, now King William IV of England, had sent me an invitation to be present in London at the Coronation, but Josiah (whose wife was expecting her second child) was present at the Exmouth celebrations.

With Josiah and his family spending more and more time in Paris I decided that No.6 The Beacon was too large for me, and in 1829 (when I was sixty eight) moved to a smaller house in Louisa Place with my devoted friend and companion Mrs. Fanny Francklyn (Josiah's cousin). Little Ellin Hoye was my maid – the three of us would travel to get her to my house at 23 Harley Street in London and occasionally to Paris. It still took three days by coach to London, and by sail and coach about the same time to Paris.

I feel as though I have known Exmouth and Littleham all my life since I first came here with Horatio over forty years ago. I have made arrangements to make it my final resting place – the churchyard of SS Margaret and Andrew looks very peaceful and I will have good company in the southeast corner overlooking Castle Lane.

Frances Nelson's grave in the church of St Margaret and Andrew, Exmouth.

CHAPTER TWENTY TWO

THE MEDIUM'S STORY

Sunny Bay is the name given to the smart society area of Exmouth at the foot of the town overlooking the harbour. One of my acquaintances was a fascinating woman called Mrs. Marianne Starke – the celebrated tourist – then a resident with her aged mother at No.11, The Beacon, near Miss Longford's Library. She was the authoress of *Travels in Europe* and gave what we called 'tableaux vivants', much, I regret to say, in the same style as Lady Emma Hamilton. A number of individuals placed themselves upon a stage in the exact attitude and dress of the figures in a celebrated picture. Around them was arranged a kind of frame, and between the individuals thus placed and the audience, who had to be at a considerable distance, was drawn a thin veil. The effect on an observer was exactly that of a fine coloured painting. At Miss Starke's house the celebrated painting by Raphael of Mount Parnassus was thus represented in a style that astonished the crowd assembled. She used to give her *public* entertainment at Ewens Rooms. Another favourite was Raphael's Sibyls, the celebrated Fresco painting in the Church of La Pace at Rome. Her nickname was Jack Starke, since she had the idiosyncracy of wearing a man's hat and riding habit. Her Travellers' Guide was popular. She once spent a lot of time in Naples and was known as the 'Queen of Sorrento'. So much did her travels interest me that I sought in 1810 to purchase good modern maps of Portugal and Spain.

Through Miss Starke I was introduced to a French woman called Miss Hortense de Crespigny – a strange woman, who took long solitary rambles by the seashore, watching the ceaseless throb of the ocean – remaining for hours on the hissing beach, heedless of the noise of the surf and the blowing spray. She said the waves spoke to her of the future and the past. She maintained that the great deep mirrored the INFINITE and the ETERNAL and the waves on the beach edge had for her a language and a lesson, and bore tidings of the dead and the distant – the lost and the loved.

Initially I thought nothing more of this strange talent, until she predicted that Admiral Carpenter (who lived at No.23 The Beacon) would lose his young son – an intelligent, shrewd, restless boy. 'That boy will cut a brilliant figure in after life' was the remark of a gentleman who had been captivated with his apt and courteous answers, 'we shall hear of him by the time he's thirty.' Miss de Crespigny looked at the lad steadily and then slowly murmured, to the amazement of those who listened 'He will never live to be thirty: he will never live to be twenty: he will never enter his teens. Early doomed! Early doomed! Poor fellow.' A few weeks later the young boy killed himself accidentally by sliding down the balustrade from the third to the basement storey. He overbalanced and fell headlong.

Secondly, she told a sad widow called Mrs. Hussey that her long lost husband was alive and would return to her, which he did. He had been fishing in the Channel and had been captured by a French privateer and lodged in a French prison. Eventually he was freed and returned to his grieving 'widow'. So Miss de Crespigny's fame grew and I determined to see whether she could help me. This is how what followed was recorded for posterity in the locally published *Memorials of Exmouth*:

Time rolled away, but left uneffaced the singular conversation which had preceded little Carpenter's demise. This, 'ere long, reached the ears of a lady then residing at Sunny Bay, remarkable alike for her sorrows, and the uncomplaining spirit in which she sustained them – Viscountess Nelson, widow of the hero of Trafalgar. However bright may be the lustre which distinguished services throw around the memory of Lord Nelson, – however conspicuous his name may stand on the roll of fame as a successful naval commander – there is in his private life much to condemn and deplore. He was a most unfaithful husband to a generous and confiding woman; he was a most careless protector of one who loved him fondly and truly – who linked her fate with his when he was poor and comparatively unknown – who was spotless in her own character and conduct, and whose life by indifference, ingratitude and neglect, was steeped in unimaginable bitterness. She, the victim, lived in comparative neglect and obscurity.

Of Nelson it may be said that his slavish subserviency to the meretricious arts of an unprincipled woman – *the wife of another* – is a matter of history. His fame as a hero remains. But in dwelling on his private life, marvellously diminished is the respect which we would fain bear him as a man.

But Lady Nelson loved him – loved him in spite of long years of indifference and desertion – cherished his fame – was proud of his exploits – tried to forget past neglect, and to recall only that period in her life when he was the attached and devoted husband.

Anxious, beyond measure, was she to ascertain whether at the last he remembered her; was sensible of the injustice he had done her; and had written or spoken aught indicative of reviving affection. To this end, and with special reference to Hortense de Crespigny, she had again and again consulted Mrs. Marianne Starke. Now Mrs. Marianne Starke viewed the reserved and melancholy foreigner with unmitigated abhorrence. Not content with deriding her pretensions, and designating her as an imposter, Mrs. Starke charged the unfortunate Hortense with treasonable designs.

"Avoid her, Lady Nelson," so ran Mrs. Starke's diatribe, "Avoid her as you would infamy. She can tell you nothing. She is an unprincipled *charlatan.* Nay, more, she is a spy. How comes it for though I am wholly indifferent in a general way to the sayings and doings of my neighbours, I have made myself mistress of hers – how comes it that she receives no letters? Whence happens it that, though continually writing, she posts no letters through the Sunny Bay office, but takes them herself to Exeter, and despatches them from thence? A journey of twenty miles to post a letter! Whence this precaution? Why this reserve? Where there is mystery there is iniquity. She's a spy; and is at this very moment, such is my firm conviction, under Government *surveillance.* Have nothing to do with her. She can tell you nothing that has reference to the late Lord Nelson. How should she? She does not know him even by name."

"Miss de Crespigny", remarked the Viscountess, with stately dignity, "is a well read and intelligent woman."

"She's a desperately wicked one," said Mrs. Starke, pointedly.

"And your advice is?"

"Shun her."

And this advice being counter to her own previous determination, the widowed Viscountess heard, and forthwith disobeyed. An interview was speedily arranged at the foreigner's cottage; and early on a bleak and gusty morning Lady Nelson might have been seen wending her way towards Shepherd's Walk. The usual greetings over, and her visitor appearing unable or unwilling to announce her errand, Hortense led the way by an enquiry. "Your ladyship wished to see me on a matter of a private nature, and I venture to ask its object?"

"It relates mainly to myself," was the reply.

"Command me. I listen."

A pause of some moments took place before the widowed lady broke silence. "Referring to- to- to your *extraordinary* and *acknowledged* powers, did" – was her question put, with moistened eyes and quivering lip, "did Lord Nelson make any – the slightest mention of me the last few days of his life?"

"He did not."

"Was I wholly forgotten?" was the next inquiry, shrieked rather than uttered, so great was the emotion with which it was accompanied.

"No, a letter was written to you some eight days before he went into action."

"I never received it," was Lady Nelson's response; "no, believe me, I never received it."

"Is it likely that it should have been permitted to reach your hands?" returned the foreigner, in her usual calm, impassive tones.

"Its tenor? Oh! Let your answer be quick – its tenor?" cried the widowed Peeress, anxiously.

"Kind, respectful, and affectionate, in the highest degree."

"Could I but credit this!" said Lady Nelson, earnestly; "could I but credit this! How it would soothe a heart riven with regrets!"

"Why should your ladyship seek me, may I ask," said the foreigner, abruptly and sternly – "unless you credit me? This interview is not of my proposing."

"True," returned the elder lady, "true; I do credit you; but I have friends who – who – "

"Represent me as an impostor and a *charlatan* – Mrs. Starke among the rest. I am thoroughly conversant with their insinuations; but I disdain answering her or them. Will your Ladyship for a brief moment listen to me? You shall yourself test the truth of what I am now asserting."

"I shall live and die here" was Lady Nelson's answer. "I am attached to this little seaport; oh, yes; much and deeply attached to it. Its quiet calms me. Its retirement screens me. In Sunny Bay less observation is attracted to my sad history. Yes, here I shall pass the remainder of my days."

"A *portion* of them," returned the foreigner, emphatically; "a portion of them. The quiet so grateful to you, will not always be yours. You will witness a frightful contest – you will be present at a revolution."

"Impossible! with my habits and predilections! – quite impossible."

"You will be," resumed the other, in a low but authoritative tone, "in the very midst of the fray, and be surrounded with all its horrors. And the day – mark me well – will be one of the most bitter and agonizing of your chequered life."

"Am I, then, to perish by violence?"

"No; not a hair of your head will be injured."

"And yet that day will be one of sorrow and suffering?" said her ladyship musingly.

"Of agony," was the reply; "intense and unmitigated. And when it dawns, as it assuredly will" – the triumph with which this remark was uttered was remarkable – "I do not ask your ladyship to think of me and to credit me; the scene around you and your own heart will compel you to do both!" A low, mocking laugh closed the sentence.

The great hero's widow seemed paralysed. Lost in thought, she eyed her companion in silence for some moments; and the quivering of her lips and the tremulous motion of her head, showed that she was deeply moved. Replying to her look, Hortense said calmly and proudly "I will not detain your Ladyship longer; I have done."

"Oh," exclaimed the peeress, her usual self-possession over-borne by the firmness and decision of her companion, "Oh, in mercy be more explicit."

"I have done."

"A few words of explanation – only a few – a single sentence."

"I have nothing to add."

"But hear me – pray hear me; can no persuasion – no inducement – no pecuniary consideration be suggested, which would influence you? I have means, ample means; these I should not scruple to use if "

"You mistake me altogether," interposed Hortense, coldly and proudly. "My wants are fully supplied. I have nothing to wish – nothing to ask – nothing to receive from human being. I desire neither countenance nor sympathy from my kind."

"Is there nothing I can offer?" persisted her generous and gentlehearted visitor.

"Our interview is ended," was the reply; and with frigid courtesy Hortense conducted Lady Nelson from her humble apartment.

Mrs. Starke was furious; and the more, because Lady Nelson resolutely withheld all details of the foreigner's conversation.

"Be satisfied," was her sole comment, "the import of the interview is singular enough. But not even to my son will I disclose its bearing. For the present I hold it sacred."

Some time later Miss de Crespigny quitted Sunny Bay. She had, it appeared, sat up the whole of the previous night burning papers; and at four in the morning had started for Exeter. Thence, without pausing for refreshment, she had posted to Plymouth. At that busy seaport all trace of her was lost. The comments occasioned by her flight were curious. Some held that she was crazy; others that she was a spy in the pay of Lord Sidmouth. Some affected to consider her to be an agent of the French Government, and busily employed in reporting English news to the Emperor's cabinet.

Altogether, there was a mystery about her which none could fathom. And what added to it was a statement made by a most respectable party, and who could apparently have no motive to mislead, that during a short visit to London he saw a person enter the Foreign Office, in Downing Street, who, he could swear, was no other than Miss De Crespigny. He recognised her at once. But she was on this occasion attired as a man. And from this strange assertion he never varied. Meanwhile, marvellous changes took place. The Emperor was driven from his throne. Peace again visited Europe. Time sped on. The Bourbons were restored and expelled. At last the elder branch of that dynasty was driven from the throne of France. The three frightful days of July drew on! and the horrors of a revolution were once more rife in the streets of Paris. And Lady Nelson was present, and in the very thick of it. The son of the mistress of the hotel where she resided was shot almost in her presence. The rifles of the combatants penetrated the room where the youthful members of her family were sitting. The servant who was waiting on them was shot dead by their side. The gendarmerie searched the house with extraordinary keenness and rigour, because they were assured some member of the Polignac ministry was concealed in it, and because they knew full well the intimacy that had subsisted between 'the Duchess de Berri and

Miladi Nelson.' Searched it was, repeatedly, minutely, distressingly, but no Polignac had, or was likely *then*, to have made it his place of refuge. *Grief possessed the household.* It was, as had been foretold her one of the most wretched days of the widowed Peeress's chequered life. She had buried her son, her only child, him who had been so true to her in all her trials, for much of her past sorrow and neglect. It was a bitter hour, for she had never deemed it possible she should survive him.

But the question still remains unanswered – where was MISS de Crespigny? and who was she? An enigma to this hour!

The undress uniform coat that Nelson wore at Trafalgar. Under the left epulette the hole made by the musket ball which caused his death can be seen.

CHAPTER TWENTY THREE

'THE CUB' MY MARRIAGE – JOSIAH'S FINAL ACCOUNT

I had sailed the *Thalia* to Portsmouth arriving in October 1800, and the ship was paid off a month later, so that I was able to meet my step-father, his mistress and her husband on their arrival at Yarmouth on 6 November. This strange party had left Leghorn in July in midsummer heat, escorting the Queen of Naples and her Court. Nelson had remained inactive at a foreign Court for far too long, and the London papers had made their disapproval evident. The travelling circus had meandered overland by coach through Florence to Ancona (where Nelson vainly hoped to embark with a Russian squadron), thence to Trieste, where everyone was unwell. Eventually they reached Vienna and were all presented at the Imperial Court. Mr. Franz Joseph Haydn, an elderly composer of music, brought them a copy of his solo cantata for voice and pianoforte called 'Ariadne in Naxos'. He played it and Lady Hamilton inevitably sang – the 'Nelson Aria.' The Queen then retired to take a cure at Baden with her large ensemble of Courtiers. The circus reached Prague in late September, went thence to Dresden and Hamburg and across the North Sea rather ignominiously from Cuxhaven in the *King George* mail-packet. In pouring rain it seemed to me to be a sad and inauspicious return as I met them in their bedraggled finery – Lady Hamilton wore an amazing Sicilian outfit of muslin bordered with the words

'Nelson' and 'Bronte'. I was sickened by this aggressive adulation. I could not understand how my shrewd, intelligent step-father could be taken in by such a childish display!

Mortified and angry at the scene I encountered of my father-in-law even more firmly in the clutches of the siren from the Court of Naples, I predictably behaved very badly that evening in Yarmouth. As usual I drank too much and made my feelings evident – that my mother was being most shamefully neglected by Nelson's public display of affection for someone else's wife. At one of the great welcoming banquets given to Nelson on the way to London, I pushed back my chair and walked out of the room saying 'I can't bear to see that woman in my mother's place.' Although I had not seen the 'Tria Juncta in Uno' for over six months nothing had changed. The complaisant husband, the strident mistress and my poor, besotted, dearly loved step-father it was all as it had been at the Court of Naples. Nothing had changed except for Lady Hamilton's figure.

For some time after her arrival in Town in mid November she referred to me as 'The Cub' in conversation and in correspondence and to my poor mother, cruelly, as 'Tom Tit' in reference I suppose to her busy gait. This shows the innate vulgarity of the woman. Nevertheless I hovered in the wings of this sad little drama, still fascinated by the siren, still hoping for my step-father's love and approbation (and of course, another command). Afterwards I learned that Lady Hamilton had written to her new friend Mrs. William Nelson on 26 February 1801 'Tom Tit at same place Brighton. The CUB is to have a frigate the *Thalia*. I suppose HE will be up in a day or so. I only hope he does not come near me. If he does, not at home shall be the answer. I am glad he is going. I hope never to –'.

I hoped against hope that my mother and her husband could hold their marriage together in the face of the facts. It was clear that since Sir William did not appear to care about (almost encouraged) his wife's infidelity, Nelson expected my mother to be equally complaisant. He was shocked when, quite rightly, she refused to be a party to such a deception.

My mother and I were almost strangers as I had not seen her for seven years. Now I was a large young man of twenty, cocksure, over confident, and for a time our relationship was difficult. At Christmas, as a Post-Captain on half pay, I was hoping for another command. Despite my overt hostility to his affair, Nelson, to his credit, wrote to his friends at the Admiralty on my behalf for a recommissioning of the *Thalia*, or another command at sea.

Several things happened simultaneously early in that dreadful New Year. During January my mother and step-father parted. Even so, she wrote to him 'I wish my dear Josiah was with you. He never writes, so much the better for he can never be accused of making mischief', which showed how our relationship had sadly deteriorated.

Nelson had been made Vice Admiral of the Blue on New Year's Day, and appointed to command the famous Spanish prize of St. Vincent – the 112 gun *San Josef* – with Thomas Hardy as his Flag Captain.

I realised in spite of my boyish innocence that Lady Hamilton was carrying a child. It certainly was not her husband's and presumably was Nelson's, conceived that summer in Malta or in Syracuse. An unkind stupid remark of mine made in temper as a result of this terrible revelation was passed on to my step-father. I had watched him going up the side of his ship – one-armed in blowing weather (difficult enough for an able two-armed man at the best of times) – and had said aloud that I hoped he would slip and break his neck. Naturally this cruel remark was repeated until it reached him.

I am my own worst enemy.

My mother now accepted the harsh brutal facts – that she had been abandoned – with her usual dignity and calm. I did not know her well enough to estimate her secret feelings, but I could guess at them. She left Town in February for Brighton with her good friend Elizabeth Locker, whose father, dear old Captain William Locker (Nelson's original 'sea-daddy') had recently died. My mother had always had a soft spot for this nice old man, who had been Governor of the Royal Hospital for some years past.

I moved in a fairly fast set in London. I had some prize money, my service half pay, and no commitments and used to meet the Prince of Wales from time to time. He asked me in his usual licentious way about the happenings at the Court of Naples and about the Hamiltons. Later Nelson got to know of our frivolous conversation and wrote to his 'inamorata' 'Recollect what the villain (HRH) said to Mr. Nisbet *how you hit his fancy.*' The Prince was planning to have dinner with the Hamiltons and my stepfather was beside himself with jealousy, since he was absent with the Fleet on the south coast. Eventually Lady Hamilton refused to dine with the Prince, let alone sing for his pleasure with Mrs. Banti the Italian singer. Old Sir William was all in favour of a musical soirée with the Prince. I tried to see Lady Hamilton too, but got fobbed off on each call.

Late in February Nelson had hopes for me at the Admiralty for the *Thalia* – and very kindly settled up my large wine bill for £152.10.0*d* through Alexander Davison, his Agent. On 4 March he wrote to my mother just before he sailed on the *St. George*,

> Josiah is to have another ship and to go abroad if the *Thalia* cannot soon be got ready. I have done *all* for him and he may again as he has often done before wish me to break my neck, and be abetted in it by his friends who are likewise my enemies but I have done my duty as an honest generous man and I neither want or wish for any body to care what become of me, whether I return or am left in the Baltic. Living I have done all in my power for you and if dead you will find I have done the same, therefore my only wish is to be left to myself and wishing you every happiness. Believe that I am Your affectionate Nelson & Bronte.

My mother obviously was deeply hurt by this final brutal letter of farewell particularly as Nelson suggested that it was mainly my fault that his marriage had come to an end. He could not see or understand that I loved him for what he had done for me in the last fourteen years – I had been his son (not, it is true, a particularly good one) – but when he abandoned my fine mother for that big, coarse handsome 'femme fatale' and flaunted her to the Fleet and to the whole of the world – then I truly started to hate him. Nevertheless my mother was much aggrieved with me. She knew too about my visits to see Lady Hamilton. I dined with her on occasions when Nelson was in the Baltic fighting the great but pointless battle of Copenhagen. I wished I had been there with the *Thalia*.

Nelson wrote to Admiral Troubridge on 27 April 1801 from his flagship the *St. George* in Kioge Bay en route to the battle of Copenhagen

> My dear Troubridge, Although I do not care if I was dead and damned yet I cannot be sorry that he (Captain Nisbet) is not to have the *Thalia* or

some other good ship. His failings I know very well. His mother wrote me a threatening letter that, if I did not go directly and get her son made a Captain that she would not only ruin Nisbet, but try to injure me all in her power and I am sorry to say that Commissioner Coffin is at the bottom of it and gave her a private letter of mine to him in which I said of Nisbet what I thought and wished naturally to try and mend his conduct by telling him. Thus you will see and I wish Lord St. Vincent to see it too, that it is not for the service but hatred to Captain Nisbet for removing Mr. Colquitt from the ship [the *Thalia*] and to try by alarming me, to frighten me to recommend her son. I therefore hope that a person who I never injured but who has done everything to injure me and by threatening letters to make me do an act, will never be employed or promoted by the present Board of Admiralty. The motives must strike you and the Earl [St. Vincent] most forcibly and will point out what is proper to be done.

By then Admiral Nelson's mistress had borne him a bastard and he was beside himself with love of the child and its mother. He was totally unbalanced and his behaviour to my mother was iniquitous. She was incapable of making any threats to him or to anyone else, and he knew that full well. Poor Nelson.

In September I visited my step-father in Deal and told him that my mother was still angry with me as being a part cause of the breakdown of their marriage. I also asked him whether Admiral Troubridge had any possible command for me, and he promised to try again on my behalf!

That year was truly my personal year of disaster. I had irrevocably fallen out with my dear step-father through my own shortcomings at sea: I had quarrelled with my mother because she thought that if I had been truly a 'good' step-son to her husband, their marriage would have survived: I had been dismissed as the 'Cub' from the Hamilton ménage because of my juvenile attentions to Lady Emma and my obvious protective support of my mother. Finally after the *Thalia* was paid off it looked as though the Admiralty would give me no further sea service. What an appalling year!

Early in 1802 I was again in Town and called to see Admiral Sir Edward Berry and called at John Tyson's, who had been in Malta badly ill with fever. He had been trying to send agricultural implements and seeds to my step-father's small property in the Duchy of Bronte. He had also been lending his own capital to Nelson to help get the Bronte estate going. Originally he had been purser of the *Alexander* and was made secretary to the Admiral when we were both at the Court of Naples.

One of my best friends was Thomas Bladon Capel, who was signal-lieutenant on the *Vanguard* with my step-father, fought at Aboukir Bay, and visited Naples in the *Mutine* with William Hoste. Thomas took the French Admiral's sword back to the Lord Mayor of London. He had met Lady Hamilton and drove round the streets of Naples with her whilst she wore a bandeau inscribed 'Nelson and

Victory'. Thomas had a distinguished career, became Admiral of the Blue and a Baronet. He stayed my friend even when I left the Navy, and in my Will I have left him £100 as a small token of our friendship.

When a biography of my step-father was being published, the authors solicited material for inclusion. As a result my old commander Lord St. Vincent sent a letter he had written to his sister Mrs. Ricketts on 22 January 1807. 'My dear sister, Upon reflexion it appears best to send you the only letters I can find relative to Captain Nisbet and to authorise you to assert in my name that Lord Nelson assured me that he owed his life to the resolution and admirable conduct of his step-son, when wounded at Tenerife and that he had witnessed many instances of his courage and enterprise. Yours most affec. St. Vincent'.

I stayed on Naval half pay until 1825, having secured a year's leave of absence in France on private affairs. My uncle Walter Nisbet of Nevis, who had married Anne Parry of Denbighshire, had returned to England, and I frequently met them and their family of two sons and a daughter. Although the Nisbets were well known for their family rows and litigations over wills, they always extended a warm welcome to me at their house in Berners Street.

Soon my mother and I were totally reconciled. Nelson's death at Trafalgar brought us together and we lived together for the rest of our lives in a variety of places. She took a house in Exmouth, which particularly suited me because I could berth my yacht in the harbour. My mother and I agreed that the local girls were exceptionally pretty!

My mother was always a very generous person. When she realised that I had the makings of a business financier, over a period of years (1808-1819) she gave me several thousand pounds to fund a business in Paris. On the new Bourse I made a market in Foreign investments and in French Rentes of stocks and Government funds and Consols. I had many wealthy influential friends, and my mother was well acquainted with the Princess de Joinville, the Duchesse de Berri, the Prince and Princess de Castelcicala, and many others in high society. She often paid my wine bill, and she purchased a chariot for me (18 October 1820) costing £143. 17s. But I paid for all my yachts myself, even the rather costly *Transit* in 1819.

I have always liked the Fair Sex, but living comfortably at home – a spoilt only son – had dulled my appetites. For years my mother had been urging me to marry – not only for my sake but for hers as well, since she wanted grandchildren around her.

Every family has their legend and the Nisbets have theirs! The Herbert family of Nevis (my maternal grandmother was Mary Herbert) came from Wales. As a result my mother had known for many years the family of Herbert Evans of Eaglebush and Kilveymount in Glamorganshire. (He was a Welsh country clergyman). Their daughter was one of my mother's many godchildren, and was christened 'Frances Herbert' Evans. She came to live with us in Exmouth as companion-housekeeper to my mother. She was a remarkably sweet and pretty girl.

The Nisbet family legend runs like this

Captain Nisbet resided with his mother after Lord Nelson's demise and her daily prayer to him was that he would marry. 'Now my dear son, do marry: there is Miss Okes, and Miss Ducarel and Miss Turquand, all fine girls and fine fortunes: my dear Josiah, why don't you marry?' To this strain there was a daily da capo, but apparently in vain. The Captain was proof against all the blandishments which his mother contrived should be brought to play against him and held on the even tenor of his course in single blessedness. One evening, however, the Viscountess turned from the persuasive mood to the authoritative, and after dwelling at some length on her favourite subject, rose into this noble peroration – 'Josiah, I your mother lay my commands on you to marry.' 'Madame' (I am reputed to have answered) 'Your commands are obeyed' pointing to the very pretty girl, her ladyship's companion, who sat blushing by her side. 'Lady Nelson, there by your side is Mrs. Nisbet: Fanny, my love, kiss your mother.'

The legend went on to say that we had been married secretly in Littleham Church (a few hundred yards away, and secrecy in a small town is not possible) and had our wedding breakfast in Sidmouth. Apparently I had ridden to the church on horseback and bribed the "jarvey not to split"! Then we had dined at Sidmouth together and I had sailed off alone to Brixham and then to France in my yacht.

It is true I had been courting this pretty girl for some time. We were married at Littleham Parish Church on 31 March 1819, and my mother signed the Register. We lived happily, partly in Exmouth, but mainly in Paris. She was a keen sailor and accompanied me on many of my cross-channel trips. She enjoyed the sophisticated life we spent in Paris living on the Champs Elysées – a far cry from her Welsh homeland. My mother gave my wife many presents – a new bonnet (cost £2. 13s.), a petticoat and other fripperies, and with my consent £1,000 in Consols when we were married.

My first child, little Josiah Herbert, was born and died in Exmouth in September 1821. Horatio Woolward, Sarah and Josiah were all born in Devon sea-ports and, poor things, died in infancy. Frances Herbert was born in Paris on 6 February 1822, Mary in Paris on 5 September 1826, and so too was Georgina on 1 January 1830, and thank God they all survived.

Apart from my early years with Nelson from midshipman to frigate captain, my marriage to my Fanny must rank as the happiest years of my life.

My mother lived with her memories of my step-father. She never complained of his treatment of her nor of his unfaithfulness and final desertion. She had the excellent portrait of the Admiral painted for her by Lemuel Abbot. She had the wonderful Presentation Vase from Lloyds, and she had a miniature of Nelson in a casket from which she was never parted – at night she used to sleep with it under her pillow. She always looked at the miniature with great affection, kissed it and put it back in the safe place where she kept it in the daytime. She used to show it to my little daughter, and cried a bit as she did, saying 'When you are older, little Fan, you too may know what it is to have a broken heart.'

Fanny portrayed by Henry Edridge *c.* 1810.

CHAPTER TWENTY FOUR
THE BYRON FAMILY

George Gordon Byron, the 6th Baron – that brilliant, gifted, but flawed man – came into our lives in a strange fashion.

After a tour of Europe he had published *Childe Harold's Pilgrimage*, which made him famous and the darling of London Society. That was in 1812, and three years later he was married for the second time, to Miss Annabella Milbanke. Sadly this marriage lasted scarcely a year, although his only child Augusta Ada (who later married the Earl of Lovelace) was born on 10 December 1815. Byron separated from his poor wife a month later and left England.

His travelling 'circus' consisted of seven servants, five carriages, five horses, a monkey, a bulldog, a mastiff, nine live cats, three peafowls and some hens, a library of books, a vast quantity of furniture, trunks and portmanteaux. They arrived in Geneva on 24 May 1816, met his friend Percy Bysshe Shelley and Mary Godwin, rented the Villa Diodati, and he started an 'affaire de coeur' with Claire Clairmont.

During his intermittent sojourns in Geneva, Byron wrote a long poetic drama called 'Manfred'. When he visited Madame de Stael at Cappel in 1819 he made a violent attack upon Geneva and the Genevese. Rocca, the husband of his hostess, replied 'C'est bien vrai, milord, mais qu'est-ce que vous aviez à faire dans une telle caverne d'honnêtes gens?' (Very true, my lord, but what had you to do in such a den of worthy folks?).

Josiah, his wife Frances Herbert, their new daughter 'little Fan' (born in Paris in February), a babe in arms, and I were visiting Geneva, where we met Lord Byron and his entourage. Josiah's love of the sea extended to rowing on Lake Geneva, and Lord Byron insisted on not only coming with us, but rowing us as well. Possibly because of his lame leg, or a slightly choppy sea, the boat gave a lurch, and little Fanny was shaken from the nurse's grasp and fell overboard! Quick as a flash 'milord' Byron leaped overboard and immediately rescued the smallest of the three Frances Herbert Nisbets (fortunately he was a strong swimmer) and presented her weeping and wet to her mother, exclaiming as he did so 'Receive thy child! She hath been baptised in sorrow.' Shortly afterwards Lord Byron took up the cause of Greek Independence and sailed to Missolonghi, where he died of fever.

During our family sojourn and holiday in Switzerland in July 1822 we stayed for several weeks in Lausanne and my three granddaughters much enjoyed the

George Gordon Byron, the 6th Baron.

paddle boat steamer trips on the lake. Whilst we were there Lady (as she became) Louisa Hardy gave me a special evening soirée on the 6 July. She has always been a beautiful woman but I believe her sympathies, unlike her husband's, have not been truly towards me.

Lady Byron (Annabella Milbanke) and her daughter came to live in Exmouth and became neighbours of mine at No. 19, The Beacon. It was called 'Chapmans Beacon Hotel' and was run by Mr. John Bastin, a churchwarden (who wrestled in his spare moments with the champions of England). Ada Evangeline was six years older than my 'little Fan' and we continued to be friends with the poor abandoned Lady Byron for a number of years.

CHAPTER TWENTY FIVE

LIFE AND DEATH IN PARIS

After the downfall of Napoleon at Waterloo the Allied armies swept into Paris under the Duke of Wellington, and by 1815 the English nobility were back there again, almost as though no war between the two countries had ever taken place. For a variety of reasons I found myself there as well, although some people thought it a trifle odd that the widow of the Victor of Trafalgar should be in the capital city of the Old Enemy!

My son Josiah was still on half pay as a Naval Captain and had become a successful businessman in Paris. The first savings bank opened there in 1818, followed by the formation of joint stock companies, and a fine new Bourse was built in 1826. Over a period of a few years I loaned, or rather gave, Josiah quite large sums of money. Although I travelled a great deal to Bath and Exmouth and to Paris, and did not stint myself on clothes, I nevertheless lived well within the handsome pension provided by the country. In November 1808, when I was in Bath at No.2 Bennett Street, I gave him £1,000, again in November 1812 from Exmouth £1,000 in 4% Consols, and in September 1813 another £1000 in 4% Consols when I was staying in Teignmouth. This gave him enough working capital for his investment business.

In 1823 Josiah applied to the Admiralty for 12 months leave of absence to go to France for his private affairs, and thereafter made Paris more of his home than my house in Exmouth. My granddaughter Frances Herbert was born in Paris on 6 February 1822, Mary on 5 September 1826 and Georgina on 1 January 1830. I was there on each occasion to help their mother. Josiah's other small children, Herbert Josiah, Horatio Woolward, who died aged 5, and Sarah were born in Devon and died in infancy – poor little things – and were buried in Versailles. Little Josiah died in Exmouth after one month in this life. We lived in great style on the Champs Elysees since Josiah's investments in French Rentes and other public funds were paying him excellent dividends.

I had learned the French language on Nevis and had kept in practice with the many French officers who came from the governors of Martinique and Guadeloupe to see my Uncle Herbert. I was the interpreter for all their meetings up to the time of my marriage to Horatio. That linguistic ability, my love of French cuisine and wines and my interest in French haute couture enabled me to live in French Court Society for many years.

Many of my friends in London after my husband's tragic death had connections in Paris – Lady Knight and her daughter Cornelia Knight, and those indefatigable travellers, the Prince and Princess Castelcicala, the Neapolitan Ambassador and his wife, who had been in London since 1801. Dear friends of mine introduced me in Paris to Court Society, in particular the young Duchesse de Berri, who was so tragically widowed in February 1820. Charles Ferdinand, her husband, was assassinated by Louvel, the Journeyman saddler, late of the old Imperial Guard, in front of the Opera. I had first met the Duchesse when she was in exile at Sir George Lee's property, Hartwell House, near Aylesbury. That was in the period 1810-1814, when King Louis XVIII was nearly 60 very jovial and very fat. She had married the Duc, who was the second son of the Comte d'Artois (Louis' brother who afterwards became King Charles X on the former's death on 16 September 1824). The Duchesse Marie Caroline was born in Naples in 1798 and lived there and at Palermo with her aunt, and was educated at the court of her grandfather Ferdinand, King of Naples. It was ironical that I should become such a great friend of this young Neapolitan Princess, since Naples has been indelibly imprinted in my mind as the 'dangerous place' where Horatio was seduced from his duty by that Siren. The Duc de Berri had been secretly married in England in July 1808 to an English girl called Amy Brown, who bore him two daughters. On his violent tragic death my friend, Marie Caroline, more or less adopted the young Comtesse d'Issoudun and the Comtesse de Vierzon. She had two surviving children of her own, a daughter called just 'Mademoiselle', and the young Duc de Bordeaux. The Duchesse had a chateau at Rosny, near Mantes, and an apartment called the Pavillon de Marsan or the little Chateau, in the Tuileries, and I would visit her there frequently. She never meddled in politics, but was the doyenne of the Arts in Paris. The new Gymnase theatre was under her protection and called 'Theatre de Madame'. She had the most vivacious face you can imagine, with a very direct and frank manner. She was always up at 6 a.m. then went to Mass and took a ride or long walk. She was the Queen of Elegance and her daily purchases were announced in *Le Moniteur*. She gave many audiences, was most charitable, visited hospitals, and industrial ateliers, encouraged small artists in their little studios, and was perhaps the most popular person in Paris. I persuaded Josiah to change his rented house to the Quai D'Orsay near the Tuileries so that I could more easily meet Marie Caroline, and he could berth his yacht more conveniently.

I was also a great friend of the Princesse de Joinville, related to the House of Orleans and a cousin of the Duchesse de Berri. The de Joinvilles I had met originally at the French Embassy in London in 1815, where poor Kitty, the Duchess of Wellington was also present (who also became a good friend of mine). Both of us had been deserted by our famous husbands and we were both talented watercolour painters! I visited her at Stratfield Saye several times during the period 1817-1820 after the Nation had granted that country estate to her. She told me how mean the Duke was, that he allowed her only £500 a year, and when she asked for an increase to £670 he refused it. Her two sons Lord Douro and

Charles were both at Eton. Although she was shy, a poor hostess, badly dressed very touchy and sensitive (and also shortsighted) – quite my opposite – we liked each other. She knew the Duc de Berri before his marriage and also the Duc de Broglie, and of course our mutual friend the Duke of Clarence. All the young folk adored her and she had a great affinity with them. From time to time we met at Cheltenham but she spent most of her life retired at Stratfield Saye. Her best friend however was Maria Edgeworth.

With my Court friends I would go shopping only to realise that "la dernière mode de Paris" was quite different from across the channel. All the hats, bonnets, robes, mantles, caps, turbans, pelisses that I wore seemed to M. Herbault, the high priest of the Temple of Fashion, to be 'passée de mode'. I bought from him a pretty 'peignoir à la neige', and a 'chapeau de dernier gout'. 'Lingerie à la mode canezus'. My 'robes de matin' I purchased from Mademoiselle la Touche. After that I could face the Duchesse de Berri and the Princesse de Joinville with more confidence! The prices were reasonable by London standards – 320 francs for a crepe hat and feathers, 100 francs for a 'chapeau negligé de matin', 200 francs for a 'chapeau à fleurs' and 85 francs for an evening cap composed of tulle trimmed with blonde and flowers. The 'costumier' Leroy & Tuloua in the Rue de Richelieu was particularly popular with visiting English ladies for his robes. Madame Beauvais and Mademoiselle Coro at 77 rue Sainte Anne were known for their 'chapeaux'. The Rue Vivienne shops were even more reasonable for hats, caps and bonnets. They sold there – the elegant little modistes – transparent muslin prettier and cheaper and quite suitable for summer wear. There were a number of good 'coiffeurs' – I recall M. Ashthley, Lambert, Butties and Tellier. I always tried to make the best of my hair and the French 'coiffeurs' took a lot of trouble to please.

Shortly after I met Lord Byron in Geneva in 1816 I was delighted to find that the men in Paris were wearing 'La Cravate Lord Byron'. He would have been amused!

I met Jules, Prince de Polignac, in London before he was recalled from the Embassy of the Court of St. James to become Prime Minister of France. The Prince had married two English brides – the first was a Miss Campbell, and the second was Lord Radcliffe's daughter. All the French nobility in exile found our young English ladies quite irresistible. The Prince's ministry followed that of M. de Martignac, M. de Labourdonnage and M. de Villele. After the Restoration in 1815 the monarchy never seemed to achieve the stability which Napoleon, for all his grandiose ambitions, had imprinted on the French. The Prince's Hotel in Paris was on the corner of the Rue des Capucins. For a number of years he was the most influential man in France and eventually, the most hated. I tried to keep out of the political scene. I could imagine what Horatio would have thought and said about me if he had been still alive! Meddling in politics indeed!

It was a very gay society after the long sad wars, and the Hotel d'Angleterre in the Place du Palais Royal was the scene of many 'routes' and balls. One danced waltzes to the music of Courtin and de Bourle and strange (to me anyway) dances called la Cosaque, la Montferrine, le Pas Russe, la Boulangerie and la Galopade.

More familiar dances were la Gavotte, l'Ecossaise and l'Anglaise. We listened to M. Aubet's inspiring music and went to watch Marie Taglioni's wonderful dancing at the Opera – so graceful, a poetical and lyrical style of dancing not seen before.

Besides the Coronation in 1825 there were other grand occasions, at most of which I was present. The wealthy Rothschilds bankers gave a great Ball in March 1821 and the Duke of Northumberland, then the English Ambassador in Paris, gave another gala affair in June 1825, a week after King Charles X's coronation.

At the Grand Jubilee in February 1826 10,000 pilgrims came to Paris. There were many processions and afterwards many balls and other events.

The Champs de Mars was used for military reviews and tattoos and watching the French veterans drill and reform. I wondered how Kitty's husband broke the Old Guard at Waterloo.

At the beginning of 1829 my friend the Duchesse de Berri gave a masked ball on a theme of 'Mary Stuart'. The French have ever had a romantic attachment to our Hibernian cousins. The English Ambassador's wife came as Anne Boleyn. Lady Vernon, Lady Cambermere and the Marquess of Huntley were there. There were three separate orchestras and no less than ten 'salons de danse'.

The society salons of Madame Recamier, the Duchesse de Duras, Madame Ancelot and Madame Vigée-Lebrun were the most illustrious and entertaining during my many years spent in Paris. At the Sorbonne there were lesser soirées with Mmes. Grizot, Villemain and Cousin. Josiah and his wife and I enjoyed ourselves. By now his French had become colloquially very sound and his bride, who came from Wales, soon learned the elegant French language. In the evening we would go to the Tivoli Gardens, which we thought much superior to our Vauxhall gardens in London. My daughter-in-law and I in demi-toilette would go for an after dinner promenade, wearing a simple robe of organdie with long sleeves 'à canezou' of net, a light scarf, a pretty 'chapeau de paille de ris', quite suitable for a visit to the Tivoli or to a theatre, but not perhaps for the Opera.

The English Ambassadors in Paris, the Duke of Northumberland and Lord Stuart of Rothesay, his successor, and his wife, and Mr. Hamilton, the Secretary, were always very polite and helpful to me on my visits to the French capital. The English travellers in Paris, there for a short visit, usually stayed at the Hotel Meurice, but the Countess of Blessington, Colonel and Madame Crauford, the amusing and original Lord Yarmouth, the amiable and kind hearted Lord Lilford would usually rent a smart hotel from impoverished French aristos. In the Anglo-French society of the late Twenties I met Colonel Leicester Stanhope, Sir Francis Burdett, Lora Darnley, Lord Charlemont and Lord Landsdown. Most of the English Court visited Paris at one time or another. Mr. T. Steuart, nephew to Sir William Drummond, was an original and clever man whose brilliant, and often cruel, sallies would convulse his audience. But then society responds to witty cruelties – a sign of our times.

The Duchesse de Berri, as royal patron of the Arts in Paris, took me many times to the theatre and opera, which were performed either at Le Francais, the

Paris, 1789 – a city of Revolution.

Odeon, the Opera in the hall of Rue La Peletier, or Les Italiens in the Salle Fauvart. And of course there was the Opera Comique in the Salle Ventadour. Signor Rossini conducted his operas 'Moise', 'Le Comte Ory' and 'Guillaume Tell' in the period 1826-9. Perhaps his most popular opera 'Il Viaggio à Reims' was sung at Les Italiens opera house. Monsieur Talma and Madame Duchesnoir sang at Le Francais, Mademoiselle Georges at the Odeon, and Messrs Nourrit, Levasseur and Madame Damoreau at the Opera. At Les Italiens one listened to M. Sontag, Pasta and Rubino. There Madame La Malibran sang 'Desdemona' superbly and the part of Ninetta in 'La Gazzaladra' and in 'La Cenexentola'. The famous singer Grizi taught my little grand-daughter 'Little Fan' how to sing.

M. Eugene Scribe wrote no less than 150 pieces of music for the Duchesse Theatre de Madame. He also wrote 'Avant, Pendant et Apres' mainly about the Revolution, which was played at the Vaudeville Theatre. We saw the famous Mademoiselle Mars, that celebrated actress, in 'Valerie' and 'Henri III'. She lived in an elegant Hotel in the Rue de la Tour des Dames. At the Porte St Martin we saw 'Sept Heures' with Charlotte Corday's role acted by M. Dorval. Also 'La Maison du Rempart' at the Theatre des Nouvautés, a frightening play about the Parisian mob during the War of the Fronde. In 1827/8 a famous English acting troupe came to Paris with all the famous London actors and actresses. There were Chippendale, Burnet, Kemble, Kean and Macready, and Misses Foot and Smithson. They played mainly Shakespeare. I remember 'Hamlet' was their last performance. Miss Smithson fell in love with the composer M. Berlioz, married him and stayed on in Paris!

It is a period when great French painters are appearing on the scene, and I go to their ateliers and galeries to see works by Gerard, Ingres, who has just returned from Italy, and Delacroix, who carries the standard of Romanticism in French Art. I have seen miniatures by Augustin, and other paintings by Lany, Isabey and Grevedon – far removed from my modest daubs.

Victor Hugo has published his 'Odes and Ballades' and writers such as Alexandre Dumas, Alfred de Musset and Alfred de Vigny are now very famous. There are many interesting excursions to be taken in Paris. The authors' quarter is known as "Pays Latin" and Josiah purchased early volumes there for his library.

Josiah would take his family to see the curiosity shops on the Quai Voltaire and in his carriage – three generations of us – to the Bois de Boulogne, to the Jardin des Plantes, and to see the elegant hotels of the 'noblesse de l'ancien regime' in the Faubourg St. Germain.

Early in November 1827 Josiah was visiting a business acquaintance and had brought his yacht up the river *Rhone*. We arranged to meet him in Lyons. Rather to my surprise an English Milord and his lady were staying at the same hotel. Lady Bunbury, who was a niece of Mr. Charles James Fox, and her husband General Sir Henry Bunbury, were making the grand Tour of France. They and their three young sons were staying in Lyons, and over the course of several days we – Josiah's wife and myself saw a good deal of them. We had Admiral Lord and Lady Keith as friends in common, so we had a lot to talk about. I think they thought that I chattered on too much!

One happier link in the chain with the Nelson family still remained when we encountered the Matcham family in Paris. George's business in France and Spain was more easily administered from Paris. They called me (not to my face of course) the 'Little Viscountess', and frequently they came to drink tea with me in the afternoon. I believe George and Josiah helped each other in the financial world.

George and Catherine Matcham, almost as restless as I am, had been living in Paris in the Rue Cadet since 1818. It was a large house let to them by a French Marquis. They were very friendly by now with my daughter-in-law. I was able to do the Matchams a favour for their son-in-law, Captain Blanckley, for which they were most grateful, as I shared the same banker with them, a M. De Lisle at No.3 Rue Blanche.

To the observant eye there had been signs of disquiet in Paris for many years and unhappiness with the various governments under King Charles X. Josiah reported to me early in 1830 that the Parisian Bourse was getting panicky, that trade accounts were being suspended, ateliers were being closed and companies were stopping payments. There had been ominous signs of disorder at the Review of the National Guard in April 1827 when the crowd shouted 'Down with the Ministers'. My friend the Duchesse de Berri had left Paris some time before to meet her Royal family of the Two Sicilies – her father, step-mother, and her sisters – in Lyons. They went on to the Pyrenees, so she could not give me any news.

A proclamation by M. de Polignac acting under orders from King Charles X proscribed the 221 deputies in August 1829 and then dissolved Parliament. Commerce declined, government employees quit their posts, the theatres and opera were forsaken. Shortly afterwards the deputies were re-elected. In July 1830. Parliament was dissolved again. Comte de Peyronnet, was then Secretary of State. The main journals and papers were then forced to close by edict because of their fierce criticisms of the government and, by inference, the King and Court. The *Courrier Francais*, the *National*, the *Globe*, *Tribune des Departemens*, *Constitutional, Journal du Commerce* (Josiah's favourite!) *The Times, Revolution, Sylphe* and *Figaro* – all were closed down. M. Mangin, Chef de Police had to obey the severe orders in Council and the presses of *The Times* and *National* were destroyed.

Josiah at this time, in early July, was unwell with a heavy summer cold. Despite the best medical care he developed pleurisy or perhaps dropsy. We were living together in a fine house between the Champs Elysées and the Quai Voltaire. My daughter-in-law was taking turns nursing him with nuns from a neighbouring convent. But their devoted care was not enough and on 9 July my dear and only son – Nelson's 'son-in-law' – died peacefully, surrounded by his family. We were all desolate and wept bitterly, and I feel that I now have little left in this life.

Meanwhile Paris was in a state of Civil war. Lady Caroline Capel was shot at by the mob. After a cavalry charge in the Rue Croix-des-Petits Champs several people were killed. Gunsmiths, such as M. Leduc and M. Lepage, were raided for their weapons. M. de Polignac's house on the Boulevard des Capucines was attacked and badly damaged. Lancers charged in the Place du Carrousel near the Tuileries. The Place de Grève in front of the Hotel de Ville became a scene of carnage and the Place de la Bourse became a battlefield. Citizens barricaded the streets and soon nearly 5,000 'citoyens' were in arms. The English in Paris took refuge in the Embassy near the Rue St. Honoré and in the Hotel Meurice. The King's Swiss Guards bravely defended their barracks in the Tuileries and were savagely attacked by a mob of students. The Faubourg Saint Antoine was the scene of another pitched battle.

In our sad house, we were waiting for Josiah's body to be removed for burial alongside his three children lying in the English cemetery at Versailles. The nuns had lighted candles and were saying prayers for his soul, on their knees by his bed. They were chanting a prayer when suddenly a large excited mob broke into the house and invaded the darkened room, shouting and screaming threats. They shot one of my servants dead on the spot, since they suspected me, a known friend of the Duchesse de Berri and the Prince de Polignac – the 'miladi Anglaise' – of sheltering supporters of the unpopular regime. The courageous sisters went on with their prayers, unmoved by the violence around them. Eventually the brave 'citoyens', having murdered one innocent man, and awed by the death scene of Josiah's lying-in-state, left the building to take part in the popular coup d'état called afterwards 'les trois jours de juillet'.

After all this confusion and horror I did not leave the centre of Paris, but moved to Lawson's Royal Hotel. With difficulty I arranged for undertakers to remove Josiah's body – (there were 800 people killed and 4,500 wounded in the bloody riots) – to disinter his three poor little children from their graves in Versailles, and ship the four bodies to Exmouth. That was difficult enough in all conscience. My pretty namesake, my daughter-in-law Frances Herbert Nisbet, now sadly widowed, collected her three daughters, disguised themselves as French peasants, escaped out of Paris in a farm cart and made their way courageously back to London.

One of my melancholy tasks was that of writing in answer to the many letters of sympathy, on special black edged mourning writing paper. To Captain Montagu, late commander of the *Hector* under Admiral Man, who lived in the Rue Richelieu, I wrote on the 22 July 'Viscountess Nelson presents her compliments to Captain Montagu and begs he will accept her thanks for his kind offer of assistance under the late afflicting circumstances, but everything was so well ordered and connected by his widow that nothing was left for the interference of either or any of her friends.' Indeed my erstwhile companion and mother of my grandchildren has been a tower of strength in these wretched times.

'Aux Armes Citoyennes.' Parisian drama in the streets.

At the beginning of August a French schooner-rigged pilot boat arrived in the harbour at Exmouth with its sad cargo aboard – the dead bodies of Josiah and the three young children. The ship arrived at the Temple Steps earlier than expected, consequently no preparation had been made to receive the bodies. The Custom House officer rose to the occasion and had them removed to the house of Mr. Edmund Webber on the sea front. It was a circular house called Beach Castle and thereafter known as Corpse Castle. All the bodies were subsequently re-interred in Littleham churchyard.

My friend Marie Caroline left France at the same time as I did with her father-in-law King Charles X and her nine year old son, the Duke of Bordeaux – the legitimate pretender to the throne known as Henri V. For the sake of peace the throne had been handed over to Louis Phillipe. Charles X, the Dauphin and Duke of Bordeaux abdicated and renounced their claims. Towards the end of August the Royal Family, now including the Duchesse de Angouleme, took ship from Cherbourg on the American vessels the *Great Britain* and the *Charles Carroll* for England and sanctuary in Lullworth. Ironically, once there, Charles X purchased Marie Caroline's best silver service table ware from her because in the confusion the Court in exile only possessed a silverplated set! They spent two months at Lullworth before going north to Edinburgh, which has harboured many French Royal families before.

So my dozen years of living intermittently in the gayest capital in Europe with my only son and my grand-children ended in tragedy. In a way I am glad to be back in the still water of Exmouth and Brighton, but the sad and desperate anxieties remain with me. All I have left now are memories of the happy life on Nevis and time spent with my dearest husband, Horatio Lord Nelson, England's famous Admiral.

Ferry boat from Brighton.

CHAPTER TWENTY SIX

PRINCE WILLIAM'S STORY

My father, King George III, determined when I was a young child that as his third son, I should have a career in the Royal Navy. This, despite an education by a cleric Dr. John James Majendie, and a soldier Major General Bude, a Swiss in the service of the Hanoverian army. Accordingly in May 1779, when I was fourteen, I embarked on board the *Prince George*, Captain Robert Digby's flagship, initially as an Able Seaman. After a cruise in the Channel and the relief of Gibraltar I was rated midshipman on 18 January 1780. There were various stories about me at the time – as a midshipman being remarked on by a captured Spanish Admiral, of a fight with a Marine Lieutenant Moodie, and a quarrel with a midshipman named Sturt. All these stories were mainly true as I inherited the proud, intolerant attitudes of our family. Still in the *Prince George*, after mildly discreditable adventures in London, we sailed to New York, transferred to the *Warwick* and then the *Barfleur* under Lord Hood to the West Indies. I was described at the time as a very fine lad, tall (not yet as bulky as I became later on) with the protuberant blue fishy eyes and heavy features of the Hanoverians. My father thought I looked 'noble and most glorious' and my ambition was to become an Admiral. As a midshipman and then later as a captain I became authoritarian, German style, with little responsibility but I think I was popular.

On the *Barfleur* in the narrows off Staten Island I met 'the meerest boy of a captain I ever beheld, full-laced uniform, waistcoat with flaps, of very old fashioned cut. His lank fair hair was unpowdered, and he wore a stiff Hessian pigtail of extraordinary length.' This was the captain of the 28 gun frigate the *Albemarle* called Horatio Nelson. I was 17 and he was 24 and he had been to the North Pole, Far East and Central America. We became firm friends, partly of course on his side out of respect for my father. Lord Hood warmly recommended Nelson's knowledge and experience to me and Nelson prophesied that I would be a disciplinarian and a strong one, but also 'a seaman which you could hardly suppose.' The *Albemarle* sailed with Lord Hood's squadron in the West Indies, but the French fleet escaped us. When the squadron returned to London, Lord Hood took Nelson to a levée at St. James and introduced him to my father, and so I met him again. For the next two years I made frivolous travels in Germany and Italy getting into many scrapes with gamblers and the opposite sex (to whom I was always attracted!) In the summer of '85 I passed my examination for lieutenant and sailed on the *Hebe*, and in the following March was appointed to command the 28 gun *Pegasus* frigate and came under Nelson's command on the West Indian Station, where we resumed our friendship. The Admiralty in its wisdom had made Isaac Schomberg my First Lieutenant, for whom everyone including Nelson had much respect, since his record and experience were far superior to mine! One of the problems with Princes, especially Hanovenan Princes, is that we are used to getting our own way. All my lieutenants and especially Schomberg, were poorly treated by me and were on the verge of mutiny. They all wanted transfers out of my ship and Schomberg felt himself so much persecuted that he demanded a Court-Martial. Nelson was on the horns of a dilemma – he liked me and I was his Prince – but he knew Schomberg to be a capable officer who should not be broken. The *Pegasus* was sent to Novia Scotia via Jamaica. Schomberg was superseded and returned to England, where he was promoted to be First Lieutenant of Lord Hood's ship the *Barfleur*. Later on, Nelson sent me a long letter in which he rebuked me for my intolerant attitude to Schomberg, particularly as I had criticised Lord Hood's decision. It is surprising that my august Father did not intervene: it is also surprising that my friendship with Nelson remained strong, and continued to flourish.

Nelson wrote home and described me: 'our young Prince is a gallant man: he is indeed volatile, but always with great good nature. There were two balls during his stay [Dec. 1786] at Antigua and some of the ladies were mortified that HRH would not dance with them ... He has his foibles as well as private men, but they are far over balanced by his virtues.'

On Nevis Island Nelson had met a young widow, niece of the President, John Richardson Herbert, and had fallen headlong in love with her. It was a curious situation because under Admiralty orders the *Boreas* and the *Pegasus* had arrested several American ships bringing trade goods to Nevis. All the traders of Nevis and St. Kitts were up in arms with this honest little naval captain. President Herbert, one of the richest men on the islands, stood to lose the most, but promised bail for Nelson if and when the American captains took their case to court. He believed Nelson was only doing his duty and deserved support. In due course I met his bride-to-be and found her to be both intelligent and attractive. I insisted on becoming the Father of the Bride and giving away Mrs. Frances Nisbet to my friend Captain Horatio Nelson at the wedding ceremony. During their long courtship of eighteen months (caused by the President's impending retirement to England) I often chaffed Nelson and accused him of being already a husband and keeping it a secret. He answered me 'I certainly am not married' and I told him that he must have a great esteem for Mrs. Nisbet – not 'the thing' which is vulgarly called love. To which he replied 'No, I wont make use of *that* word,' which was considered rather fast. One used more discreet words such as 'admiration' and 'esteem'.

Of course all the island communities, Jamaica in particular, showered hospitality on me, and to a lesser extent on Nelson who wrote 5 May (1786) 'If you had considered I was a sailor, and what should I do carrying a wife in a ship and when I marry I do not mean to part with my wife.'

In due course on Sunday 11 March 1787 Nelson, aged twenty eight, and his bride of twenty-five [actually twenty-seven] were married at a grand ceremony in the President's house of Montpelier on Nevis. All we naval officers were in full dress uniform. I danced with the handsome young widow and wrote of her to Lord Hood 'I found a pretty, and a sensible woman and may have a great deal of money, if her uncle, Mr. Herbert, thinks proper: poor Nelson is over head and ears in love. I frequently laugh at him about it. He is now in for it: I wish him well and happy and that he may not repent the step he has taken.' I congratulated Nelson on 'having borne off the principal favourite of the island ... which statement all the naval officers present agreed with.'

A few months later when the *Pegasus* under my command (considered by many authorities one of the best-disciplined ships to come into Plymouth) was paid off, Nelson and his bride came to the festivities to celebrate my safe return. Nelson too had been paid off and was on the beach and like all dedicated naval officers, desperate for a command. He wrote to me several times. He even suggested that his wife, whom I admired, should become a Lady in Waiting at Court.

Shortly after that, on 20 May 1789, my father created me Duke of Clarence. Together with my other brothers we started our long struggle to unseat our father and form a Regency.

Meanwhile I had command of the *Andromeda* which spent a year in the West Indies. On her return to England I was given the *Valiant*. At the end of 1790 I was promoted to be Rear-Admiral after eleven years in the Navy. In my more candid moments I knew that I did not deserve this title, when post-captains such as Nelson, with twice my ability and experience were unemployed. The main problem for Nelson was Lord Hood who had had the misfortune to tell him that a ship was impossible because 'The King was impressed with an unfavourable opinion of him [Nelson]'. I was not aware of this situation as I was at sea. My father must have been advised that Nelson was to blame for the Schomberg and my other problems in the West Indies in 1786-8. My father was *not* informed that Nelson was my friend and had behaved at all times with honour and propriety. He remained my friend until his death.

Nelson's sad letters still came to me. 'My not being appointed to a ship is so very mortifying that I cannot find words to express what I feel on the occasion'. Although I wanted to [help] I had no influence with the Admiralty despite my rank, and I never went to sea again. It was represented to my father that I would be at risk! But I had been at risk in the last eleven years, nine of them in active service. Nelson wrote to me about social conditions in Norfolk, about average earnings and Ale-House licences. Eventually to my great pleasure the Admiralty awarded the *Agamemnon* to Nelson early in 1793 and I asked him to take Joseph King, formerly boatswain of the *Boreas*, latterly with me on the *Valiant* with him, 'One of the best boatswains I have seen in His Majesty's service.' Earlier I had written to Nelson 'Never be alarmed, I will always stand your friend.' It probably never occured to him that I had such little influence with the Admiralty. In 1793 I was an unemployed Admiral and Nelson wrote to his wife 'I am sorry he is not employed. What does it matter to him whether the war is right or wrong. As an officer who I would wish to see rise in the esteem of his country I wish he was at sea where I am sure he would acquire honour.'

During the Mediterranean campaign he and I exchanged letters. After the Spithead mutiny I wrote 'Pardon my gloom over the state of the fleet at Spithead, during a War, for a whole week in a complete state of Mutiny ... and Ireland in open rebellion awaiting French invasion. I have a very large stake in this country and a family of young children to protect ...' I had formed an attachment to a London actress called Mrs. Jordan who lived with me at Bushey Park and bore me several children – the young Fitz-Clarences.

Nelson wrote to me from St. Vincent's fleet 'To serve my King and to destroy the French I consider as the great order of all, from which the little ones spring: and if one of these little ones militate against it (for who can tell exactly at a distance) I go back to obey the order and object, to down with the damned French villains.'

Later that year (17 September 1797) I wrote to Nelson from Dover after his assault on Santa Cruz

> I congratulate you with all my heart upon your safe arrival at last covered with honour and glory. As an old friend, I cannot but lament the very severe loss you have sustained in losing your right arm. I hope your health is good and that you are gone, as I am informed, more for the purpose of joining Lady Nelson than for the re-establishment of the constitution in which I am doubly interested both as a friend and as one who is anxious to see the country have restored to her a brave and excellent Officer. Excuse my anxiety as it proceeds from friendship and admiration of your public character and I must request you will allow Lady Nelson to write to me how you are and when you will be able to be in London, that I may be one of the first to shake you by the hand. My best wishes and compliments attend you and Lady Nelson and ever believe me, Dear Sir, yours sincerely, WILLIAM.

I received from Nelson an answer in his laboured left hand

> Sir, I trust your Royal Highness will attribute my not having sent a letter since my arrival to its true cause – viz, the not being now a ready writer. I feel confident of your sorrow for my accident: but I assure your Royal Highness that not a scrap of that ardour with which I have hitherto served our King has been shot away.

I still had delusions that I might become entrusted with the executive management of the Admiralty and in due course become Lord High Admiral.

After Nelson's stormy home-coming, lengthily overland (most out of character, not sailing home with dignity), the only member of our family who expressed an interest in meeting him was my eldest brother, the Prince of Wales (who had an eye for Lady Hamilton). At a levée in the winter of 1800 my father was very brusque with Nelson and asked perfunctorily after his health and was not interested in his answer. I know that my morals cannot stand investigation, nor can those of my brothers, but Nelson was a National Hero and John Bull expected his morals to be beyond reproach. Nevertheless our friendship, though strained, still continued. Before the ill-fated levée I allowed him to watch the procession of Peers to the House of Lords from my apartments. He wrote to me a few days before his last battle.

After his tragic and perhaps inevitable death at Trafalgar, I attended his magnificent funeral and remarked to his brother-in-law 'I am come to pay my last Duties here, and I hope you and I shall never meet on such a like occasion.'

During my stay in Brighton my friends at my private 'Court' often discussed our feelings after Nelson's death on the *Victory*. One such occasion was reported back to Lady Nelson by Mrs. Fitzherbert, my close friend, after a visit by Mrs. Creevey; 'She gave me an account of the Prince's grief about Lord N.'s death and then entered into the domestic failings of the latter, in a way infinitely creditable to her [i.e., to Lady N.] and skilful too. She was all for Lady Nelson and against Lady Hamilton who, she said (hero though he was) over power'd him and took possession of him quite by force.'

I continued to see his widow, by now the Duchess of Bronte, from time to time on her brief visits to St. James. In 1827 I received a letter from Paris from her which begged me to consider the merits of a relative of Admiral Nelson. Captain Blanckley was George Matcham's son-in-law (Matcham being married to Nelson's sister), so I answered from the Admiralty (9 June) how I could not forget the many happy hours that I spent at Nevis with her Ladyship – and would see what I could do for Blanckley.

When eventually I succeeded to the Throne in 1830, I visited Brighton and stayed at my elegant new Pavilion. In September I paid a call on Admiral Holloway's widow and also on the Duchess of Bronte. She was staying at a hotel called The Ship in Distress on the Kings Road. Over its porch it had a picture of a wrecked ship and the words 'By danger we'er encompassed round/ Pray lend a hand, our ships aground.' After my visit the landlord changed its name to the Royal Sea House Hotel!

At Christmas my old friend from Nevis left her card for me at the Pavilion. Earlier that year she had returned from Paris with her dead son Josiah in the face of the July revolutionaries – a brave woman. I never saw her again although I was represented at her funeral the following year.

In Brighton, views of the Royal Pavilion and Mrs Fitzherbert's house.

EPILOGUE

Admiral Sir William Hotham, Nelson's old commander in chief in the Mediterranean, visited Fanny on 4 May 1831. She had just reached her 70th birthday and was grieving over Josiah's sudden death in Paris the year before. He recorded that she was in great dejection of spirits, her son was gone and four of Josiah's seven children dead in infancy, and her beloved daughter-in-law dangerously ill with inflammation of the lungs. Sir William recalled seeing Fanny dancing a Minuet with Horatio on Nevis previous to their marriage.

Fanny died two days later in her London house, No.26 Baker Street, Portman Square, attended by her cousin and close friend Mrs. Fanny Francklyn. She had made her Will on 18 April at No.23 Harley Street, with her maid Ellin Hoye as witness. She left the interest of two instalments of £1,200 each to Mrs. Nisbet (her daughter-in-law) for life, the principal to her favourite grandchild Frances Herbert Nisbet (little Fan). A legacy of £100 went to her friend Miss Elisabeth Locker. The total estate was under £4,000 as she had made over considerable sums already to Josiah and his wife. The Executors were Lord Bridport and General Egerton.

Fanny died peacefully with the same dignity that she had shown all her life – and with the memories of the happy carefree days on Nevis when she was being courted by her dashing little Captain.

One curious incident happened a day or so after her death. Lady Bridport (Charlotte Hood née Nelson) suddenly appeared at Fanny's house, bustled her way in, – and carried off two large porcelain vases representing Lord Nelson's battles, which had been given to Fanny by Lord Spencer when First Lord of the Admiralty. These had been specifically left to young Fanny, her grand-daughter. Mrs Nisbet quite correctly made such a fuss and to-do that the vases were eventually returned to her for her children.

Fanny was remembered by the grand old Admiralty families. To her funeral came Sir Thomas Masterton Hardy, now an elderly Vice-Admiral, Nelson's Captain of the *Victory* at Trafalgar. So too came Lt. General Sir Charles Bulkeley Egerton who had married Rear Admiral Sir Thomas Troubridge's daughter. Thomas had admired both Horatio and his wife, detested Lady Emma Hamilton and refused to visit Merton. Lord and Lady Bridport represented the Samuel Hood family. George Lord Vernon represented that fine old naval family. Sir William Hotham and many old Admirals who remembered Fanny appeared on this last occasion. The Nelson family were represented by Horatio's brother William (now Lord

Nelson) and Charlotte his daughter (Viscountess Bridport). Josiah's friend the Hon. Thomas Bladen Capel, Admiral of the Blue, also paid his respects.

The Times notice of Friday, 13 May 1831 stated that a long line of carriages was present in the funeral cortege of the late Viscountess Nelson. Doubtless the other famous sea Lords sent their representatives too – the Spencers, the St. Vincents, the Collingwoods, the Parkers and the Saumarez families.

Fanny was buried in a handsome vault in her beloved Littleham at the church which she attended so frequently – SS Margaret and Andrew. Her daughter-in-law commissioned a fine tablet by Turnerelli, of white marble with inverted torches carved in high relief at each side of it. On the top of the actual slab a weeping woman kneels resting her head despairingly on her right hand hard by a couple of heraldic urns, over which a palm branch is laid. On one of these urns is a shield with three boars' heads, a boars' head above as a crest and the Nisbet motto 'Vis Fortibus Arma'. On the other is a Viscount's coronet with the capital letter N and painted arms upon a lozenge. Her tomb is in the south chancel aisle upon the eastern wall in the south corner of the church. The inscription on the tablet reads as follows:

Sacred to the memory of
Frances Herbert,
Viscountess Nelson – Duchess of Bronti
Widow of the late Admiral – Lord Viscount Nelson
and to her son Josiah Nisbet Esq.
Captain in the Royal Navy
whom she survived eleven months
and died in London May 6th 1831 aged 73 years
This humble offering of affection
is erected by Frances Herbert Nisbet
in grateful remembrance of those virtues
which adorned a kind mother in law and good husband.

Fanny's daughter in law made one error – Fanny Nelson was aged 70 when she died, having been born in 1761 on Nevis. On the tomb itself the inscription reads:

Beneath are deposited the remains of Frances Herbert Viscountess Nelson, Duchess of Bronte aged 73 (sic) who departed this life May 6th 1831. Also Josiah Nisbet aged 50, died on the 14th of July 1830 and also of his four children Horatio Woolward, Herbert Josiah, Sarah and Josiah all of whom died young.

Fanny, Josiah's widow, continued to live for a time in Paris, where her three surviving daughters were educated. After they were married she returned to England and died in Cheltenham on 15 January 1864. She too lies buried near Josiah in Littleham graveyard.

The eldest child Frances Herbert Nisbet (little Fan) married in London on 12 December 1846 William Johnstown Nelson Neal, Midshipman, Barrister and Recorder of Walsall (1839-1893). They had six children. She called one of her daughters, Ada Evangeline, after Lord Byron's daughter. William's father was Dr. Adam Neal, physician Extraordinary to the Duke of Kent. He practised in Exeter from 1814–24, where no doubt he met Josiah Nisbet and his mother. Curiously enough Dr. Adam Neal wrote a pamphlet on the nature and properties of Cheltenham spa waters, which was so unfavourably received that he left that town shortly after. Dr. Josiah Nisbet's report on the medicinal properties of Nevis spa water was greeted more favourably when he wrote it in 1768. Both men studied medicine at Edinburgh University. Little Fan died in 1898.

The second daughter Mary Nisbet married at Dover 22 August 1848 Charles Frederick Thruston of Talgarth Hall, Merioneth, who became High Sheriff in 1860. They had seven children. Mary died in 1915.

The youngest daughter Georgina married on 10 April 1849 Captain, later Vice Admiral, George Butler Mends RN. They had eleven children and she died in 1904. Their eldest son, born 28 December 1851, became Brig. General Horatio Reginald Mends. Mrs. Finney (née Neal) one of Fanny's great-grand-daughters owns an *étui*, a watercolour of Fanny's exquisitely painted with roses. Her fine embroidery can be seen in the initials of her kerchief.

In Josiah's will, in which he left substantial sums to his wife and surviving children, he remembered his Nisbet cousins, Emilia, Caroline Lockhart, Walter's second son, also named Josiah, a Woolward boy in the West Indies, and his wife's relations in Glamorgan, including Christopher Maxwell Talbot. He left legacies to his Naval friends Admiral Capel, and George Lord Vernon.

Thus ended the most famous Eternal Triangle drama of the late eighteenth/ early nineteenth century. Horatio Nelson threw away – almost carelessly – the first true love of his life. He lost his friends' respect, and eventually his life at the age of forty-seven at Trafalgar. Glamorous, tawdry Lady Emma gained several passionate years of notoriety, sank into obscurity, and died unmourned in a foreign grave. Fanny, despite her constant ill-health, outlived the other two partners in the Triangle. Her long, interesting, dignified life masked her constant grief at the loss of her husband to another woman. Nevertheless she had her only son Josiah, her grandchildren, many friends in two countries, and her memories to console her. Of the three she was the only one to come out of the affair with honour.

The Rev. A. S. Woolward was a descendant of the Bath Doctor of the same name, who said to the ailing Horatio in Bath 'Pray, Captain Nelson, allow me to follow what I consider my professional duty. Your illness, Sir, was brought on by serving your King and Country, and believe me, I love both too well to be able to receive any more [payment].'

On Trafalgar Day, 21 October 1930, the Rev. Woolward caused to be placed a wreath on Fanny's tomb with the inscription

To the memory of Viscountess Nelson,
a good woman and a faithful wife.

EPITAPH
BICENTENARY OF NELSON'S WEDDING IN NEVIS

11 March 1987 was the 200th anniversary of the wedding of Nelson to Fanny Nisbet. Montpelier, where the reception was held, exists now as a hotel and is owned by English proprietors who appropriately marked the day. At Morning Star there is a Nelson Museum where visitors are welcome.

In celebration of the occasion a ballad was composed:

> The winds of chance have filled the sails
> And brought *Boreas* to the Isle,
> Where Fanny Nisbet, widow lives
> In graceful but provincial style.
>
> She keeps house for her Uncle there –
> He is both rich and gracious:
> Josiah is her four year old
> Montpelier House is spacious.
>
> See now the Captain come ashore
> Desiring to marry
> (As he had several times before)
> But now was courting Fanny.
>
> Fanny thinks him very strange
> He does not speak much ever:
> His eyes are fixed on wars to come
> And small talk he has never.
>
> Yet on marriage he is bent
> And Fanny can't deny him
> (Only Bonaparte himself
> Would ever dare defy him.)

Sing heigh, sing heigh for glory
Waiting for her groom,
He never doubts his vision –
It is glory or the tomb.

The wedding at Montpelier
Will be remembered long –
All Nevis helps to celebrate:
With feasting and with song.

The Duke of Clarence is a guest,
He is a future King.
His presence at the wedding seems
A nobly gracious thing.

Two hundred years have come and gone,
Since Fanny was brave Nelson's bride –
And she remains his only wife
In spite of later passion's tide.

And here at old Montpelier,
The memories abide
Where a brave young English captain
Took Fanny for his bride.

We cannot know how much she helped
To set him on his way –
But here's to Fanny Nelson
As we celebrate the Day.

Robert D. Abrahams

CHRONOLOGICAL SUMMARY

1722 Edmund Nelson born in Burnham Thorpe.

1724 William Woolward, sea captain, married Anne Smith, widow, on Nevis.

1730 William Hamilton born.

1739 War of Jenkins Ear between England and Spain.

1745 Jacobite revolution under Prince Charles Edward.

1747 Josiah Nisbet born 7 August to Walter and Mary Nisbet née Webbe.

1756 French took Minorca – Admiral Byng executed.

1758 Horatio Nelson born 29 September to Rev. Edmund Nelson and Catherine née Suckling.
      William Hamilton first marriage to Miss Barlow.

1759 Year of victories – Quebec, Minden, Lagos, Quiberon Bay.

1761 May. Frances Herbert Woolward baptised, daughter of William Woolward and Mary née Herbert.

1763 Mary Woolward died.

1765 Emma Hart born – later changes name to Lyon.

1768 Rev. Edmund Nelson's wife and mother died, leaving eight children. Josiah Nisbet qualified as Doctor at Edinburgh.

1769 Dr. Josiah Nisbet Apothecary in Coventry.

1771 Midshipman Horatio Nelson joined *Raisonnable* on 1st January.

1772 Severe hurricane on Nevis island. Nisbet and Lockhart family in Bath.

1773 Nelson in *Racehorse* on North Pole expedition 'nephew to Captain Suckling'.

1776 American War of Independence started – Nevis sugar planters suffered.

1777 9 April, Nelson made Lieutenant, joined *Lowestoft* to Jamaica station.

1778 Nelson made Post-Captain of *Hinchingbrooke* frigate, then the *Janus*.

1779 27 February, William Woolward died of tetanus. Fanny Woolward married Dr. Josiah Nisbet 28 June.

1780 Nisbets took ship to England. Josiah Nisbet born in Salisbury.
      Nelson in Nicaraguan campaign.

1781 Dr. Josiah Nisbet, Fanny's husband, died in Salisbury 11 October. Nelson convalescent in Bath.

1782 De Grasse, French Admiral, captured St. Kitts and Nevis island. James and Richard Nisbet Assemblymen on Nevis. Nelson commanded the *Albemarle*.

1783   Treaty of Versailles, Nevis island returned to British rule. Nelson met Prince William. December Fanny returned to Nevis with young Josiah to keep house for Uncle Herbert. Nelson visited France.

1784   Nelson captain of the *Boreas* sailed to Leeward Islands. Brother William was Chaplain.

1785   Fanny met Capt. Horatio Nelson on Nevis island. Fanny's aunt Sarah Herbert died.

1786   Fanny became engaged to the 'little Captain'.

1787   Prince William was 'Father of the Bride' on Nevis at the Nelson-Nisbet wedding 11 March. May, Nelson sailed *Boreas* to Portsmouth. Fanny, her uncle and cousin sail 'home' on *Roehampton*.

1787–93   Captain Nelson 'on the Beach' lived with Fanny and Rev. Edmund mainly in Norfolk.

1789   Storming of the Bastille. French Revolution started.

1791   Emma Lyon married Sir William Hamilton.

1793   18 January, Uncle Herbert died in London, left legacy to Fanny. Louis XVI executed. February, England declared war on France. Nelson commanded the *Agamemnon* 64 guns. Josiah joined his step-father as midshipman Mediterranean campaign. 14 September, first visit to Court of Naples. Nelson & Josiah met the Hamiltons. November Nelson visited Tunis. Fanny in lodgings at Swaffham in August, stayed with Lady Walpole in December, then to Bath with 'Our Father'.

1794   Fanny went to Bristol and Bath with her father-in-law, met Lord & Lady Hood. Siege of Bastia & Calvi. Josiah fought well, and Nelson lost his right eye in the land battles. In March captured the *Ca Ira* and the *Censeur*. Fanny went to Plymouth, Exeter in the spring.

1795   Lord Hood retired from being C in C Mediterranean Fleet, became Governor Greenwich Hospital. Nelson off Genoa, Leghorn, gazetted Colonel of Marines.

1796   Sir John Jervis new C in C Mediterranean. Nelson made Commodore, transfered to the *Captain* 74 guns. 19 February Bath Fanny went to Mrs. Western's Great Rout. August, Fanny in Lyme Regis. November, Fanny & 'Our Father' in Bath until March 1797.

1797   Nelsons bought Round wood House near Ipswich. Louisa Forster married Captain Edward Berry. 14 February Battle of Cape St. Vincent. Nelson in the *Captain* distinguished himself, received Order of the Bath. April Fanny at James Tobin house, Berkeley Square, Bristol. 27 May Nelson gazetted a Knighthood. 25 July Josiah Nisbet saved his step-father's life at battle of Santa Cruz.

Josiah promoted from 1st Lieutenant on the *Theseus* to command the *Dolphin* in August. Nelson wounded, lost his right arm, returned to Bath, re-union with Fanny. Promoted to Rear Admiral Of the Blue. October, Duncan's victory over Dutch at Camperdown.

1798   21 March Nelson made Will in favour of Josiah and Fanny. Nelson sailed
         in *Vanguard* in April for Mediterranean. Josiah in *Dolphin* took 3 prizes off
         Lisbon, praised by Earl St. Vincent. 1 August, Nelson brilliantly defeated
         French, Battle of the Nile. Took battered squadron into Naples. Father
         and step-son fell in love with Lady Emma Hamilton. Josiah commanded
         La Bonne Citoyenne, visited Naples August/September. Blockade of Malta
         for two years. Fanny spent summer at Round Wood, Winter in Bath. 2
         October, Lady Emma wrote to Fanny. 16 October, Fanny attended Victory
         Ball at Ipswich. Fanny painted by Mr. Daniel Orme. 22 November, Fanny at
         Court with Countess of Chatham. 5 December, Nelson returned to Naples.
         December Josiah made Post-Captain, Nelson and Hamiltons in Palermo.

1799   Nelson inactive at Court of Naples. Josiah commanded the *Thalia* 36
         gun frigate in many escapades and scrapes. Nelson's flag aboard the
         Foudroyant; made Duke of Bronte. Josiah sent to Constantinople with
         Turkish Ambassador in January. Off Malta and Palermo in rest of year;
         took several prizes. Summer, Autumn Fanny at 92 Sloane St. London.
         Fanny went to Court with Walpoles on 4 June. November at 54 St. James
         Street.

1800   The Keeper & the Bear. Queen of Naples, the Hamiltons' and Nelson's
         overland journey from Naples started 15 July. Arrived Yarmouth 6
         November. Josiah captured more prizes, in trouble again sailed *Thalia* to
         Madeira in May, and back to England for refitting December. Fanny went to
         Court with Lady Hood and Nile Captains and met Queen on 14 November.

1801   February Horatia born to Nelson and Lady Emma Hamilton. Nelson made
         Vice Admiral of the Blue. 2 April, Battle of Copenhagen. Nelsons sold
         Round Wood. Fanny left for Brighton with Elizabeth Locker – April in Bath.
         Nelson wrote farewell letter to Fanny, who kept on Somerset St. London
         house. Nelson returned to Yarmouth 1 July from Baltic. 1 August, attacked
         Boulogne. Nelson bought Merton Place for himself and Hamiltons. 21
         August, Fanny at 66 Wimpole St. December Fanny wrote final letters to
         her husband.

1802   2 March, Josiah dined with Hamiltons. Nelson's grand tour of Britain with
         the Hamiltons. 20 April, Fanny at 16 Somerset St. Portman Square. 26
         April, Fanny to Bath to be with 'Our Father'. 26 April, Rev. Edmund Nelson
         died at Bath. Brig named after Fanny *The Lady Nelson*.

1803   6 April, Sir William Hamilton died. Nelson started blockade of Toulon
         July in *Victory*. Fanny at 54 Welbeck Street London – attended St. James
         Court. Fanny rented house at Clifton, near Bristol. Britain again at war
         with France. Nelson appointed to C in C Mediterranean Command in the
         Victory. Admiral Samuel Reeve died.

1804   Fanny in Bath much of the year. Nelson gazetted Vice Admiral of the
         White on St. George's Day, made new Will. Napoleon became Emperor of
         the French. England at war with Spain.

1805 French plundered Nevis island. Fanny in Bath during the spring. Fanny in Bath ill. 21 October, Battle of Trafalgar, Nelson died in action. 4 November, Fanny arrived in Bath – play presented *Nelson's Glory*. 7 November, Lady Walpole wrote to Josiah with condolences. 9 November, Lord Barham wrote to Mr. Pitt for peerage for Fanny. 3 December, Battle of Austerlitz.

1806 9 January, Nelson's funeral at St. Paul's. 23 January, Death of Pitt. Napoleon declared Britain in state of Blockade. January – March Fanny in London 36 Weymouth St. 6 February, Fanny wrote to Admiralty Board re Pension. February – October litigation re Nelson's estate. May – June Fanny in Bath. 16 June, Fanny in Great Malvern. 14 July – 20 October Fanny in Clifton.

1807 Slave Trade abolished in the British Empire. Admirals Troubridge and Louis died, one in Malta, the other at sea. 28 February, Fanny in Exmouth. 26 March and 19 November, Fanny in Exmouth. Paid sub. Naval Asylum for girls 4 guineas. September, Fanny in Bath. 8 October, Fanny in Weymouth, met the Pinneys, went to Exmouth by 19 November.

1808 Peninsular War began. Wellington won Battle of Vimeiro. 22 July, Exmouth Fanny paid Wright the Taylor for a new suit of livery. Admiral Alexander Ball died on Malta. 21 November, Fanny was in Bath at No.2 Bennett St. She paid Josiah £1,000 in 4 per cent Consols.

1809 Battle of Coruna, Sir John Moore killed in action 16 January. 29 January, Fanny in Bath at 8 Russell St. 25 March, Fanny sent bills to Mr. Joseph Thomas from Bath. 20 July, Fanny in Exmouth. 22 September, Duel between Castlereagh and Mr. Canning. Sir William Beechey painted Fanny.

1810 23 January, Fanny in Exmouth. Litigation in Nevis on Nisbet estate. 29 January, 8 Russell St. Bath Fanny received Nelson Vase. 18 June, Regency commenced. Attempt on life of Duke of Cumberland. 10 August, Fanny in Exmouth – Josiah to Dartmouth by sea. Bill for £66 for wine protested. 29 August, Lord Hood's grandson married Lady Charlotte Nelson. King ill for two years.

1811 27 April, Fanny at 3 Queens Square Bath, sent Anne Nisbet £50. Luddite Riots. Admiral Collingwood C in C Mediterranean died.

1812 Regency Act expired. Napoleon retreated from Moscow. August-November Fanny in Exmouth. 10 November, she paid Josiah £1,000 in 4 per cent Consols.

1813 Duke of Wellington beat French at Vitoria June 21. 1 September, Fanny in Teignmouth. Paid Josiah £1,000 in 4 per cent Consols.

1814 11 April, Napoleon abdicated. Summer the Czar, Marshal von Blucher in London – Fanny went to Serpentine Festival. Lady Emma Hamilton died of drink and poverty in Calais.

1815 Fanny took No.6 The Beacon in Exmouth. 23 January, met the Pinneys there. Napoleon escaped from Elba. Battle of Waterloo, 18 June. 16 October, Napoleon exiled to St. Helena. Frances Herbert Evans became Fanny's companion.

1816   5 April, Fanny in Exmouth. 17 July, Fanny in Teignmouth. 1 September, 22 October, in Torquay. 25 November, Fanny and Josiah arrived in Exmouth from Torquay; she sent Anne Nisbet £25. Admiral Lord Samuel Hood, Governor of Greenwhich Hospital, died aged 90.

1817   8 February, Fanny sent Anne Nisbet £40. Fanny in Paris.

1818   Matcham family lived in Paris, met Fanny & Josiah there. Part of year Fanny in Bath at No.8 Russell St. 20 June, Fanny in Exeter paid Mrs. Anne Hawkins £200. 25 December, Fanny and Josiah went to Exeter.

1819   31 March, Josiah's marriage to Frances Herbert Evans in Littleham. 17 June, Fanny bought a petticoat for her daughter-in-law. 2-12 August Fanny met Duchess of Wellington. 15 August, Fanny gave Josiah £1000 for his wife. 16 August, "Battle" of Peterloo. Josiah's new ship "Transit" in Exmouth harbour. 1-6 October Fanny in Southampton. Fanny sent Elizabeth Locker £40. Baron Thomas Fremantle died at Naples. 27 December, Exmouth, Fanny ordered Hogshead white wine and new bonnet for her daughter-in-law.

1820   29 January, King George III died. 18 October, Fanny in Exmouth. Paid £143.17s for Chariot for Josiah. Admiral Cornwallis died. 10 February, little Horatio Woolward Nisbet born in Exmouth – died later on in Paris. Fanny spent most of year in Paris. 14 February Duc de Berri assassinated in Paris.

1821   31 January, Fanny and Josiah gave grand dinner & Ball in Exmouth. 5 May, Napoleon died at St. Helena. George IV crowned, 19 July. Queen Caroline died 7 August. 24 July Coronation celebrations in Exmouth. 18 September, young Josiah Herbert Nisbet born and died in Littleham aged 17 days.

1822   6 February, Frances Herbert Nisbet born in Paris Fanny present. In the spring Fanny & Josiah & family met Lord George Byron in Geneva – went rowing on the lake. Most of the year in Paris, met Matchams.

1823   Josiah on half pay – lived in Paris with family & Fanny. Lord St. Vincent died aged 90 on 13 March. Lady Byron took up residence in Exmouth.

1824   Fanny in France most of year. Charles X became King of France. Fanny's Bankers in London bankrupted by defaulting partner. September/October Firm paid up in full.

1825   Fanny in France most of year. Josiah Nisbet RN placed on Retired List, remaining on half pay.

1826   5 September, Mary Nisbet born in Paris. Fanny visited France most of year.

1827   Fanny spent most of year in France. Fanny wrote to Prince William, Duke of Clarence of behalf of Matcham's son-in-law. 5-7 November, with Josiah and family in Lyon, France, Fanny met Gen. & Lady Bunbury.

1828   Fanny owned No.26 Baker St. Portman Square house. Mrs. Fanny Francklyn was her companion. She spent part of the year in France.

1829   Fanny owned house at Louisa Place in Exmouth, spent part of year in France with Josiah.

1830   1 January, Georgina Nisbet born in Paris during Fanny's visit. Josiah died in Paris 14 July – during Revolution. Fanny sent the bodies of her son & grandchildren back by ship to Exmouth. 26 June, King George IV died. Louis Phillippe became King of France after the July Revolution. September King William IV saw Fanny in her Brighton hotel. At Christmas Fanny called on the King at the Pavilion.

1831   Duchess of Berri visited Bath. Charles X of France refugee in Lullworth. 4 May, Admiral Sir William Hotham visited Fanny. Fanny died 6 May at Baker St. house, and was buried at Littleham. Rear Admiral Sir Edward Berry died.

1833   Anne Nisbet and George Matcham died.

1834   Abolition of Slavery on Nevis.

1836   Vice Admiral Baron James Saumarez died.

1837   Queen Victoria succeeded to the throne.

1839   Vice Admiral Sir Thomas Hardy died.

1840   Queen Victoria married Prince Albert.

1846   12 December, Frances Herbert Nisbet married William Johnstown Nelson Neal in London.

1848   22 August, Mary Nisbet married Charles Frederick Thruston at Dover.

1849   10 April, Georgina Nisbet married Capt. George Bulter Mends RN.

1854   France and Britain declared war on Russia.

1864   15 January, Josiah's wife, Frances Herbert died in Cheltenham aged 72 and was buried in Littleham.

BIBLIOGRAPHY

Viscountess Frances Nelson's letters in MSS are to be read in various archives the British Library, the Bodleian Library, the National Maritime Museum, the Nelson Museum Monmouth, etc. Some of her letters were sent to the early publishers Clarke and M'Arthur, and to Sir Harris Nicolas. Mr. Alfred Morrison's collection provided further letters. Many others were unfortunately destroyed by her husband and son before the bloody battle on Tenerife.

The excellent biography of Nelson by Carola Oman (1947) provided useful background material. G. P. B. Naish's *Nelson's letters to his wife* and E. M. Keate's *Nelson's wife* were equally valuable. The Bristol University Archives have an interesting collection of West Indian Plantation seventeenth and eighteenth century diaries and logbooks: they produced intriguing details of the young Frances Woolward; of the Nisbet family and of their relatives the Webbes, Pinneys and Tobins.

The Nisbet Family History Society (in particular Mr. Richard K. Nesbitt, the President, Mr. David Nisbet Wilson, Peter Nisbet and Rupert Nisbet) provided the links with the sugar planters of Nevis to the old Scots clan.

The dramatic events that befell Fanny's family in Paris derived from a variety of diaries, and her life in Exmouth from the local studies library there.

The Public Record Office, Kew, provided information about Josiah Nisbet's naval career and his Captain's log of the SS *Thalia*. There are several of his letters in the British Library MSS collection. The Navy Records Society publications contain further letters.

Charles Beresford and H. N. Wilson, *Nelson and his Times*
G. Lathom Browne, *Life of Nelson*
Robin Bush, *The book of Exmouth*
Cann & Bush, *Newspaper extracts from Exmouth history*
J.S. Clarke &'Dr. J. M'Arthur, *Life & Services of Horatio, Viscount Nelson*
Casimir Delavigne, *Evenements de Paris, 1830*
E. R. Delderfield, *Exmouth Milestones*
Dictionary of National Biography
M. Eyre-Matcham, *Nelsons of Burnham Thorpe*
Everitt-Webb, *Memorials of Exmouth*

Hilda Gamlin, *Nelson's Friendships*

The Gentlemans Magazine

Mrs. Joyce Gordon's, *Nevis, Queen of the Caribees*

John Gore, *Nelsons Hardy and his Wife*

Elsa V. Goveda, *Slave society in the British Leewards*

E. M. Keate, *Nelsons Wife*

A. T. Mahan, *Life of Nelson*

J. Marshall, *Royal Naval Biography*

Kathleen Manchester, *Historic heritage of St. Kitts – Nevis – Anguilla*

A. Morrison, *The Nelson & Hamilton Papers*

E. Moorhouse, *Nelson in England*

G. P. B. Naish, *Nelson's letters to his wife* (Navy Records Society)

The Nelson Society publications

The Nisbet Society

Sir Nicholas Harris Nicolas, *Despatches & Letters of Lord Nelson, Notes and Queries*

V. L. Oliver, *Caribbeana* and *Monumental Inscriptions of the B.W.I.* Carola Oman *Nelson*

Richard Pares, *A West Indian Fortune*

Geoffrey Rawson, *Nelson's letters from the Leeward Isles*

Jack Russell, *Nelson and the Hamiltons*

Percy Sadler, *Paris in 1830*

Robert Southey, *Life of Nelson*

A. P. Watts, *Nevis & St. Christopher*

W. J. W. Webb, *Memorials of Exmouth*

Other Nelson biographies by Tom Pocock, David Walder and W. C. Lane.

Diaries by Louisa Emilia Bunbury, Francis Lady Shelley, the Wynne sisters, etc.

Record Offices and local History libraries at Exeter, Bath, Portsmouth, Monmouth, Norwich, Ipswich, Exmouth.

Newspapers inc. *Trewmans Exeter Flying Post*, the London *Morning Chronicle*, *Morning Herald*, *Morning Post* & *Gazeteer*, the *St. James Chronicle* etc.

The National Maritime Museum, Greenwich; the Hood, James Western MSS etc.

Public Record Office, Kew; Co. 184, 186, 187, Captains log SS *Thalia*

British Museum MSS 34, 988, 28, 233, 337

Admiralty Navy Board Bounty Papers, No 3028 etc.

Naval Historical Library, Ministry of Defence, London SW6

INDEX